THIS MOMENT: REFLECTIONS ON LEADING, LEARNING, LAUGHING AND LIVING

DEAR JENNIFER -
What A great pleasure
it is working with you on this
important project. I hope that
you enjoy my book.

All the best -
JESSICA

THIS MOMENT: REFLECTIONS ON LEADING, LEARNING, LAUGHING AND LIVING

Jessica C. McWade, Ed.D.

ISBN-13: 9781544182223
ISBN-10: 1544182228

DEDICATION

This book is dedicated to my wonderful husband Walt Kuklinski, dear sister Pat McWade and her partner George Rozalowski, sons Zack McWade and Jackson McWade, so many good friends and colleagues and, of course, Mikey for their love and support over the years.

I would also like to thank my publishing and editing colleagues Ken Lizotte and Elena Petricone of the Emerson Consulting Group, Inc. for their considerable expertise as well as Sarah Madey for her gracious Foreword.

TABLE OF CONTENTS

PREFACE

I like to write, especially on the road. I like to travel, too, so I have ample mobile moments to reflect on leading, learning, laughing and living.

It would be convenient to say that a friend of mine encouraged me to compile some of my blog posts and newspaper columns over 16 years into a book, but that didn't happen. I simply looked at all that material one day – the passion, joy, frustration and chronicle of events that it depicts – and decided to tackle this project. The book you are reading is the result. I hope you enjoy it.

This work comes at a time – a singularly distressing moment – when our very definitions of leadership, dialogue, fairness, decency and, yes, sanity are being questioned. Maybe a small project of this nature can help salve the wounds and inspire us to care about how we lead and are led, how we learn and teach, and how we make time to laugh, live and love amidst all the coarseness and turmoil.

I often feel like I've been looking for leadership in all the wrong places, and I'm hardly alone. That's because the standard-issue titans, executives, politicians, athletes and celebrities we treat as leaders these days too often let us down. And yet, why should this surprise us?

After all, we routinely put ambitious, accomplished and technically savvy lawyers, financiers, engineers, surgeons and salespeople in leadership positions and, somehow, expect them to succeed without much if any real leadership orientation and training. We put people in charge of other people without sufficient evidence of their ability and, more important, their willingness to engage in the messy business of human behavior. Too bad for them and for us all. It's colossally self-defeating and downright pathetic that so few of our institutions invest in educating, training and inspiring their people to lead – and to follow. Our military is a notably wonderful exception.

I learned over the years that there is a profound difference between leaders and those who just happen to occupy leadership positions because, perhaps, they are good at making money or garnering votes. Yes, it really is about separating the contenders from the pretenders.

My great joy has been to find real leaders across all walks of life and around the world, in community service, social justice, education, health care, media, the military and, yes, even rare examples of remarkable leadership in business and politics, too. The deeds of some of these extraordinary individuals are showcased throughout this book in recurring profiles entitled, "Now That's a Leader."

The men and women featured in these stories responded well to their leadership moments. They rose to the occasion and did the right thing, often selflessly. We never know when and how we will be called to lead and serve. We might miss the moment completely if we are too self-absorbed with money or ideological wet dreams or otherwise distracted by the endless demands on our time made by things that simply do not matter.

That is why this book is entitled, *This Moment*. We certainly live in a toxic, perilous moment, seemingly at the nadir of effective national leadership. So, in this challenging context, when will you seize the moment to be a helper, healer or hero? Will it be this moment, right now?

I have also incorporated another series of vignettes throughout the book entitled, "It Really Happened." I do not merit any autobiography, for sure, but I have been fortunate to experience many things around this wonderful world of ours in personal, corporate, military and academic life, some of them funny. Since humor is essential to a life well lived and a crucial part of the humility that decent leaders and human beings possess, I take time out here and there to tell some lighter stories. This moment in time warrants all the humor we can muster. We have today at the highest levels of government too many angry, selfish, humorless and, arguably, soulless people determining the fate of our planet. Let us never forget the power of humor and narrative to put them in context and, perhaps, take them down a notch or two. It was Langston Hughes who once wrote, "Like a welcome summer rain, humor may suddenly cleanse and cool the earth, the air and you." Besides, as Robert DeNiro said in the movie *Analyze That* (2002), "I'm just trying to levitate the situation."

I'm also pleased to share with you some of my photography – except the shots I'm in, of course – including images of young LeBron James in his first professional game, a Shinto procession in Tokyo, joyous musicians in Cuba and, good grief, a rogue elephant charge in South Africa.

My first motivation with this book is to pay tribute to our next generation, the young adults who look at the world we are handing them and ask, "Is this the best you could do for us?" So many of the sharp, inspiring young adults of today simply do not share many of the blind fears, prejudices and hatreds that seem more abundant in older generations, including my own. They just want to get on with it and to focus on what really matters. They are far from perfect, of course. We hear all the complaints about Generation X and the Millennials but, frankly, much of this is the customary nonsense that older generations always say about their daughters and sons. Count me in with the young people, for they will show us the way. Perhaps some of the lessons in this book – organized around themes of leadership, wisdom and judgment, justice, global, communications and media, creativity and culture, education, and economy and business – can be of help to them.

That is why I asked a remarkable friend and colleague named Sarah Madey to write the Foreword to this book. It is for her, my sons and the brave, determined face of our younger generations – shortchanged by our ghastly shortsightedness – that I offer this work.

Jessica C. McWade
Princeton, MA
February 2017

FOREWORD

I n one of my first client-facing roles as a recent college graduate, I – wearing a fresh, new client-worthy suit – traveled by car with Jessica for a meeting in what was once one of this country's great mill cities. Nearing our destination in the heart of the downtown area, I looked around and saw distressed homes, dilapidated buildings and faded signs hinting at much livelier times. As I sat looking out the window, imagining this city in its better days, Jessica started talking about it, as if she could read my mind.

She told me how incredibly vibrant this city had become. She remarked on its diverse international community, which led to the growth of dynamic art, music and food scenes. Left and right, she pointed out exciting things to see – a new brewery, a historic mill museum, a restaurant serving African cuisine. Very quickly, she brought me to the realization that this was a city on the move. A city I'd very much like to explore. A city that I almost entirely dismissed.

I reflected on this moment – when she and I looked at the same scene, but saw it so differently. As if we had been in two separate cities. On that day – and on many days since then – Jessica enabled me to see things that I was looking at, but failed to notice. And thus began one of my life's greatest lessons – a lesson on perspective. On thoroughly consuming each and every moment. On looking beyond the surface and uncovering the beauty and truth in what was, what is and what could be.

And what an enduring and relevant message it is, especially given the uncertainty of the times in which we live. Have we ever needed perspective and the ability to find truth more than now? When it's easier to become wrapped up in and warped by the media's portrayal of what's real, wrong and right than it is to tune it out and remain purely objective. Messages of hope and despair are delivered in a rollercoaster-like fashion through a deafeningly loud, multi-channel surround-sound system. Perspective not only feels important, but necessary.

Sure, it would be far easier to simply wait for the dark clouds to pass. To accept that we may be in a holding pattern – or worse. But instead, we are witnessing the true empowerment of the people. Through social media, even the most unexpected leaders are given a platform on which to loudly and freely express their voices and inspire their audience, cutting the legs out from under the fear-based rhetoric. The more resistance we face, the greater our response – with true leaders and calls for justice rising loudly amidst the clutter.

Just as Jessica helped me see the greatness in what I initially perceived as a depressed city, we need to help one another extrapolate the good and work unequivocally toward it. Today's generation – that is, anyone who embraces that we live in a rapidly changing, forward moving, global society – refutes the idea that we must merely accept things as they are, powerless in our words and actions. We see what is and, despite the chaos, sustain hope and maintain a complete faith in the world's ability to deliver on our high expectations of what can be. Settling in and sitting back simply will not suffice. We are instead driven by the idea that we *can* impact real change, that our responses and our attitudes can make or break us – and we won't be broken – and that it's not just the future we're fighting for, it's *our* future.

Time and again, we witness first-hand people who are leading a movement and do not even recognize their actions as leadership. This is leadership in its truest form. Jessica has captured instances of leadership spanning cultures, industries, eras and interests. She provides much-needed perspective and guides readers to a path of discovering more from life's everyday moments. Those instances, the good and the bad that so often pass us by, unrecognized by the untrained eye as an opportunity to find beauty, to dig for truth, and to learn and gain new perspectives.

So what is next? More reasons than ever to keep on fighting for what we believe in. There are countless ways to have our voices heard and people, like Jessica, will continue to inspire and guide us toward greater meaning and purpose.

As Jessica applauds people and principles in all their glorious forms in her masterful compilation of a life well traveled and spent, we applaud you, Jessica. You wrote about your friend Rich Wilson in January of last year, as I'll now say to you: "this world is a better place for your vision and courage." *I* am a better person for your passion, your leadership and your friendship. Keep leading the way, my dear friend.

Sarah E. Madey
Boston, MA
February 2017

CHAPTER 1

LEADERSHIP

Saturday, January 21, 2017

Contenders, Not Pretenders

S erious leaders know how to confront difficult challenges while giving people perspective, hope, optimism and potential solutions.

JFK did just that in 1961 when circumstances were much darker than today. Kennedy spoke at the height of Cold War mania – with duck-and-cover drills and existential fears of nuclear winters – and at a time when despots ruled many countries, pollution swelled before the Clean Air and Clean Water Acts, our cities were starting a decades-long decline before their renaissance, crime rates grew before their substantial declines in more recent years, women were second-class citizens, African-Americans were being lynched and gays and lesbians were savagely persecuted.

Nonetheless, our new President in 1961 – certainly no saint himself – encouraged us by saying that, "The energy, the faith, the devotion which we bring to this endeavor will light our country and all who serve it – and the glow from that fire can truly light the world."

Yes, serious leaders know how to balance heat with light.

Saturday, March 5, 2016

The Playbook

Havana

We used Castro's playbook for too long. Fidel has outlasted 11 US presidents in part because he turned our decades-old embargo against us, using it to blame the evil gringos to the north for just about everything gone wrong with his country. Sure, our initial fanaticism about Castro in the 1960s and '70s can only be seen through the rabid Cold War lens of the time to be understood. Nonetheless, the embargo helped turn a tinpot dictator into a cagey, defiant global figure who too often seemed to be playing a winning hand against us. We let misplaced ideology and the appeasement of a small but politically potent cadre of anti-Castro, Cuban-American voters distort our decision making and, in the process, we helped keep the Castros in power. Irony knows no bounds.

There is much to love about this future US ally, alive as it is with gracious and talented people, world-class health care, a vibrant music scene, seemingly endless possibilities for the future – and that rum, too. My sister Pat and I are fortunate to be here as Cuba starts its emergence and just weeks ahead of visits by President Obama, the Tampa Bay Rays and the Rolling Stones. Still, one wonders whether this opening to Cuba should have been 15 or 20 years earlier. If we actually believe in the freedom of markets and movements, why have we been so reluctant until now to help open Cuba up and let the fresh air of trade, technology and tourism cleanse this nation of the Castros' authoritarianism? Those who peddle building walls and stifling the flow of commerce and ideas are almost always working from fear, anger and hatred and, as a result, too often using the other guy's playbook.

The Afro-Cuban Jazz Matanzas band played for us one magical afternoon in Matanzas, Cuba.

Tuesday, January 19, 2016
Now That's a Leader: Rich Wilson
Kangaroo Island, Australia

Rich Wilson is a truly inspiring individual. In an age marked by far too much braggadocio from armchair warriors and paper tigers, Rich demonstrates real courage. He completed the last (2008-2009) Vendée Globe, a challenge where participants sail around the world solo, non-stop and without assistance, aboard his *Great American III* as the oldest competitor and only American. He's now preparing for the next race this year. Far more people have climbed Mt. Everest or been shot into space than have completed this, perhaps, the most grueling athletic event on the planet.

I first became aware of this rare breed of intrepid solo circumnavigators when my friend Dennis and I had the honor of working with Sir Robin Knox Johnston on NATO duty in Norway many years ago. In 1968-1969, Sir Robin was the first person ever to sail around the world single-handed. He is also quite the character. Folks like Rich and Robin march to the beat of their own drummers and leave the rest of us to question what we are doing to be extraordinary.

More important, Rich is paying it forward. He is giving real meaning to his already remarkable accomplishments with his www.sitesalive. com K-12 educational initiative. Sites Alive provides platforms and curricula for students to follow and interact with field research projects and adventure challenges such as the Vendée Globe and learn about science, math, leadership, teamwork and life.

I know Rich from our work with Sea Education Association (SEA), reading his fine book on the 2009 Vendée Globe, *Race France to France: Leave Antarctica to Starboard* (2012), while here facing the Southern Ocean, the fifth and most violent of the world's oceans. Rich wrote of this mysterious and majestically deadly body of water that it is a "dreaded expanse of gales and cold, albatross, sleet, hail and icebergs, of massive seas unchecked by obstructing land, and all the while a mostly unrescuable distance from any reasonable expectation of help."

As I sit here in the comfort of an armchair, occasionally shifting to keep Antarctica to starboard, all I can say is, "Thank you, Rich." The world is a better place for your vision and courage. Rich's inscription in my copy of his book reads, "Dream your dreams and then go live them." Well, what are we waiting for?

Thursday, December 17, 2015
Buffaloed
It takes many things to build great organizations. Discipline is one of them. That's what makes the Buffalo Bills franchise so painful to watch, especially under Coach Rex Ryan. Just when they need mental toughness and personal accountability the most in game situations, they devolve to foolish, overly aggressive, pseudo-tough-guy penalties time after time after time. It's so predictable that it's boring.

Physical toughness gets you to the NFL; mental toughness and emotional intelligence win championships. Coach Ryan and the Bills should not be so indifferent to sloppy, self-defeating penalties and the dubious characters who constantly commit them. The loyal, long-suffering Buffalo fans deserve better. As a Patriots follower, however, I'm delighted that discipline, mental toughness and accountability do not seem to be priorities for the Bills.

Friday, December 11, 2015
Keep Them Wanting More
Detroit
Orson Welles was the big star of the Oliver Reed-directed film, *The Third Man* (1949), right? His Harry Lime character seemed to overwhelm the role of his long-time collaborator Joseph Cotten, who played the perpetually perplexed Holly Martins. But, guess what? Welles appeared on screen for under 10 minutes. Ten minutes! And he didn't appear at all until halfway through the film.

We spend the whole time anticipating Welles' appearance, eagerly awaiting his every word and deed. There's a lesson here for all of us in knowing how best to manage our presence; in achieving a substantive "less is more" approach that, well, keeps people wanting more. Too many folks in leadership positions talk too much and cheapen the value of what they're saying. Their discomfort with silence or rejection of other people's voices produce volumes of BS that drown out their legitimately important messages.

When it comes to leadership rhetoric, keep it lean and meaningful. Encourage people to listen to you by keeping them wanting more.

Friday, August 21, 2015

Now That's a Leader: Khalid al-Asaad, RIP

The blood-thirsty bastards killed him. The Medieval malignancy known as ISIS butchered Khalid al-Asaad earlier this week for the "crime" of trying to protect the precious antiquities of Palmyra, Syria. The pathetic men who lead this criminal band seem to fear everything, from reminders of the past found in the Palmyra UNESCO World Heritage site to any positive and productive possibilities for the future. Theirs is solely the realm of ignorance and destruction.

For decades, Asaad, dubbed "Mr. Palmyra" by scholars, curated and chronicled Palmyra's many historic treasures. Most recently, as the ISIS plague descended upon his beloved town, he and his colleagues secreted many of Palmyra's most precious artifacts to other parts of the country for safekeeping. Asaad wouldn't tell these gangsters where the goods were hidden, so this gentle, 83-year-old man was tortured, beheaded and defiled.

How far would any one of us go to protect our history and civilization? Khalid al-Asaad never even had to ask that question.

Friday, May 29, 2015

Sepp Blatter Must Go

Sepp Blatter will likely be re-elected today as FIFA president. This is a terrible shame, for Blatter has lorded over a global kleptocracy for many years and it's finally catching up with him. The criminal cases now underway from US legal authorities are only the start of a rolling snowball of such gigantic proportions that even Blatter will not be able to avoid it.

Just wait until the Swiss authorities complete their investigation of FIFA's awarding of the 2018 World Cup to Russia and the 2022 tournament to Qatar. The former is a nation indifferent to "the beautiful game," where players of color compete at their own risk. The latter is a nation that has never fielded a serious World Cup team. What they both share, of course, are bundles of money that President Putin and Emir Al Thani were only too happy to "share" with FIFA officials. Perhaps there is no better proof of Blatter's ultimate demise than being vigorously defended yesterday by a thief of breathtaking arrogance, Putin himself.

Mr. Blatter, the best way to protect FIFA and world football and to prevent some of what is about to justly cascade in your direction is to resign – quickly. Otherwise, your sponsors like Coca Cola, Visa, and McDonalds will inevitably force your hand.

Friday, May 15, 2015
Liked or Respected?
Fast Company tells us there are seven habits likable people share. I've always rejected the ludicrous binarism that has people ask, "Would you rather be liked or respected?" My answer has often been "both," if possible.

Great leaders know how to be firm, tough and decisive, as well as decent human beings. I was often perplexed in my corporate days observing colleagues in power positions who thought that acting like jerks made them seem tougher, somehow. No, it just made them seem like jerks. And people don't want to work for jerks, especially gifted, talented people who have employment options.

That's why some of *Fast Company's* seven habits such as listening, authenticity and relationships to name several, define leadership by any other name.

Sunday, December 7, 2014
Talent Variations
What a joy it was to discover the movie *Copying Beethoven* (2006) last night. The film had me reading more this morning about the moody maestro. It seems that in 1819 Anton Diabelli, an Austrian music publisher, editor and composer, had asked fellow composers to create variations of his rather mundane, unremarkable waltz. Beethoven resisted the invitation, concurring that the piece was hardly adequate. Four years later, however, Beethoven debuted his *Diabelli Variations, Op. 120* as the masterpiece it was. Today's *Wall Street Journal* calls it "one of the two greatest sets of piano variations in classical music history."

We all know that talent is among the essential arbiters of successful performance. And yet some hiring organizations seem unwilling to discern among talent levels. They buy into the view, more or less, that people are interchangeable parts regardless of wide variations in underlying talent and motivations.

Some bosses don't want to hire people smarter than they are, or they suppress their most talented employees because of their own insecurities. Some organizations settle for budget-conscious mediocrity and, sadly, never realize the difference between, say, Diabelli's "cabbage patch," as Beethoven dubbed the original, mediocre waltz, and the subsequent product of real talent.

Saturday, November 29, 2014
Cast Them and Let Go
Peggy Noonan reminded us in today's *Wall Street Journal* what made the late Mike Nichols so effective. The Hollywood and Broadway director and comedy giant, who died this week, once told Noonan that he didn't direct movies; he cast them. Isn't that key to successful leadership? Great leaders are unafraid to hire, develop, reward and promote the best possible talent. They excel at leading people who may be smarter and more creative than they are. They create the conditions for success (vision, strategy, resources and communication) and then get out of the way and let the talent flourish.

Wednesday, November 5, 2014
Don't Forget the People
Raleigh
The passing of Boston's former Mayor Tom Menino reminded me of one of his constant admonitions. Tom would always tell leaders never to lose sight of the people they are privileged to lead. He never did. Too bad that we have so many characters in leadership positions today who think they are bigger than the people they purport to lead. I watched the once-great Mayor Kevin White act this way during his later years in office, to the detriment of his legacy. A vital lesson for any leader is to possess sufficient humility to know that your success starts and ends with the success of your people.

Saturday, October 4, 2014
Drive-By Bullet Points
It used to be said in the Cold War that there were two ways to fail to communicate: say everything, as in the "white noise" of the United States, or say nothing, as in the "black box" of the Soviet Union. Well, India's Prime Minister Narendra Modi combined the two and still said absolutely nothing to us in a speech today at the Council on Foreign Relations.

He excelled at making glancing references to every issue known to humankind, offering superficial, promotional statements about each one, and then moving on to the next glossy item. Call them "drive-by bullet points." Perhaps he felt he owed us nothing, having been feted to a rock-the-house, sellout crowd the night before at Madison Square Garden.

Great leaders score real points embracing the intelligence of their audiences and not trying to spin them with counterproductive, intelligence-insulting bullshit.

Saturday, July 12, 2014
Now, Repeat after Me
Chattanooga
Effective leaders understand that they are communicators in chief. The more unwilling or unable people in leadership positions are to communicate and repeat their organization's vision, objectives, strategies and key developments in a respectful, timely manner, the less effective they will generally be as leaders. Such communications cover not only their spoken and written words but, more important, their behaviors, too. Too many leaders routinely and even wantonly corrupt their communications by saying one thing and doing the opposite.

I recall walking toward a senior officers' meeting with my Fortune 200 CEO-boss many years ago. I urged him to repeat the core-strategy points he had raised with the senior team a month earlier. His response: "Look, I said it once and I don't want to have to say it again." Oh, excuse me, I thought to myself, I forgot for a moment that you are God. This gentleman typified the "world revolves around me" reluctance, if not truculence, some top executives exhibit when it comes to exercising one of their prime leadership responsibilities.

In vivid contrast, Alan Mulally knew he had to change the rotting culture at Ford Motor Company when he assumed the helm in 2006. He understood the essential role of communication – in word and deed – in undertaking that daunting challenge. *The New York Times'* columnist Joe Nocera wrote recently that among Mulally's many gifts was accepting that he owned the responsibility to repeat the message using varied approaches, facts, stories, examples and media, with a commitment to repeat, repeat, repeat. "Once he [Mulally] had his vision for the company formulated," Nocera wrote on June 27th, "he repeated it at the start of every meeting, whether the audience was Ford executives, securities analysts or journalists. Ford had been notorious for changing its business plan every six months. That stopped under Mulally."

Leaders in waiting should take note of Mulally's example. First, develop a clear strategic direction. Next, be unrelenting in repeating your course. After all, it takes people – especially smart people who have to break down their own stubborn, preconceived notions – many exposures to the same message before they actually hear, understand, internalize and act on it.

Monday, January 6, 2014
Now That's a Leader: Barb Stegemann
Barb Stegemann understands dollars and scents. She helps farmers in Afghanistan convert their opium crops into fields of rose, orange-blossom and other essential oils used to craft fine fragrances. In 2010, she purchased $2,000 worth of oils from an Afghan farmer on her personal Visa card, unable to secure a loan from predictably timid banks. With the help of a Toronto perfumer, she then created the 7 Virtues brand. Stegemann is assisting Afghan farmers held captive by the drug trade to find their dignity and earn some small measure of economic freedom. Indeed, her company has invested over $100,000 in Afghanistan to date.

Stegemann's firm has also designed lime tree, bergamot and amber fragrances from Haiti as well as a politically intriguing blend of grapefruit oil from Israel and lime and basil oils from Iran for a scent called Middle East Peace. Her products can be found in Lord & Taylor and Hudson Bay stores and other retailers who know a good brand story when they see it. Stegemann and Afghan traders such as her business partner, Abdullah Arsala, certainly do pass the smell test. They deserve our thanks.

Sunday, August 4, 2013
The Soul of Success
A Gallup survey finds that 70 percent of Americans are not fully engaged in their jobs or worse. No kidding. This owes, in part, to an appalling lack of leadership in organizations. Sure, there's plenty of celebrity, management discipline and professional expertise in business today. Lots of hubris, too.

What's missing, however, are sufficient numbers of men and women able and willing to engage in the long-term, messy business of leading people. Without effective leadership, organizations fail to reach their full potential, atrophy, and even die. Why isn't this obvious truth understood by boards of directors and others who place in positions of power people simply unqualified to articulate a galvanizing vision, build effective teams, open lines of communication, create conditions of trust, spur creativity, lead by example and develop their people personally and professionally?

Thursday, May 9, 2013
The Power and Peril of Personal Brands
How will Manchester United handle the departure of legendary manager Sir Alex Ferguson? Here's a classic case of a personal brand that is so thoroughly conflated with the institutional brand that the individual's departure creates more-than-the-usual difficulties. No matter the global strength of the Old Trafford brand – and this is the wealthiest sports franchise in the world – Sir Alex's news will affect the franchise's appeal, though only in the short term. It will certainly make life difficult for his immediate successor, and it'll get even worse if Ferguson decides to meddle or maintain a high media profile as a new board member. The best breaks are often the cleanest ones.

Monday, April 15, 2013
A Penney for His Thoughts
Miami
Hiring Ron Johnson as JC Penney CEO 17 months ago seemed like a good idea. After all, he was grounded in practical success with Target and rocketed to fame as Apple's retail guru. Now, he's gone. A spectacular bust. Penney is mired in difficulties that hedge fund manager

Bill Ackman, who handpicked Johnson to revitalize the dormant Penney brand, never saw coming.

Johnson's confidence and intelligence were sufficient to the task, no doubt. Was it hubris, however, that had him believing his success at Apple had more to do with his brilliance than with the off-the-charts-popular Apple products he was selling? Undoubtedly. As they say, intellectual intelligence gets you hired and emotional intelligence (or the lack of it) gets you fired. Those unable to discern between the two – and that seems to include Ackman and the Penney board – too often pay the price. The problem is everyone else pays it, too.

It Really Happened: Margaret Thatcher
British Prime Minister Margaret Thatcher had to cancel a trip to Boston to receive an award from the World Affairs Council in the mid-1980s. Months later, a small delegation led by Council Chairman and global figure Charles Francis Adams presented the award to Thatcher in person at the British Embassy in Washington DC. Upon greeting Mr. Adams, Thatcher mischievously looked at all of us and exclaimed to him, "You're Charles Francis Adams? THE Charles Francis Adams?" Scurrying to find her husband she said, "Dennis, take my photo with Charles Francis Adams!"

Of course, Thatcher knew well the identity of her visitors, but cleverly used the moment to break the ice. This despite the fact that John Adams, Mr. Adams' great grandfather many times removed, had a little something to do with ousting the British from America.

Monday, February 25, 2013
Using History Wisely
One of my favorite graduate courses ever was Uses of History taught by the legendary scholar of the US Presidency, Dick Neustadt. *The Financial Times'* columnist Andrew Hill reminded us on February 11th that an organization's history can be used wisely to move it forward. Hill invokes Don Young's new book, *Enterprise Rules: The Foundations of High Achievement – and How to Build on Them* (2013), to underscore the importance of the leader role in detecting signals – especially weak ones that nonetheless convey strong meaning. Having the ability and willingness to discern

historical patterns can help a leader build on history. Hill adds, "People weak in this ability – and therefore unable to learn from history – will never be good strategists and are unlikely to make good leaders in a complex world." Sure, this is Santayana redux. It's also exactly right in a Global 2000 world that remains obsessed with myopic, short-term, finance-above-all-else performance.

Thursday, January 31, 2013
Where's Pink Floyd When You Need Them?
Chicago
Luke Johnson declares in today's *Financial Times* that, "An enterprise must be about more than just the money." In reviewing Whole Foods Co-founder and Co-CEO John Mackey's new book, Johnson buttresses his point by writing that, "Happier and better trained staffs are more productive" and "a constructive corporate culture helps generate innovation and growth." This is what sets places like Zappos and SAS apart, in my view. In Johnson's words, if profits and cash "are the exclusive purpose of an undertaking, then it is less likely to succeed, less likely to endure – and less fun." Go ahead, monetize this!

Sunday, January 20, 2013
Weaving it Together
Longtime Baltimore Orioles' manager Earl Weaver passed away yesterday. Say what you will about him – apparently he could be a real pain – but the man knew how to assemble, motivate and coordinate teams. Key to his success was an uncanny ability to stitch together great, good and average talent – not just All Stars – into high-performing ensemble casts. He knew how to play to people's strengths, minimize their weaknesses and create an outfit where each player's talent could be appreciated and maximized.

Friday, January 18, 2013
Now That's a Leader: Sergio Marchionne
It's easy to criticize the large number of poor leaders today who happen to occupy leadership positions. Let us count the ways, right? Chrysler/ Fiat CEO Sergio Marchionne may be an exception. He told NPR today

that the first thing to disappear in decaying organizations is support for employees and their work environment. It's likely that this is more than rhetoric and that Chrysler's turnaround has much to do with the prime directive of leadership, which means getting the "people thing" right.

Friday, January 4, 2013

Leading Means Communicating

Finding great leaders is an elusive exercise, often because we look for leadership models in all the wrong places, such as politics and sports. Great leaders – those who are effective in real, operational terms on a day-to-day basis – know how to communicate in both word and deed. Alicia Clegg's *Financial Times* piece yesterday points to research on leadership and language at the University of Lausanne.

Key tips for wannabe leader-communicators? Set high but achievable goals, demonstrate authenticity and moral conviction, understand your audience, use metaphor and narrative to paint vivid pictures of the present and future states and ask rhetorical questions. So here's a rhetorical question: Why are so many people in leadership positions so bad at these things?

Tuesday, December 11, 2012

CEO-Speak at Walmart

We just finished a Council on Foreign Relations conference call with Walmart CEO Michael Duke. His remarks and answers to questions were hideous examples of vapid CEO-speak. He's doing himself and his organization a disservice with such rhetorical empty calories. When asked about protestors outside his appearance in NYC's Pratt House right now, he said something about people not accepting the scale and success of others. His comments on sustaining values and corporate culture included talk of a "recognition banquet" featuring a rendition of the company's pep-rally song.

Duke otherwise failed to mention the toll on the Walmart culture and professed values exacted by its Foreign Corrupt Practices Act violations in Brazil, China and India, let alone serious bribery charges in Mexico, until he was asked about them. He spoke with what had to be false pride about "women's economic empowerment," "healthy eating," "consumer transparency," and other issues in which Walmart has a horrible track record. So for leaders out there and those who support them with strategy, training and speechwriting, it's long past time to move beyond the bullshit. People are too smart for it, and they deserve better.

Sunday, August 26, 2012
Now That's a Leader: Bobby McFerrin
Rhinebeck, NY
Vocal improvisation is a useful metaphor for business and even life. I participated in an improvisation camp with Bobby McFerrin and his colleagues here this weekend. Of all the learning or reminders of lessons already learned, two essential points rose to the top. First, listen! Too often, we're planning what we're going to say (or sing) at the expense of truly hearing others. "Understand the sonic landscape before you jump in," McFerrin told us. Join the "conversation" if you have a contribution to make and, otherwise, be quiet. Second, know your stuff. Improv is not just random nonsense. It builds on knowledge, discipline and practice. Ella and Coltrane improvised so well because they were experts in their craft. "You need to know the structure before you can fly," McFerrin associate Joey Blades told me. Just imagine the power of applying these two McFerrin lessons to the infinite number of ridiculous business meetings.

Sunday, November 13, 2011
There's Hope
Minneapolis
The never-ending merry-go-round of horrible leadership examples continues to spin out of control these days. And yet, two shining examples emerge amidst the heinous Penn State scandals, long-overdue departures of George Papandreou and the contemptible Silvio Berlusconi and the foolishness of Herman Cain and most of the field of US Presidential candidates.

Dover Air Force Base mortuary employees James Parsons, Mary Ellen Spera, and Bill Zwicharowski had repeatedly tried to tell their supervisors about gross malpractices at the nation's largest military mortuary. As is too often the case in these situations, their concerns fell on deaf ears. The predictable inclination to protect one's institution and one's career suffocated the revelations of these brave individuals. Somehow, these three persistent professionals went outside the chain of command to express their legitimate concerns and, well, justice has now been served. Unlike Joe Paterno, Mike McQueary and the entire Penn State crowd, these brave three transcended institutional insularity and rose to their leadership moment.

Then there's retired NHL veteran Theo Fleury. He was one of those scrappy guys you hated when he played for opposing teams, but his recent work underscores that this man is a leader. He wrote the best-selling novel *Playing with Fire* last year, in which he spoke to the pain of longstanding sexual abuse at the hands of a criminally deranged coach and that coach's enablers. As the Penn State scandal unfolds for the next year and more, Fleury is an important, informed voice on the subject of sexual abuse in sports. His work with kids recovering from these unspeakable crimes is certainly to be commended.

Folks like Theo Fleury and the Dover whistleblowers should make us proud as we nonetheless feel such profound shame about so many others – insulated and invidious – who dare think of themselves as leaders.

Wednesday, November 10, 2010
So Why Does This Happen?
San Diego
We were pleased once again to attend The College Board's annual Inspiration Awards luncheon last week in Washington DC, honoring three truly excellent schools. We listened to remarkable young people from Green River High School in Virginia Beach, Hogan Preparatory Academy in Kansas City, and Medgar Evers College Prep School in Brooklyn declare their passionate commitment to careers in public service and their desire to run for public office – and even, as several of them said with a twinkle in their eyes, to be President of the United States.

The event was thrilling and inspiring in the extreme. It gave us great hope for our nation's future, a sentiment expressed well by former Congressman Kweisi Mfume (D-MD) who said after the ceremony that, "It's good to know who's on the battlefield and who's coming behind you. Given what we've seen from these young people today, there can be no doubt about our future." Well, maybe.

The problem is the enormous gap between the earnest, honest and public-spirited orientation of these young scholars and leaders – who truly want to rock the world – and what we actually get from the adults who purport to lead us. As I listened to these young people, occasionally with tears of joy in my eyes, I simultaneously conjured images of the "me first" blind ambition of a Mitt Romney, Andrew Cuomo and Carly Fiorina or the utter lunacy of a Sharon Angle, Christine O'Donnell, Joe Miller and, yes, Sarah Palin and asked myself, "What have we wrought?" Or better still, "What have we rot?"

How can we the people help these extraordinary kids avoid the selfishness and rancid divisiveness that personifies public life today? Sure, most of these great young people will ultimately avoid elective office – as so many sane people do, much to our peril – and make amazing contributions in the education, non-profit and business sectors. That's wonderful, but we need more of them running for Congress, governorships and other public offices. The climate that we have created in Washington DC these days – a litter box that's ours to own – will find many of them turning their backs on politics just when we need them most. What a shame. More important, what a peril.

We just assume that youthful idealism, passion and reason will eventually get beaten down by the "system." Somehow the so-called "real world" is supposed to enter stage right and coat these wonderful young people with the thick syrup of doubt, unreasonableness and cynicism. Well, enough already! Hasn't the "system" proven to be so catastrophically broken that it's time we embrace new ways? These kids can show us the way if our politicians would just get out of the way. I'm going to hang onto the memory of these young people during the next two years of bitter, vindictive stalemate and mind-numbing selfishness of this election season.

Tuesday, July 13, 2010
Five Lessons from LeBron
Thanks, LeBron. The utter crassness in how you chose to announce your defection to the Miami Heat has given us a powerful "teachable moment" in matters of decency, communication and leadership. Here are five lessons I'm considering this week:

1. *Don't Blame The Younger Generation:* Too many LeBron critics are ascribing his epic lack of grace, civility, respect and humility to the way it is with young people in today's selfish celebrity age. This is preposterous. Good people of any age know how to do the right thing, or at least know how to find out how to do the right thing. LeBron's boorishness last week owes instead to the fact that he inhabits an imaginary world, which has been exacerbated by bad advice coming from childhood buddies at his LRMR firm. He needs to find a mentor with wisdom, and real fast. If you find yourself blaming young people then, well, you're getting old. The wisdom and grace of so many young people today are a source of great inspiration.

2. *Don't Sink To His Level, Dan Gilbert:* Cleveland Cavaliers majority owner Dan Gilbert took LeBron's bait and absolutely choked on it. His Thursday night diatribe in reaction to LeBron's actions was an embarrassment to his city, his team, his fans and himself. Sure, anyone subjected to what LeBron did to that guy deserves to be outraged. However, he should have had the presence of mind to wait until the morning to react. The lesson for us all is not to send any e-mail or letter in a state of rage. Gilbert will be living that one down for many years to come. Perhaps he, too, has nobody to help him achieve perspective beyond himself. "You bet, boss, it's a great letter. Go get 'em." And wasn't Gilbert the guy who grossly enabled LeBron's behaviors over the past seven years in the first place?

3. *Where Was Pat Riley In All Of This?* Should that source of wisdom and sanity LeBron so clearly needs have been esteemed Miami Heat President Pat Riley? Why not? He can't shrug it off as having been none of his business until LeBron joined his team. What he has to realize is that LeBron's actions discredited Riley and his Heat franchise, too. And even without preventing LeBron from hurting himself with that putrid Thursday night made-for-television non-event, Riley certainly had responsibility for the garish, out-of-control Worldwide Wrestling Entertainment-style introduction of the new "Big Three" in Miami on Friday. For some of us, that spectacle was worse than the Thursday night TV event. What were these people thinking?

4. *Manage Expectations Carefully*: One should learn at an early age to underpromise and overdeliver. Here's the self-anointed "King" who after seven years in the league has yet to win a championship. Here are the biggest of the Big Three ever, also self-proclaimed, who've yet to play a game, let alone win a championship. I'll take Bill Russell and his 11 championships any day of the week.

5. *Stay Out Of It, Jesse Jackson*: You are only heaping embarrassment upon embarrassment and, in the process, making matters worse. Jackson consistently fails to understand that leadership is not the same thing as publicity.

This was likely LeBron's first game as a pro at the old UMass Summer League in 2003.

Tuesday, March 24, 2009

Ambition for the Public Good?

Los Angeles

New York Attorney General Andrew Cuomo is about as politically ambitious as it gets. And that's saying a mouthful today. Oh, alright. It does get worse. Sorry, Newt.

The benefits of some of Cuomo's past, highly publicized interventions into, say, the college financial aid market seem unclear and may have done more harm than good. If his particular brand of publicity-seeking populism can be somehow linked more to the public interest and less to his own ambition, however, it may be just what we need.

Cuomo has now set his sights on AIG. Specifically, he is methodically asking each of the AIG mega-bonus recipients to return their loot and, so far, he is doing so in private. We learned today that nine of the top 10 bonus recipients have coughed up the dough at Cuomo's urging, returning $50 million to the US Treasury. How would you like to be that one holdout?

One conjures in Cuomo an excited Jack Russell Terrier with an unrelenting, biting clutch on the metaphorical cuff of these bonus babies. His example illustrates, however, how certain leadership styles can be just right for the times. Cuomo has found his time and he can now do some real good. Go for it, General.

Sunday, March 22, 2009

This Is When It Counts

Los Angeles

It's easy to be personable, professional and effective in good times, whether in leadership or customer-service settings. The true test comes when times are tough, which means right now in this darkening economy. The problem is that we mortals tend to hunker down in a defensive crouch at moments like this, just when we need to open up wide to people, promises and possibilities.

Richard gets this point. He's a Virgin America gate attendant at Boston's Logan Airport. When he noticed my quandary this morning in being unable to locate a *Sunday New York Times* – it was so early that they had not yet arrived at the gate's lone shop – he approached me, smiled and said, "I can go back through security and get a *Times* for you." This cost his employer nothing, and yet it has earned a loyal customer in me. It's a mindset that just seems so utterly lacking elsewhere among the legacy US carriers. Those employees are every bit as nice and professional as Richard, but there is little in their organizational cultures, climates, training and reward systems to do what Richard did for me. In fact, there are probably company rules prohibiting it.

Now is the time when we must rise above ourselves and not submerge under the weight of fear. Best leadership practices these days include staying on strategy, clarifying matters for our teams when we know the facts, honestly indicating when we do not know the facts and attempting to discover them, utilizing self-awareness (if we have any), practicing situational awareness and listening skills, rewarding our best people, avoiding reckless decision-making in the name of short-term budget-cutting, being visible and available and modeling the behaviors we expect from others. Yes, it's difficult, but that's the job. Nobody said it was easy. Richard certainly gets this point.

Saturday, October 11, 2008

Now That's a Leader: Martti Ahtisaari

The world is a far better place for the likes of former Finnish President Martti Ahtisaari. He is not exactly a household name in the United States, but he should be. I will trade you one Ahtisaari for 10,000 Paris Hiltons. Finally, this global mediator par excellence received his just reward yesterday with the announcement that he has won the Nobel Peace Prize.

Ahtisaari has been on the front lines of peacemaking for decades, from Namibia and South Africa to Banda Aceh and Kosovo. He now heads the Crisis Management Initiative based in Helsinki. This good man reinforces the essential value of discipline, maturity, patience and creativity in the name of peace. These qualities stand out in stark contrast to the boorishness, arrogance, hate-mongering and propensity for needless war found in too many of those who purport to lead us today. There are better ways, and they are available to us in the work and wisdom of Nobel Laureate Martti Ahtisaari.

Wednesday, October 1, 2008

Terry Francona and Servant Leadership

It is generally agreed that the modern servant leadership concept has one founding father, the big thinker, author and consultant Robert K. Greenleaf. Servant-leadership rejects power-centered authoritarianism and underscores the leader role in achieving organizational goals by serving the needs of others.

In his 1970 essay, "The Servant as Leader," Greenleaf wrote of the differences between leader-first and servant-first leaders:

> *"The difference manifests itself in the care taken by the servant-first to make sure that other people's highest priority needs are being served. The best test, and difficult to administer, is: Do those served grow as persons? Do they, while being served, become healthier, wiser, freer, more autonomous, more likely themselves to become servants?"*

Over the years, Ken Blanchard, Stephen Covey, Peter Senge, Margaret Wheatley and others associated with the Greenleaf Center in Westfield, Indiana have refined the concept into a full-fledged movement whose leadership tenets include listening, empathy, self-awareness, humility, teaching and stewardship all coupled with a commitment to helping people grow. Yes, they would have called all of this "sissy" stuff back in my Fortune 200 days.

The Boston Red Sox manager Tito Francona would seem to be the embodiment of servant leadership. He knows it's simply not all about him. Mediocre players such as Francona often become superb managers because they embrace – and maybe they have no choice but to embrace – the precepts of servant leadership. Everything Tito does works to steward organizational resources by letting talent emerge, repair and grow. He maneuvered endlessly this season to orchestrate, integrate and heal a revolving cast of frequently injured players, putting himself in front of the media so that his players could concentrate on baseball. Yes, some managers happily hog the media spotlight – Ozzie Guillen, anyone? – because they crave the attention. With Tito, however, one gets the sense that he does so to serve the needs of his players.

It is clear why Larry Bird, Magic Johnson, Michael Jordan and other superstars find it so difficult to succeed as coaches. They have always been leader-first inclined and likely lack the orientation let alone the disposition to "serve" others. Servant leaders like Tito Francona are superstars in their own right, however, which two World Series rings over the last four seasons surely underscores.

Terry Francona will always have a special place in the hearts of Red Sox fans. Boston celebrated two World Series Championships under Tito's leadership.

Monday, September 29, 2008
Vision: The Credibility Test
Visions must tell us where we are going as organizations and why it matters. At best, visions create vivid, compelling and directionally useful portraits of some future state and our role in achieving or creating it. Well beyond the empty rhetorical calories of "maximizing shareholder value" exist some visions that are truly inspired and inspiring. One such example is the Johnson & Johnson subsidiary DePuy Orthopaedics, whose vision is "restoring the joy of motion for patients around the world." That says it all, elegantly.

Vision statements run into trouble when they do not stretch people far enough or, conversely, when they stretch them too far. There is a fine line between strategically placing one's reach just ahead of one's grasp and simply tilting at windmills with Don Quixote-like impossibility. Here is where wisdom governed by facts makes all the difference.

Let's consider two presidential clarion calls in this context. President John F. Kennedy told a joint session of Congress in 1961, "I believe that this nation should commit itself to achieving the goal, before this decade is out, of landing a man on the moon and returning him safely to Earth." Jim Collins and Jerry Porras called such visions "Big Hairy Audacious Goals (BHAGs)." Yes, these visions are ambitious and daunting, but they also perform essential energizing, mobilizing and focusing roles. Why? Because they are doable. Kennedy and his aides knew that the science supported the possibilities of a safe moon landing and return.

Collins and Porras also emphasize the role that specificity plays in successful visioning. They wrote in 1994 that "Kennedy and his advisors could have gone off into a conference room and drafted something like, 'Let's beef up the space program' or some other such vision statement." The specificity of landing on the moon and returning safely captured the public's imagination and the line added last minute to his speech that the United States would do so "before this decade is out" lent urgency to that specificity.

When President George W. Bush called for a $1.2 billion Hydrogen Fuel Initiative during his 2003 State of the Union speech, he offered America what, in the abstract, was a wonderful vision of our energy future. The President subsequently dropped this vision from speeches and policy formulations because, well, the facts suggested it was not practical or even particularly doable.

Yes, we all like the idea of clean hydrogen-powered automobiles, but as Professor Robert Muller of UC Berkeley said last July on *On Point Radio*, the scientific community was not able to get to the President or his political advisors until after the 2003 announcement. They ultimately told the White House that in liquid form hydrogen has less energy than gasoline by a factor of four. Furthermore, hydrogen is not a fuel source, per se. You have to make hydrogen, and making it costs substantial amounts of money and requires widespread new infrastructure that also costs substantial amounts of money. Plus, it takes coal or gas to manufacture hydrogen, emitting considerable carbon dioxide into the atmosphere. Hydrogen cars may not pollute, but the processes used to create the hydrogen itself are enormously polluting. We will someday arrive at a point when hydrogen cars are possible. They are simply not possible on any meaningful scale right now or anywhere near a 20- or even 30-year horizon.

Visions need to be rooted in the doable and vetted by the people who know how to achieve them. Kennedy's vision animated a specific cause and moved us forward. Bush's vision caught our fancy, but smashed upon the rocks of reality. Kennedy's informed vision was credible. Bush's uninformed vision detracted from his credibility. It's all a question of knowing how far to stretch and whether, in the final analysis, the vision is real enough to encourage anyone to try to stretch that far in the first place.

Saturday, September 6, 2008
Leadership and Humility
Senator John McCain's bravery under unimaginable circumstances as a prisoner of war in Vietnam is so far beyond the call of duty that, well, words could never do it justice. Those of us with relatively easy military careers really have no idea what heroes like McCain endured.

The history of one of the proudest and most distinguished of American naval families – the McCains – is also worthy of our utmost respect. I have met the Senator on several occasions. The first time was in 1992 at Maine's Bath Iron Works for the christening and launching of the guided missile destroyer *USS John S. McCain*, named for his father and grandfather who were both admirals.

That said, Senator McCain's appalling choice of a vice presidential running mate raises severe questions about competence, let alone leadership. Chief among them is humility. One of the most difficult moments during Charlie Gibson's ABC-TV interview with Governor Sarah Palin was when she told him that she "didn't blink" when asked by Senator McCain to be his running mate. Wouldn't and shouldn't any otherwise thinking person blink, take a deep breath, pause for reflection and reach for an extra dose of humility – if they have any – at the prospect of being just one heartbeat away?

Why is it that some people in leadership positions think that we expect them to be superhero cartoon-panel perfect? Are they lacking that much self-awareness to attempt to hide that they are human? Ironically, Sarah Palin scores political points for being below average because, mysteriously, we are somehow supposed to see ourselves in that reflection? And she didn't blink? Excuse me?

Deborah Ancona, Thomas W. Malone, Wanda J. Orlikowski and Peter M. Senge stressed the power of personal humility in the best of our leaders. They wrote in a *Harvard Business Review* article last year, "In Praise of the Incomplete Leader" that, "It's time to end the myth of the complete leader: the flawless person at the top who's got it all figured out." They suggest that leaders can gain credibility, trust and even power when they appropriately reveal the natural and normal condition of human fallibility. I reported to some Fortune 200 CEOs who never got this point and often attempted to appear all-knowing – and failed at it. The deceit must have been exhausting. It also often prevented the executives around these CEOs from offering ideas and insights because, well, the boss already had all the answers. They never blinked, either.

With Senator McCain in Boston the night before 9/11. Yes, we were all much younger then. Here's a true war hero admired by many, though he can never be excused for subjecting us to the likes of Sarah Palin.

It Really Happened: Things Are Looking Up

An executive recruiter had asked me to interview for a senior post at the New York Stock Exchange in the early 1990s. I flew to Manhattan for the day, meeting with Chairman and CEO William Donaldson, President Dick Grasso and others. The top Human Resources guy warned me prior to my session with Grasso that the president would not be making much eye contact with me since he'd be frequently looking over my shoulder to monitor trading. After all, aren't markets more important than people? Any candidate for an Exchange vice presidency couldn't possibly be worth 30 minutes of his uninterrupted time, right?

I had a disjointed and utterly meaningless meeting with Grasso, and I subsequently informed the HR guy that the session was a waste of my time and his. I asked him why we didn't meet when the markets were closed if Grasso's OCD wouldn't otherwise let him engage in civilized behavior. I was still pretty young, but was already developing the resolve not to work with assholes. I have not always succeeded in this quest. What a pity that society too often confuses arrogant, one-dimensional jerks with being tough guys or passionate geniuses. There's nothing tough or genius about bad manners, ignorance and the lack of productivity.

Tuesday, March 18, 2008
Civilized Workplaces
Orlando

The world is filled with them. In turn, they fill the air with the noxious odor of maniacal and even deranged arrogance. Too many of us have worked for one or more of these absurd people in our careers, witnessing the true costs of their brutal pathologies and wondering why the boss and the board fail to recognize the grenade that will soon blow up in their faces. It almost always does.

This sentiment comes after so many are now dealing with the shrapnel of New York Governor Eliot Spitzer's implosion. Such self-absorbed people almost always destroy themselves but, tragically, their demise too often comes after much needless damage has been done to good people and organizations as well. Just read David Margolick's troubling article in January's *Vanity Fair* about Spitzer's arrogance, rage, selfishness and abject disdain for others, and you would think he was writing about Spitzer now, after his fall from grace and not before his abrupt resignation. So many people made past-tense references to Spitzer in the article because only one year into his four-year run, nobody wanted to work for or with him.

Why? Well, for starters, he certainly seems to fit Stanford Professor Bob Sutton's definition of *asshole*. And a pretty big one at that! As reluctant as I am to use that term in this context, it is found in the title of Sutton's book, *The No Asshole Rule: Building a Civilized Workplace and Surviving One That Isn't* (2007). Sutton's is a wake-up call for employers to understand the difference between being tough, firm and decisive and just being a garden-variety "kiss-up, kick-down" asshole. Some friction and creative tension in organizations is useful, if properly channeled. However, Sutton tells us that true assholes care little about balancing such energies in the workplace. Instead, he says people are certifiable assholes if they meet two primary criteria: 1) making others feel oppressed, humiliated, excluded and de-energized, and 2) inflicting their pain on those less powerful than themselves.

Sutton reminds us of some the very best here, such as the professional downsizer "Chainsaw" Al Dunlap. He compares them to tough, driven leaders like Intel's Andy Grove and Costco's James Sinegal, who endure over the long term and whose organizations thrive because they mercifully emerged from childhood without the need to destroy others to protect their own fragile egos.

Of course, the real test always comes when these jerks *appear* to be driving effective performance, often coated in tough talk. Here is where those distanced from the asshole, such as board members, too often protect the status quo to derive short-term gains only to find several years later an organization fearful of creativity, innovation and collaboration and a workforce shorn of morale and depleted of its best talent. Sutton quotes Google's Shona Brown, whose company "acts on its 'Don't be evil' motto by making Google a place where it simply isn't efficient to act like an asshole." Somehow, I doubt that this is actually the case at Google. Nonetheless, the many costs of abuse must be understood and even quantified in operational and financial terms in the form of inefficiency and ineffectiveness which, by the way, assholes are typically very good at hiding. By the way, Sutton calls these costs "asshole taxes." I've called them in accounting terms the "costs of abuse."

Sutton reminds us that assholes don't always do more harm than good. Calculated sound and fury has its time and place. Sutton says General Patton and Bobby Knight seem to fit the asshole definition but, on balance, they achieved conditions in which, well, people "worked their asses off" for them. Maybe he has a point, albeit he is reluctant to fully embrace it. Still, most of us would decline entering into such megalomaniacal manipulation. We'll take General Omar Bradley or Duke's Coach K anytime.

Wednesday, November 28, 2007
The Art of War
San Francisco
A quick reread of *The Art of War* (5th Century BC) can be worthwhile. As I look forward to a performance of Verdi's *Macbeth* tonight at the War Memorial here, I took time today to reread the Sun Tzu classic. I was reminded that it is as much a book about peace as it is about war. The armchair politician-warriors who seem so ready to swagger our nation into needless, reckless wars enjoy making casual references to Sun Tzu. They somehow miss the point, however, that the author was actually speaking to the hollowness of aggression. Ah, the paradox of Taoist psychology.

Sun Tzu's chapter on Strategic Assessments offers five tools for measuring success in war and peace, each of them with actual and metaphorical value: 1) the way, 2) the weather, 3) the terrain, 4) the leadership, and 5) discipline. Of course, it is the inspiring, aspiring vision found in "the way" that is too often missing from most organizational pursuits these days. With the appropriate "way" in place, Sun Tzu tells us that the people "will share life and share death without fear of danger." It would be nice.

It Really Happened: Ninoy Aquino
The Benazir Bhutto assassination attempt reminds me of the tragic killing of Ninoy Aquino in 1983. I was just getting involved in The World Affairs Council of Boston at the time, which I was later privileged to lead, and was invited to a small farewell dinner for Ninoy Aquino.

Ninoy was embarking on a courageous return to Manila to oppose the brutal regime of Philippine President and long-time American puppet Ferdinand Marcos. My mother and I sat with the Aquinos and found Ninoy to be a warm and wonderful person; one of those people who sincerely blends confidence with humility. We all hugged Ninoy and wished him well upon his departure that night, only to watch with horror days later his airport assassination at the hands of Marcos' thugs. I remember sharing a good cry with my mother over the telephone.

Friday, August 3, 2007
When Will We Learn?
Two DePaul University professors will release a study at this weekend's American Management Association meeting showing a serious disconnect between what businesses and students say they need from MBA programs.

America is finally waking up to the staggering costs associated with people in leadership positions who can't lead, communicate or conduct themselves in a dignified, principled manner. The ashtray-hurling John Bolton comes to mind, as do "the smartest guys in the room" at Enron. Yet, MBA students say they have little use for these so-called "soft skills." In the study, students say soft skills won't get them jobs in a market that demands ever-increasing technical and financial prowess.

Where did this notion come from that leadership, communication, listening, synthesizing and other so-called people skills are soft? There is nothing soft about them! In fact, it is relatively easy to master technical subjects, especially disciplines without much human interaction. Balance sheets and computer programs rarely talk back. Learning to respect and be respected, to trust and be trusted, however, are the hardest skills known to humankind. They are almost always the root of leadership, management, business and political problems that no amount of venture capital, engineering brainpower, creative bookkeeping or real estate flipping will ever solve.

If these technical skills are to be called "hard," then the human skills so desperately needed today should be called "harder." Much harder. That's it; let's call them the "hard" skills and the "even harder skills." Then, it won't be so easy to discount them by calling them "soft."

Language really matters when framing issues. I recall a Fortune 200 CEO reprimanding a top executive for bringing the word "intuition" into a conversation. He didn't like the word intuition because it was not serious in his mind and, if truth be told, it was also too soft and feminine for him. He said there was no room for "intuition" in any business conversation. Can you imagine? Yet this never stopped him from invoking his own "gut feeling" in conversations. Just the sound of the word "gut" gives it the requisite masculinity but, of course, says most of the same things as intuition. Remember, too, Joe Biden's apocryphal question to President Bush, "What if you're wrong about Iraq?" The President told Biden he knew he was right because he had a "gut feeling."

Saturday, April 28, 2007
Two of the Best and Brightest
It has taken me several days to reflect on the passing of David Halberstam. Few historians and journalists – few people, really – have been as insightful, inspirational and dignified as this good man. I can't claim to have known him, although meeting him, exchanging small talk and hearing him speak over the years served as reminder that eloquence, wisdom and dignity can and must remain part of speaking truth to power. Some people talk tough and perform weakly. Halberstam was a gentleman whose journalism, analysis and bravery was authentically tough.

Halberstam joined with Neil Sheehan, Peter Arnett, Malcolm Brown and others to expose the many deceptions and hypocrisies that were the hallmark of the War in Vietnam. Where are their likes today? Perhaps only the good folks at Knight-Ridder/McClatchy who, over the years, have been a powerful voice of real journalism in a media chorus that hardly questioned the basis for war in Iraq and, as was the case with *The New York Times'* Judith Miller, actually became complicit in its mindless run-up. Imagine the lessons not learned from David Halberstam.

One must also note the passing of the extraordinary cellist Mstislav Rostropovich. "Slava" fought relentlessly for human rights, freedom of speech and artistic expression at home in the Soviet Union and Russia and from his many outposts around the world. In the week that Boris Yeltsin also died, it's important to remember that Rostropovich rushed to his aid to resist the 1991 communist coup in Moscow. Those were perilous moments and Slava put his personal capital to work at time of great personal risk.

In his book, *Where Have All The Leaders Gone?* (2007), Lee Iacocca excoriates the Bush Administration, Congress and scandal-plagued CEOs. Sure, those are pretty easy pickings, since leadership in those circles is perilously below abysmal. Yet, we must continue to remind ourselves of the greatness found in people like Halberstam and Rostropovich and, with some recent posts here, General Tony Zinni, Dr. Liviu Librescu and even good-old Kurt Vonnegut. Great leaders are living and dying among us. You just have to look in the right places.

Thursday, April 19, 2007
Now That's a Leader: General Tony Zinni
General Anthony Zinni is a truly great American. Whether as a Marine, diplomat or author, Zinni personifies the tough-minded, balanced and respectful characteristics of true leadership. In his new book, *The Battle for Peace: A Frontline Vision of America's Power and Purpose* (2006), Zinni says that the US government is broken and that, for the next President, it will be time for America to "pull up its socks" and lead with judgment and wisdom.

Zinni rightly brandishes the "chicken hawks" in our government who have never served in uniform yet are so willing to send our young men and women into war in pursuit of their own ideological and commercial wet dreams. He told *On Point Radio's* Jane Clayson yesterday that these neocons had first "to earn the right to swagger." He correctly calls for a universal national service requirement for our young people to honor the latent values of patriotism and citizenship that have been so abused by politicians and ideologues.

There was a time when citizenship was taught in our schools and homes. It mattered. I recently found a 1938 letter from the Master of the Barnes School in East Boston to my maternal grandfather. It praised my mother for earning an A in every subject, but Master Chester Wilbar singled out the importance of her A in Good Citizenship. In recent years, there has been a tendency to discount and even ridicule notions of citizenship, effort and conduct. However, doesn't so much of what plagues us these days come right back to our leaders' inability or unwillingness to play well with others or to put country ahead of self? Master Wilbar had that right in 1938 and General Zinni has it right today. I'd follow him anywhere.

Monday, March 19, 2007
The Biology of Leadership
Washington DC
Business Week's review of top undergraduate business programs lauded Cornell, but added that students must, "strangely enough, take a full year of biology." Sorry editors, but there is nothing strange about it. Biology is to an understanding of leadership in the 21st Century as psychology was in the 20th Century. As leaders and followers, we are all products of our biochemistry, physiology and neural anatomy in ways that we are only now starting to fathom.

The Chilean biologists Humberto Maturana and Francisco Varela were among the first to introduce biology to the social sciences, especially in the biologic causality of emotion, cognition and behavior. Varela argued that human cognition and consciousness can only be understood in terms of the enactive structures in which they arise, chiefly the body and the physical world surrounding it. Varela co-authored *The Embodied Mind* (1991) with Evan Thompson and Eleanor Rosch and greatly advanced this mind-body thesis. Jon Kabat-Zinn's extraordinary work at the UMass Medical School to bring mindfulness into the mainstream of medicine and management through stress and anxiety reduction represents just the start of what will someday be a commonplace understanding of the links between, say, brain chemistry and impulsive, indifferent or reckless leadership.

The field of "change blindness" is one case in point. The Visual Cognition Lab at the University of Illinois does terrific work showing how and why people can't or won't see the obvious or see very different things in a common object or circumstance. The people at Koanetic Consulting use a simple "scotoma" or "blind spot" test to make a related point. They show how the brain fills in what it "thinks" it sees where, indeed, that particular object or color simply does not exist in the first place. Is it any wonder that multiple witnesses of the same crime often report seeing very different things?

So, *Business Week*, it is all about biology and Cornell's undergraduates could be much better equipped as leaders and followers because of such a "strange" curriculum.

Saturday, March 3, 2007
All That Jazz
St. Helena, CA

Listening to the Miles Davis classic *Kind of Blue* (1959) instantly evokes the man's genius. Miles' gift for quiet, sonorous "cool jazz" emerged in stark contrast to the frenzy of bebop and post-bop jazz forms in the 1950s and '60s. Yet, thinking about Miles always raises interesting questions about, well, working with jerks.

Miles could be a world-class jerk, as many who knew him have said and written. In fact, his sometimes miserable treatment of collaborators, sidemen and audiences wrapped in an almost mystical inaccessibility was branded as part of his creative persona. But was it really necessary? And do singular creative gifts merely provide some geniuses with an excuse to act like sociopaths?

Hey, we've all worked with sociopaths, right? And they're often the ones without any particular genius, too. It seems that each of us is free to decide whether we will carry the heavy baggage of a damaged boss or colleague. Maybe it's worth a short ride to conspire with the greatness of a Miles Davis. After all, John Coltrane, Cannonball Adderley and Bill Evans saw in Miles something that made it all worthwhile. *Kind of Blue* was just one astonishing result.

Music is sometimes used by thinkers as a metaphor for leadership and organizations. My thinking about the jazz metaphor was heavily influenced in the early 1990s by Albert Murray and Stanley Crouch. NYU's Richard Sennett, a renowned sociologist and first-class cellist, has also written marvelously about classical and jazz metaphors as tools for understanding societies. The hierarchical and linear nature of symphonic orchestration contrasts in leadership and organizational terms with improvisational and even nonlinear jazz forms. Indeed, many corporations embrace symphonic stricture while nonetheless competing in the latter, non-linear world, sometimes to their own detriment.

I recently came across Mary Jo Hatch's 1999 article in the journal *Organization Studies* in which she set about "exploring the empty spaces of organizing." A professor at the University of Virginia, Hatch is a wonderful scholar for, among many reasons, her ability to write well and present creatively. She uses Richard Rorty's 1989 model of metaphoric redescription to help us think of organizational cultures in jazz terms in order to break with old vocabularies and derive new understanding. In doing so, she reminds us just how readily the ambiguous, emotional and temporal aspects of jazz performance extend to working life in today's modern organization.

Monday, January 29, 2007
Manny, We Hardly Knew Ye
Manuel Rivera's stunning and embarrassing decision to withdraw his appointment as Boston's next school superintendent underscores a growing and little understood problem with senior executive hirings. Call it "the gap." There was an unacceptably long 10-month period between his selection and planned starting date. Furthermore, his selection was announced before his contract was even negotiated. Yes, it's a political process, but shouldn't the standards of excellence apply to public selections, too?

Given the cauldron that is Boston politics, 10 months is too great a gap. There is too much time for "buyer's remorse" to set in and, with it, too great an opportunity for executives to reconsider. As Donald Rumsfeld infamously reminded us, "Stuff happens!" And it certainly did in this case.

This gap between an appointment and the first day on the job also finds newly named CEOs and college presidents saying and doing things, often unaware of their new organization's history and culture, that come back to haunt them. Most executives would likely say their new job starts when they arrive. Dead wrong. Their job actually starts when their appointment is announced. That's when employees start the Google searches on their new boss fueled by gossip and media accounts.

Internal and external audiences start forming their opinions of the new leader at that moment; they don't wait for the boss to find his or her new office. During the "neither here nor there" void of finishing one job and starting another, leaders make cameo appearances at the new institution, engage in e-mail conversations, fall prey to the political agendas of employees at the new place, and start answering questions about vision, values and strategy. Whether they like it or not, these new bosses are creating their image, taking sides and making back-door decisions many months before they start their new job.

Having said this, awareness of these "gap" issues is painfully limited. Newly appointed leaders no longer have the luxury of waiting to start their new job. That job commences immediately and these CEOs and college presidents sorely need a plan to help them navigate such rocky shoals. That plan should start with a commitment to closing the gap between selection and the start of their new job.

It Really Happened: Mikhail Gorbachev

Mikhail Gorbachev met with a handful of us on the executive management team at my Fortune 100 employer in 1998, accompanied by his interpreter. Over lunch, the President reminisced about his relationship with Aleksei Kosygin. I had just read a passage in Gorbachev's book, *Memoirs* (1996), the night before in which he discussed Kosygin, the Stalin-era survivor who became Soviet Premier in the 1960s and '70s. I mentioned this passage to the President, who beamed with pride when he saw his book in my hand. Through his interpreter, he asked me to read it to the group. So, there I was, reading Gorbachev's memoirs to Gorbachev as he listened intently to his account of younger days.

Wednesday, November 1, 2006
Board Stiff

Maybe, just maybe, the American Red Cross is starting to understand the dilemma of underperforming boards. Red Cross board governance has been a particularly sore subject in the aftermath of 9/11 and Katrina failures. Yesterday, however, the Red Cross announced substantial governance changes including reducing its board from 50 to 20 members by 2012. Fiduciary boards over 20 (or so) people are generally too large, unwieldy, and seem to create an environment where members are not really expected to roll up their sleeves and get to work.

Board members with money, well-known names, and organizational titles are essential, of course. However, non-profit boards must add to this business-as-usual approach by also giving thought to the balance and diversity of experience, creativity, opinions and skills needed to engage in what Harvard professor Richard Chait calls "generative thinking."

Chait tells us that non-profit boards display three forms of governance: fiduciary, strategic and generative. Most boards play useful fiduciary roles. According to Chait, however, boards must also engage strategically and, at their best, in truly generative ways by providing lucid, insightful and creative wisdom about the organization's place and opportunity in the world.

Tuesday, January 3, 2006
Reading Really Is Fundamental
Isn't it time we start demanding the leaders we need and not ones we seem destined to deserve? Intellectual curiosity and a passion for reading and listening are central to effective leadership. Why then do we continue to put people in leadership positions who epitomize anti-intellectualism and seem to revel in their unwillingness to read, learn and grow?

"I don't think anyone anticipated the breach of the levees," President Bush said recently about the consequences of Hurricane Katrina. Excuse me, Mr. President? Many thousands of people knew the risks posed by the levees from the *Times Picayune* and other sources. Check out the October 2001 issue of *Scientific America* entitled "Drowning New Orleans," which absolutely foreshadowed current events. Here's the blurb: "This 10-page feature article by S.A. Contributing Editor Mark Fischetti describes the causes of the ever-increasing vulnerability of New Orleans to a major hurricane." The article summary in the table of contents reads as follows: "A major hurricane could swamp the city under 20 feet of water, killing thousands."

Say what you will about President Clinton, but his voracious intellectual curiosity is an essential leadership requirement. Otherwise, we have people in office merely play-acting as leaders with consequences that can be damaging in the extreme. President Bush likes to play the anti-intellectual "good old boy." He really loved saying, "I don't do nuance." Without nuance, however, the world is reduced to simplistic comic-book notions of good and evil. The Middle East might as well be called the "Middle Nuance" and the President's startling ignorance of that region's history has plunged us into an abyss from which we will not recover in my lifetime.

Friday, May 27, 2005
The Cost of Abuse
Boston Business Journal

The controversy over John Bolton's confirmation as United Nations Ambassador reveals a tragic blind spot in our understanding of leadership. Politicians, boards of directors and others who appoint senior executives to public and private leadership positions too often equate bluster and bombast with true effectiveness. They fall victim to believing that crude, uninspiring and repugnant interpersonal behaviors are simply part of being tough. They couldn't be more wrong.

The tendency among some boards of directors and executive search firms to confuse bravado with bravura can catapult into leadership positions people for whom and with whom nobody wants to work. The "take no prisoners," fear-based leadership style may make for great storytelling – and it may even produce some short-term results, too – but at what cost?

How much scorched earth in the form of wasted opportunities, productivity losses, employee defections, retraining costs and outright errors must be sacrificed at the altar of one individual's hubris, insecurities or disregard for quaint notions of dignity, professionalism and manners?

Isn't it time to separate the justifiable search for leaders who are tough, firm, decisive, and driven from would-be leaders who are excessively difficult and draining of an organization's morale, productivity and creative energy? True leaders understand that they are merely temporary stewards of an enterprise, a vision or a public trust.

How many of us have seen organizations wither on the vine of out-of-control egos who fail to understand that it's not about them. Of course, that is until the board of directors or others in authority finally realize that these individuals are actually the ones impeding long-term progress.

Sunday, November 10, 2002
Hold the Phone
The Boston Globe

Emperor Nero chose the wrong instrument. Instead of fiddling around, the doomed chief executive of Rome Inc. should have returned his phone calls.

Absurd, you say? Of course, but hardly more ridiculous than executives who routinely damage their brands by ignoring their phone calls, letters and email messages.

Character is a core competency today. After all, didn't Enron stress a commitment to four values – communication, respect, integrity, and excellence – in its last annual report? Didn't ImClone tell shareholders in its 2001 annual report, "We want to ensure you that management will endeavor to justify your confidence"? And didn't the former Tyco chief executive once write to shareholders, "I promise that we will stay focused on the business goals that matter most"? So how can customers, shareholders, and employees assess management character? Try sending a letter.

Poet Robert Browning wrote, "We find great things are made of little things." Small behaviors really can predict larger ones. That's why coaches, conductors, and commanders alike all sweat the details. Chief executives who are indifferent to their calls and mail will probably have equally indifferent customer service departments. That's why great organizations will be increasingly led by executives who balance hunger with humility in their roles as temporary brand stewards.

This point hit home recently when the general manager of The Balsams Resort returned my call within three hours. When I expressed gratitude for his courtesy, he said, "We return calls. That's The Balsams brand." He understands his duty to personify the Balsams brand in both words and deeds. Just consider the alternative. Let's assume a typical Fortune 500 chief executive receives 50 letters, e-mails, and calls each weekday. If that chief executive ignores 40 items every day, she or he has created more than 10,000 brand-damaging impressions in one year.

Jack Welch always told GE executives to put the market first. Several years ago I received a response letter from the former GE CEO. No doubt it was prepared by Welch's handlers, but the letter was prompt and certainly seemed personal. Welch's reputation has been cut down to size recently, but at least he had front-office systems in place to protect the GE and Jack Welch brands.

So, why do some executives fail to answer the call? First, consolidations have created enormous and unwieldy organizations that are disengaging from the market. The sheer size of the organizations also insulates them from the consequences of self-inflicted brand erosion, at least in the short term. Size matters, of course, but not when it becomes dysfunctional. Just look at the popularity of airlines such as JetBlue and banks such as Port Financial. They're building great brands by balancing the benefits of size with the accessibility and agility needed to satisfy customers.

So what's a CEO to do? Being busy is certainly no excuse. President Bush seems busy these days, but the White House answers his mail. The best executives use response management systems to save them time and aggravation. Talking about values is easy; living them is difficult. The gap between talk and action defines effective leadership and helps measure an organization's character. Don't believe me? Try calling or writing some top executives, and see who calls back.

Sunday, June 30, 2002
A Failure to Communicate
The Boston Herald

What's in a word? Plenty, especially if it's the "L" word. The word "leader" is about as loaded as a drunken sailor, and just as unpredictable.

That's because our culture automatically confers the title "leader" on anyone in charge. We routinely impose leadership expectations on our elected officials and the engineers, lawyers and financial executives who run our businesses. Are they leaders? Well yes, some of them are outstanding leaders.

However, success as a politician, lawyer, or financier does not translate easily into success as a leader. What's worse, we treat business, sports and show-business celebrities as leaders simply because they're in the news. Regrettably, we're rarely exposed to the true leadership found every day in community service, education, health care, art, small business and military circles. In recent years, the leadership cart has been well behind the celebrity horse and, well, the view has been pretty messy. We have to hope that times are changing.

I bet the CEOs of Enron, Global Crossing, ImClone, Rite Aid, Tyco and WorldCom were all praised in recent years as great leaders. So, too, the Catholic Church hierarchy has demonstrated that leadership must be more than the product of rising to the top.

Leadership means giving voice to an organization's values and vision – personally and with complete integrity. Great leaders instinctively understand this link between leadership and communication. Indeed, the two words are synonymous in so many ways. Great leaders embrace communication – in substance and symbolism – as the only means to give voice to their vision. Organizations get stuck in neutral or worse when their top officials choose not to personify leadership in an unrelenting campaign of communicating and modeling their values, vision and expected behaviors.

There's one problem. Managers traditionally rise to the top through narrower confines of expertise, such as finance or even religious doctrine. Then, suddenly, they are thrust into a higher calling where communicating with people openly and consistently matters far more than managing budgets, blueprints or buildings. This makes some would-be leaders uncomfortable, especially as they are required to lead increasingly diverse people who may not look, think or act like them.

There are five warning signs when executives fail to lead by communicating. Regrettably, the Catholic Church hierarchy today illustrates them all. First, communication is always diminished by arrogant, autocratic, "my way or the highway" approaches. The church serves as a textbook example of how communication fails when organizations turn a deaf ear to those they lead.

A colleague once said to me that we'd survey our employees over his "dead body." His justification? "We'll just have to deal with their complaints," he said. Is it any wonder that Bernard Cardinal Law has wanted to thwart formation of parish councils? Perhaps he's not interested in what some executives label that "touchy-feely stuff."

Next, the church has a pathological need for secrecy and control. To the contrary, the best executives understand that releasing some power to employees, customers or even parishioners in an ongoing, two-way dialogue is the hallmark of successful leadership. Besides, great leaders know that secrets of public consequence do not remain secret for long in today's media-saturated culture.

Then there's the question of size. The church is an extreme example of what some global corporations have become today – too big, distracted and defensive to sustain meaningful, timely communication to customers, employees or investors. Successful leaders of large organizations understand this disadvantage. Sure, they have all the technology and staff that money can buy. However, they know that most of their waking hours must be spent communicating their vision – up close and personal. Indeed, the more time officials in large organizations spend managing things, the less successful they'll be at leading people.

And that's the next warning sign. When bosses say they're too busy to communicate, or do so only episodically, they're really saying they're too busy to lead. President Franklin D. Roosevelt, Mahatma Gandhi, the Rev. Martin Luther King Jr., Winston Churchill, and Nelson Mandela were all pretty busy, but they never missed an opportunity to communicate and personify their vision. In business, the just-retired CEO of General Electric, Jack Welch, and Southwest Airlines' Herb Kelleher found the time, as does eBay's Meg Whitman today.

Autocracy, secrecy, control, size, and time all work against effective leadership. But the problem cuts even deeper. Church leaders actually seem to fear communicating. A recent exchange on NPR's *Diane Rehm Show* said it all. Baltimore's Cardinal Keeler started his response to a question about possible pedophilia cases in his diocese with, "Well, Diane, we've gone past the time that has been allocated for me to speak with you, and something else is waiting for my attention." Cardinal, that's Baltimore, right, not Dodge City?

Top officials lose their leadership voice when they fear discussing subjects that make them uncomfortable. The church is at a clear disadvantage here, since it has declared many subjects off-limits. Remember the Reagan administration's handling of the AIDS crisis? An administration that brilliantly helped talk down the Berlin Wall had a Keeler moment, unable for years to muster the vocabulary needed to address a deadly epidemic. This dereliction of duty is being repeated right now in southern Africa, where leaders are afraid to talk about their own AIDS crisis, let alone deal with it.

Remember the line from *Cool Hand Luke* (1967) when the prisoner (Paul Newman) is knocked to the ground? "What we have here is failure to communicate." Well, what we truly have in failing to communicate is a more destructive failure to lead. The church provides a powerful and painful lesson.

Mass leadership requires mass communication, and effective communication means rising above the arrogance, secrecy, and fear that can otherwise disable leadership.

CHAPTER 2

WISDOM & JUDGMENT

Friday, January 27, 2017

This Is To Be Our "Moon Shot" - Really?

Border walls are generally a sign of fear, weakness, insecurity and even paranoia, especially unnecessary walls and particularly in modern times. Just ask the Soviet Union.

Illegal immigration across our Mexican border is a problem, for sure, but most illegal immigrants in this country enter via airports and overstay their visas. It won't be easy to erect walls around our airports. In the larger scheme of things, illegal immigration across the Mexican border has declined substantially over recent decades. Furthermore, I wouldn't place illegal immigration across the Mexican border among the Top 50 challenges facing our great nation.

Successful leaders know how to define and present real challenges and rally us to the cause as part of our shared national interests, as FDR did in mobilizing us to defeat Fascism in Europe or even as President Reagan did in imploring Mr. Gorbachev to "tear down this wall." Sane, effective leaders don't wallow in the bile of negativity or manufacture it in mendacious ways to salve their personal insecurities. Instead, they inspire us to reach for collective greatness, as JFK did in compelling us to the Moon.

Two of the great "Moon Shots" of our time remain curing cancer and developing the trillion-dollar, new-energy market. Only three nations are positioned for global leadership in the clean energy and environmental remediation sectors – China, Germany and the US We already gave China the lead in shaping Asian trade rules by abandoning the TPP this week, instead of renegotiating it. By denying climate change and continuing to sissy-fy clean energy – and I'm not an anti-oil-and-gas person – the US is now also working overtime to give China the lead in the lucrative, jobs-producing new-energy sector, which Beijing is doing with great abandon.

Sure, the smog-coated state of China's cities finally forced its hand on the need for new-energy alternatives. Beijing now unequivocally gets it, however, and intends to dominate these markets. Never mind about Putin, the 2016 US Presidential election is for China's President Xi Jinping the gift that keeps giving. Not even Xi could have imagined the US would be this stupid to retreat from clean energy and invest, instead, in a needless wall that won't work anyway.

A complete 2,000-mile wall will never be erected. Nor should it, at $7.4 million per mile. So that's $10 billion for the 1,300 miles of border without any fencing right now, assuming that the White House does not want to replace the existing 700 miles of fencing with concrete. A 2,000-mile wall would check in at $15 billion. But since when have estimates of this nature been even remotely accurate? A $15 billion price tag will easily become $30-$40 billion, and that's without considering the massive opportunity costs and ongoing operating expenses, too.

Imagine the positive impact of that kind of money on real challenges such as cancer and authentic opportunities such as new-energy markets. Besides, what will happen when immigrants tunnel under or propel themselves over the wall? Is the plan to station sentries every 100 yards with East German-style orders to kill?

We're about to waste a great deal of time and money on this inane and insane idea, diverting our focus from truly pressing matters such as China, Russia, Syria and jobs. This Great Wall of Gorgan is a metaphor for so much that is wrong right now. It's all so profoundly sad.

Tuesday, July 28, 2015
What a Shame
Our beloved Boston has well-deserved egg on its face with news yesterday that the city has withdrawn its 2024 Olympics bid. There was an inevitability about this outcome, given the disastrous, mind-numbing

combination of unbridled ego, extreme naïveté, sloppy management and wholesale indifference among the small band of self-appointed czars who delivered this Games bid to us virtually stillborn.

Boston should have competed for the Pan Am Games or World University Games first. Each of these daunting exercises would have taught us many things – including how painfully complex and expensive these quests have become – while building the necessary credibility and coalitions.

Instead, Boston and the USOC are laughingstocks globally and the former in an untenable position to compete again for an Olympic Games, at least in my lifetime. If there ever is a next time, fellas, avoid making this a private junta among a handful of guys in over their heads and let some adults run the show.

Wednesday, December 31, 2014
So Suh Me
It would be hard to find a bigger jerk in professional sports than the Detroit Lions' Ndamukong Suh, at least on the field. Suh illustrates why undisciplined teams lose more than they win. The Jets and Raiders come to mind. His suspension in the Lions' upcoming playoff game may cost his team dearly, pending his appeal. Suh's dirty, unthinking tactics are as reckless and selfish as they are predictable.

Lions' owner William Clay Ford, this is your team and your legacy. This is a reflection of your values. There should be no next time for this fool. It's time to fire Ndamukong Suh and reassert the importance of human decency – even in pro football.

Sunday, October 11, 2015
Now That's a Leader: Chef Chad Hauser
Dallas
I'm blessed to travel regularly with my son, Zack. We've shared many wonderful adventures together. Thanks to Zack, meeting Chef Chad Hauser last night in Dallas was one of them. At his Cafe Momentum, Chef Chad provides a positive, productive environment in which at-risk youth who have spent time in juvenile detention work and receive culinary, business and life-skills training as well as the mentorship and expectations of

accountability they need. We spoke at length with Chef Chad and some of his "interns," leaving Cafe Momentum deeply inspired and hopeful that leaders like Chad Hauser receive the support they need in this otherwise celebrity-soaked, greed-stained world. As we leave this morning to see the Patriots play the Cowboys inside Jerry Jones' Death Star, I'm again reminded that we're looking for leaders in all the wrong places. You may find them at the griddle instead of on the gridiron.

My son Zack (right) with Chef-Owner Chad Hauser at Cafe Momentum in Dallas.

Thursday, May 14, 2015
Huffing and Puffing
We at the Council on Foreign Relations had a conference call with Senator Marco Rubio yesterday. Ever the centrist, I was thinking I might be pleasantly surprised by a few of Rubio's foreign policy insights. I certainly don't agree with him on many domestic issues. This guy could well be President of the United States someday, however, so what he says matters. Please, I'm not inviting the predictable partisan ranting here by either of the two wings. My point is that with this audience, at least, Rubio had an opportunity to move momentarily away from the

customary red-meat-tossing, faux-machismo and Manichaean nonsense and speak in thoughtful, even-handed, and, yes, presidential terms to the vast majority of us in the middle. He failed to do so.

Sure, I agreed with him on some matters. But, predictably, every foreign policy and national security challenge he identified – what he generalized as the "broader unraveling of the global order," as if that claim is something new – was the unadulterated fault of President Obama and the other party and every solution he proffered involved tough talk, threats of military force and calls for spending vastly more on national defense. He claimed, without substantiation, for example, that the US Navy is at "pre-World War I levels." Really? I don't expect it from the whack jobs, but supposedly serious candidates need to take a break once in a while from the huffing and puffing of base-building campaign bluster and show us the right stuff as our potential commanders-in-chief. It's that important.

Wednesday, September 3, 2014
Type Hype
Human nature finds simplistic comfort in "typing" people. Maybe the right word is "stereotyping?" We all seem to want to know what somebody is before, or in lieu of, trying to understand who they are. We should be leery of any science or pseudo-science claiming that the human personality can be reduced to a set of generalized, dichotomous variables. To do so is a disservice to the complex and dynamic personality each of us possesses. We're better and far more interesting than the cages ordained by Myers-Briggs, for example; worse, such tools that flatten human experience can cause real-world consequences, opening up ways for employers to misunderstand and misuse the data when considering and evaluating talent. This is a truth especially pertinent to those of us who seem to produce different type indicators over the years.

May 24, 2014
Et tu, Piketty?
French economist Thomas Piketty's extraordinarily popular book, *Capital in the Twenty-First Century* (2013), is on my list. The central arguments in his treatise are already well known. Today's revelations by *The*

Financial Times of "flawed data" supporting his conclusions, however, subject his arguments to serious doubt.

Sure, the FT is ideologically resistant to Professor Piketty's data-rich findings of growing wealth inequality in the US and Europe and, most certainly, to his call for a wealth tax. Yet, it is unlikely that the paper's exhaustive review of Piketty's data analyses is wrong.

The FT reports that Piketty's work suffers from: "fat-finger errors of transcription, suboptimal averaging techniques, multiple unexplained adjustments to numbers, data entries with no sourcing, unexplained use of different time periods; and inconsistent uses of source data." The paper concludes that these problems "are sufficiently serious to undermine Professor Piketty's claims." Whew. Other than that, Mrs. Lincoln, how was the play?

This is all regrettable. The FT's investigation will appropriately discredit some of Piketty's arguments, although they likely still have merit in the context of today's essential conversation about wealth inequality. To be fair, Piketty chose to make so many of his spreadsheets, tables and raw data publicly available to bolster his wealth-inequality arguments and expand dialogue on the subject. It looks like he snared himself in a trap of his own making, however, assuming *The Financial Times* is correct.

So here's another reminder to resist blind allegiance to data. Suffice it to say that we must always assess data-driven arguments critically, since human beings are too often capable of errors and worse in the manipulation of numbers. There are obvious reasons now to doubt some Piketty claims, but there is no reason to use the FT's important findings to discredit the overall conversation.

It Really Happened: Breaking Bread
My sister Pat and I met the wonderfully idiosyncratic Peter O'Malley at a restaurant bar in Oak Bluffs, Martha's Vineyard. He suggested we have dinner together, enjoying as we were some excellent wine, conversation and laughter.

Peter is the co-founder of the literary magazine *Ploughshares*, and we were pleased when he told us that the award-winning poet Fanny Howe would also be joining us. The dinner started well until, that is, we dared ask for bread. The waitress told us that the restaurant did not serve bread. This strained credulity, which Peter underscored when he bellowed something like, "No bread. Really? How can there be no bread?" We were told that some customers on low-carb diets didn't like to have bread visible, a preposterous and absurd notion.

I did what anybody would do in this situation. I excused myself to visit the restroom and, instead, walked down the street to the local bakery. I purchased two loaves of fresh-made bread and secreted them back into the restaurant, fearing that the toasty, fresh-baked smell would give me away. I stealthily handed a loaf to Peter under the table and, with great subtlety and dexterity, he pounded the tabletop and exclaimed, "She bought bread. I don't believe it; she bought bread!" Of course, this was enough to alert the waitress, general manager and even some neighbors down the street. The stern general manager then visited our table and, with steely determination, promptly confiscated our bread.

Monday, March 31, 2014
38 Special
Numbers never lie. I've been hearing that pious refrain in meetings for 30 years now. The painful truth is that numbers and the people who manipulate or misuse them can and do lie – all the time. In this era of burgeoning data analytics and endless fascination with "big data," let's never forget that data without wisdom can be illusory. Evidence always works best when combined with experience and expertise.

Take the number 38. Pundits, professors and politicians have long maintained that 38 "witnesses" remained silent in their apartments as they watched Kitty Genovese's murder on the street below in Queens, NY one night in 1964. Thirty-eight witnesses did nothing to help her, or so we have been repeatedly told. It turns out that the number 38 was a junior police official's "guesstimate" in a report filed in the aftermath of the case. It was purely speculation used to decry the brutality of human apathy and, later, to codify the cottage industry that became known as the "bystander effect" or "Genovese Syndrome." Few social psychology classes in the second half of the 20th Century – and even today – were immune from the Genovese case.

Fifty years later, a clearer picture of these events has emerged in several new books and author interviews. The work receiving the most attention is Kevin Cook's *Kitty Genovese: The Murder, The Bystanders, The Crime That Changed America* (2014). It turns out that a neighbor named Robert Mozer did, in fact, scream at the assailant from his seventh-floor window chasing him away, only to have him return for a second attack several minutes later. Two individuals did call the police, who were extremely slow in responding in those pre-911 days. Another brave woman ran down the stairs to the apartment vestibule where Genovese managed to flee between the stabbings. She cradled the dying woman in her arms, awaiting the arrival of ambulances.

Yes, there is plenty of blood on the hands of certain Kew Garden residents who did nothing to help. And there is certainly empirical evidence to support the "bystander effect" or diffusion of responsibility in these situations in which people assume that others will call the police. The real culprits in escalating a false story and a bad number, however, were Police Commissioner Michael Murphy who nonchalantly passed the fabricated number 38 to the young, ambitious *New York Times'* Metropolitan Editor Abe Rosenthal over lunch two weeks later. We are now told that Murphy did so to chase Rosenthal off another story the NYPD did not want publicized. Rosenthal chose to give larger-than-life credence to the fictitious data point, with the *Times* running subsequent pieces with headlines such as, "Thirty-eight who saw murder didn't call the police." Rosenthal later published a sensationalist book on the case entitled, *Thirty-eight Witnesses* (1964).

Rosenthal used the attractive tangibility of the number 38 to build an erroneous narrative. He propelled the Kitty Genovese story globally, darkening New York City's reputation as a crime capital filled with uncaring citizens. The work of Kevin Cook and others underscores the need to examine the role of human motivation and error that too often accompanies the misuse of data.

Saturday, October 19, 2013
No to Yasukuni
Philadelphia
Japan's Prime Minister Abe deserves some credit for refusing to visit the feverishly nationalistic World War Two Yasukuni Shrine during Autumn Festival. It's encouraging to watch this uber-conservative hawk rise above

the base instincts of his political base to a leadership stature that eluded him during his disastrous first term.

Message to House Republicans: Here's an ideologue who's learned to put country ahead of narrow, petty politics. He's not doing so out of altruism, of course, but rather because he knows what works. Relations with China and South Korea are too important, and the success of Abenomics too real, to return to childish pandering.

Let's not kid ourselves. Abe is no statesman. He is cunning enough to move past the angry, hate-filled interests of a narrow-minded cabal, however, and Japan is better off for it.

Sunday, August 25, 2013
Now That's a Leader: Bouya Haidara
Our headlines reek with failings of politicians, so-called business leaders, and celebrities gone bad. It's sometimes difficult to imagine anything good about contemporary leadership. And yet, great leaders abound. These are real heroes who stand in sharp contrast to, say, the selfish behaviors of San Diego Mayor Filner. Okay, deranged may be a better word to describe his act.

Bouya Haidara had no time for any of this foolishness. As the Islamist armies of darkness descended on Timbuktu, Mali last year – ignorant, pathetic figures who only know how to destroy things – Haidara and his fellow conservationists at the Ahmed Baba Institute smuggled thousands of priceless historic manuscripts out of harm's way at night and through checkpoints manned by Neolithic thugs. Some 4,000 irreplaceable manuscripts were destroyed or stolen by these ignorant fools. However, Haidara and colleagues saved tens of thousands of these cornerstones of Malian culture. You'd certainly want to be in a foxhole with Haidara because, well, he's already been there.

Thursday, May 2, 2013
Instant Statistics
The cricket star and global celebrity Imran Khan is running for prime minister of Pakistan. He confidently told a press conference in Lahore last week that, "Eighty percent of Pakistan's leaders are corrupt." How does he know this? What study is he citing? Of course, like so many

politicians, he just made the number up and is happy to see what sticks in the media. The number may well be higher than that in Pakistan, but why won't the media, including the UK and US reporters traveling with Khan, question the basis upon which he is making this specific claim? Maybe it's because 92.7 percent of them are lazy.

Thursday, April 25, 2013
It Just Doesn't Add Up
London
The old Warner Brothers' cartoon bulldog Spike was perplexed by what he had just seen. So he pulled out an adding machine from his naked rolls of fat, examined the numbers and exclaimed, "It just doesn't add up!"

As the "big data" drumbeat continues, I'm reminded that decisions slavishly informed by numbers sometimes just don't add up. Those who worship data to the exclusion of common sense, experience, human nature, and, yes, "gut feel," can run serious risks that exact significant costs. Just witness the causal role of the young, unwise "quant jocks" and their superiors in the financial crisis. How many times I've lamented hearing that "numbers don't lie" when, in reality, the people who use and abuse them lie all the time – willfully or not.

On the other hand, data phobes who don't understand the essential role of legitimate quantitative evidence in effective decision-making run equally devastating risks. So enough with the false dichotomy between the "quant" and "qual" camps. Good leaders should have sufficient comfort levels in both domains to produce data-informed decisions mediated by wisdom and judgment. After all, data are only as credible as we mortals who enter them into the system and then interpret and apply them.

For example, the much-ballyhooed government debt and growth model developed by Professors Reinhart and Rogoff at Harvard is now found to be in error. Too bad, since some stimulus-stunting, austerity-driven choices made by European governments cited their work as inspiration – if not proof. It turns out that Reinhart and Rogoff or their people entered data incorrectly into some of their Excel spreadsheets and, well, the rest is history.

Wednesday, April 24, 2013
This Much Is True
Detroit
I just read Jerry Weintraub's homage to Paul Anka in *Vanity Fair*. It has me thinking about the vitriolic reactions to Anka's two big-band interpretations in recent years of 1980s pop songs. Lovers of tunes such as "Eyes without a Face" by Billy Idol or "True" by Spandau Ballet were incensed that some "old guy" was reinterpreting their songs. My husband Walt and I absolutely love these new, brassy, big band takes. Fans of Anka's classic hits in the 1950s and '60s such "Diana" or "Put Your Head on my Shoulder," on the other hand, were livid that their boy embraced this other music. Isn't this the problem? People get locked into one paradigm – the one they know – and shut down their capacity to be open to new possibilities. In the process, they become old no matter their chronological age. This much is true.

It Really Happened: Arafat, Havel & Guest
The Council on Foreign Relations hosts world leaders every fall when heads of state and government address the UN General Assembly. One year, a small group of us participated in an extraordinary lunch with Vaclav Havel, followed by an equally dramatic dinner with Yasser Arafat. We were leaving Pratt House to pursue our personal business between the two meetings when the door to a small room opened slightly and revealed an even smaller group of fellow Council members lunching with Fidel Castro. And we thought we were on the A-List.

Monday, March 11, 2013
Lots of Marginal Gains
South by Southwest in Austin
Nate Silver told us here at SXSW that his work in the science of prediction is popular because, as he put it, there was so much "low-hanging fruit" in his first two fields, politics and baseball. He believes those two domains – served by his www.fivethirtyeight.com blog and PECOTA tool for forecasting ballplayer performance – delivered "lots of marginal gains" from relatively modest effort. Huh? I wonder what brilliant, successful pollsters and sabermetricians think about their work before Silver's arrival.

When asked about new arenas for study, Silver listed public policy matters, such as urban planning, education, and even prison recidivism. Why? Because "these are areas with low levels of competition," he asserted before a packed audience here today. Silver said these domains offer the marginal gains he seeks. He added in this context that, "We need more data in education." Really?

We had a chance to talk after his presentation, which drew on themes from his best-selling book, *The Signal and the Noise* (2012). I offered what is painfully obvious to many folks working in higher education research and prediction these days; that institutions are drowning in far too much data with too much of it of limited value, or worse. The argument should be for better data, not more data. He agreed with this point, of course, since his central premise is to discern useful signals from wasteful noise.

I added that what's really needed are sharper, prioritized objectives and strategies from colleges and universities – and all types of organizations – that can help executive teams and institutional research professionals understand what is most important. It seems to me that before we can sort signals from noise, we need to know what matters most to our organizations and why. Leaders need first to separate wheat from chaff at the strategic level if their data analysts are to know how to discern signals from noise in specific, contextually useful ways.

Thursday, February 28, 2013
Victories over Hubris
What do wine and the piano have in common? They each cut down to size two nations that had arrogantly assumed their own greatness. The Soviet Union was convinced of its global superiority in classical music in the 1950s and '60s, at the height of the Cold War. Blinded by this hubris, they launched the quadrennial International Tchaikovsky Competition in Moscow, a competition obviously destined, they thought, to be won by them. Much to their shock, a brilliant American named Van Cliburn won the inaugural competition in 1958. The Soviets were so stunned they had lost that they reportedly needed Premier Khrushchev to approve Cliburn's victory, in real time. RIP, Van Cliburn.

This keyboard conquest is reminiscent of the similar, absolute certainty of the French in 1976 – at the Judgment in Paris – who knew their wines were simply the best in the world – without question. They considered upstart California reds and whites the equivalent of, as my husband likes to say about bad wines, the fluid used to degrease the ball joints on a Citroen. They were only too happy to pit inferior Napa Valley wines against their own in a blind tasting. Of course, in a moment that forever put Napa Valley on the map, Chateau Montelena won the Chardonnay competition and Stag's Leap won the Cabernet Sauvignon battle. The French judges, indeed the Fifth Republic itself, must have been as stunned as their Soviet counterparts two decades earlier. Hubris blinds us to possibilities, which always makes it a self-defeating proposition.

A magical moment tasting wine and dining outdoors with our friend and winemaker Dean Hewitson at one of his vineyards in Australia's Barossa Valley.

Saturday, February 2, 2013
Why Are You So Afraid?
Los Angeles
Here's yet another ballplayer with a homophobic rant. This time, it's 49ers' cornerback Chris Culliver opining that, "No, we don't got no gay people on the team. They got to get out of here if they do." No fear in that guy's eyes, huh? No brains in his head, either. I also found the predictable apology prepared by the 49ers' PR department to be even more lame than usual. It read, "The derogatory comments I made yesterday were a reflection of thoughts in my head, but they are not how I feel." Say what? Come on, folks, you need a more plausible, less laughable apology than that to cover up the fact that Culliver remains as homophobic as ever, likely learning nothing from this episode.

Saturday, January 12, 2013
Playing the Wrong Tune
He lasted nine days. Richard Dare, New Jersey Symphony CEO, resigned yesterday amid disclosures that he had pleaded "no contest" in an under-age sex case in 1996 and served 60 days in jail. My first thought was, here we go again; another stunning case of a board of directors and recruiter missing something of enormous consequence about a candidate's back-ground. No, it's worse than that. The board actually knew. Dare had been honest with them about the case and actually married the woman when she turned 18. With a perplexing inability to see how serious their brand was about to be damaged and the distraction such a choice would cause, the board nonetheless proceeded with the appointment. Yet another case underscoring the need for a Director of Common Sense in all organizations.

Thursday, January 10, 2013
Time for Some Answers
Fareed Zakaria entitles his article in the current issue of *Foreign Affairs*, "Can America Be Fixed?" He devotes the entire piece to a suffocating litany of our problems – from 5th to 25th in global infrastructure in a decade, for example – without one mention of possible solutions. If we

are to straighten ourselves out as a society, and that remains an open question, it's time to move beyond the diagnostics that sell books and deliver some substantive, tough-minded answers.

Saturday, January 5, 2013
Fools Not Suffering Fools
The New York Times' David Brooks gets it just right. I too hate the expression that somebody "doesn't suffer fools gladly." This trite phrase has always struck me as a rationalization for people in leadership positions to act like horse's asses. Obviously, leaders should hire and promote employees who are not fools. But when fools do appear, and they most certainly will in the course of events, the leader must be as fair and respectful as he or she is tough and firm.

Wednesday, March 7, 2012
Saints No More
Seattle
I've always liked the New Orleans Saints, especially when they were such colorful losers. While not surprising, revelations of an informal "bounty program," where bonuses were paid to players who seriously injured members of an opposing team is painful if not perplexing. When will people in leadership positions such as Saints' Defensive Coordinator Gregg Williams ever learn that there are principles larger than their twisted objectives and, for that matter, that these schemes are totally discoverable in our 24x7 social media world?

I was in the Super Dome in 1987 when the Saints clinched the playoffs for the first time in their then rather tortured history. Thousands of us paraded to the French Quarter that night, celebrating that the 'Aints were no longer losers. Well, they're big losers now.

Monday, April 11, 2011
Earth Calling Jacob Zuma
I've never been a big Jacob Zuma fan. Of course, it's difficult for any mere mortal to serve as South Africa's President in the formidable shadow of Nelson Mandela. Still, how can somebody agree to serve as part of the African Union's heads-of-state negotiating team in Libya and skip the

Benghazi portion of the trip? Negotiating peace means speaking with both sides, Gaddafi in Tripoli and the rebels in Benghazi.

Zuma has seen fit, however, to reap the publicity and adulation of the pro-Gaddafi forces, which almost certainly has been his aim from the start, while thumbing his nose at Benghazi. His people say he needs to return to South Africa to depart for the BRICS meeting in China. Baloney! This is too important to not have carved out a day in Benghazi and, besides, his presidential aircraft is just as capable of departing for Beijing from Benghazi. The AU's mission to Libya is nothing more than posturing and window dressing and, with Zuma's actions, has only made matters worse.

These young women on Cape Town's Victoria & Alfred Waterfront would be so much better off if their nation was led competently and without endemic corruption.

Thursday, September 9, 2010
They Just Don't Get It
High-paid jocks who just don't get it have become the norm. It's one thing for these erstwhile role models to frequent strip clubs at 3:00 a.m., brandishing firearms. I guess that's their pathetic business. It's quite another matter, however, when they turn their backs on wounded servicemen and servicewomen recovering at the Walter Reed Medical Center.

Enter three fools from the New York Mets. It seems that multimillionaires Carlos Beltran, Oliver Perez and Luis Castillo had better things to do on Tuesday than to join their teammates on an annual visit with wounded soldiers. Shades of Manny Ramirez's boycott when the Red Sox visited Walter Reed in 2008.

It's pretty clear that these beauts don't know much about much at all. At minimum, however, one wonders why their handlers failed to persuade them at least to *appear* to do the right thing. Beltran told *The New York Times* today that, "I don't know who is creating this issue. I had my own things to do, and I couldn't make it." Here's the answer, Carlos, you are creating the issue and it is manifest in your profound selfishness and ignorance.

What would guys like this see if they possessed the ability let alone the willingness to be introspective and think beyond themselves? Nothing. Absolutely nothing. Let's leave to another day why it is that some organizations (like the Mets) acquire more than their fair share of such stunningly characterless people.

Saturday, June 5, 2010
Blown Calls and Blown Wells
If only BP CEO Tony Hayward had some of umpire Jim Joyce's humanity. Hayward's firm blew a deep-water oil well in the Gulf of Mexico with devastating consequences, especially for those who lost their lives aboard the Deepwater Horizon and for the families left behind. Every time Hayward speaks, he loses credibility and only seems to make matters worse. This is what happens when CEOs sacrifice common sense and humanity enroute to the top and are then surrounded in crisis by too many lawyers, sycophants and equivocators.

Joyce blew a big call in a baseball game the other night, robbing a pitcher and his fans of a perfect game. He apologized immediately and with a level of class, dignity and speed not frequently seen these days. No hedging, no caveats and no lawyers. Yes, Hayward's challenges are far more complex and consequential than those faced by Joyce, but the need for authenticity and humanity remain as fundamentally simple as they are essential to effective leadership.

Monday, April 26, 2010
All Greek to Me
Buffalo
The rants of those who angrily slam government and rail against taxation have grown more pernicious in recent months. We the people deserve good government, but it's impossible to achieve when the evil menace

of "big government" is constantly foisted upon us by various forums for angry nativism, nationalism and nihilism. We are certainly free to question government, of course, and to be skeptical about how our tax dollars are being spent. Yet the unrelenting assault for 30 years now on the very institutions and individuals we expect to serve us well has created a self-fulfilling prophecy as well as a clear and present danger.

After all, who else but government can and should arm and protect our brave sons and daughters fighting for freedom? Who else will ensure that the airline flights we endure these days depart and land safely? Who else will pave our highways and save our wetlands? Who else will manage our public universities and community colleges? Who else will patrol our streets and extinguish our fires?

Ironically, the shrillest anti-tax voices are often the same people who nonetheless demand everything from a government they perpetually bash and, in the process, make less capable of actually delivering it. These are the same folks unable or unwilling to cite specific, meaningful examples of how to reduce the national deficit or cut big-ticket defense platforms designed to fight yesterday's Cold War.

Among the many painful lessons of the current financial debacle in Greece is what happens when citizens want it all but are unwilling to pay for it. The system collapses under its own weight.

It Really Happened: Roamin' Romans

My friend Dennis and I were walking the Via Veneto one beautiful evening in Rome. We had been working at the US Embassy supporting President Clinton's visit commemorating the 50th anniversary of the Anzio invasion and, of course, enjoying much of what the Eternal City offers. We chose a side street in search of a great bar or restaurant and discovered a lovely, out-of-the-way trattoria. We sat at the tiny bar, ordered drinks and nibbled appetizers, thoroughly reveling in the joyous nature of our fellow patrons.

When it came time to pay the bill and move on to another place, however, the bartender motioned that he could not take our lira. He called over an English-speaking patron who informed us that we had unwittingly crashed a private wedding. "So that's why we were getting blank stares every now and then," I thought. As it turned out, each side thought we were guests of the other side. We apologized and started to leave, but our new friends would have none of that. They invited us to drink some champagne, enjoy a piece of cake and dance. And so we did.

Friday, May 8, 2009

Like, Plagiarism

I unintentionally overheard a young woman engaged in a heated phone conversation the other day at the Columbus Airport. I mean, how can one help *not* overhearing endless cell phone chatter seeping into any cherished moment we actually find to think, reflect and relax.

It seems that this college student was thoroughly pissed off because she had to do a semester's worth of homework that day. Or at least that's what she said. She was supposed to create a blog on a particular subject, solicit comments and build readership over the course of several months. Now, under duress, she was copying other people's blogs and making their thoughts her own, all while waiting for a flight. It was her own flight of fancy, no doubt.

She said, "You know, it's, like, for this PR class that really sucks and, like, nobody knew we were supposed to do this." *Pause.* "Ya, it's in the syllabus but, like, nobody reads that." In concluding the conversation, she asked her friend to find somebody to do her statistics homework this summer. "Like, I'll pay them to do it, you know. I'm really, like, bad at that stuff."

I'm trying to avoid all the feelings this encounter naturally evokes, not the least of which is that somebody is paying thousands of dollars so that this young woman learns only how to beat the system. The responsibility for doing the work rests solely with her, but the responsibility for detecting that she did not do it belongs to her professor. We can only hope that the system works and may not always be so damn beatable. That would be, like, wonderful.

Thursday, March 12, 2009

Bing Bang

It was terrific to learn that basketball legend Dave Bing is running for mayor of Detroit. At long last, it seemed, the city might benefit from the discipline, integrity and high standards of this great player and good man. Bing was as dignified on the court as he has been successful as a businessman off the court. Besides, the good people of that long-besieged city could hardly do any worse than former Mayor Kwame Kilpatrick, recently released from prison for lying under oath.

Now comes the revelation that, well, Bing lied, too. He does not have an MBA degree from the General Motors Institute nor did he graduate from Syracuse University in 1966 as he has claimed. He did finally graduate from college in 1995, which is a better story and therefore makes even more mysterious why the candidate would lie about it. His more serious transgression it seems to me is in fronting a spokesman named Clifford Russell to make matters worse with statements like, "Given all the hard knocks he had gone through and the rigors of being an auto supplier, he felt he had an MBA in terms of the amount of knowledge he had acquired." This is BS, not an MBA.

So here is yet another edition of what happens even to good people when they taste political success and yet somehow feel inadequate to the task. Should we forgive Dave Bing? Likable basketball star aside, he deserves at least one more shot at the truth. Everyone is entitled to one mistake and Bing has earned our respect as an employer and civic leader. One more fib, however, may well end a promising political career before it barely started.

Thursday, January 1, 2009
Milgram Redux
The infamous 1963 Milgram experiments taught us something very painful about blind obedience to authority. Yale psychologist Stanley Milgram wanted to know why seemingly decent German citizens long supported Hitler's monstrous regime. The original Milgram research demonstrated that otherwise ordinary New Haven residents were willing to administer increasingly violent electric shocks to "learners" in another room who failed to answer quiz questions correctly. Of course, the shocks were not real. However, the participants thought they were real. People readily administered what seemed to be painful shocks to their fellow citizens because some guy in a lab coat and badge told them to do so. In the original experiment, 80 percent of participants administered 150-volt shocks and 65 percent took the punishment right up to 450 volts.

We wondered at the time how it was possible for good people to lose sight of right and wrong in the presence of authority, however twisted. Well, keep wondering. Jeffrey Burger of Santa Clara University recently replicated Milgram's study. After four decades of exposure to Vietnam, Watergate, Iran-Contra, Clinton and Monica, Cheney, Iraq, Abu Ghraib and many other abominations, polls consistently tell us the unfortunate news that Americans are far less trusting of our leaders. Still, Burger showed that 70 percent of participants delivered a 150-volt shock simply because the authority figure in a lab coat told them to do so. Sure, some of the outcome is contextual and not especially generalizable. However, there is clearly something innate in humans that finds us ready to follow obviously terrible orders from obviously horrible authority figures. This fact has long been intuitively understood and venally exploited by the likes of Mussolini, Mao and Mugabe.

Monday, December 22, 2008
Ah, the Children
Here they go again. Why is it that disgraced politicians – let's see, we have Boston's Chuck Turner and Diane Wilkerson, and Illinois Governor Rod Blagojevich among the recent bumper crop of failed public servants – always spin appropriate legal and public reactions to their wrongdoing as an assault on the people? Remember when Senator Larry Craig (R-ID) said that "a cloud hangs over Idaho" when he was caught in that Minneapolis men's room? No cloud there, Senator. Idahoans had nothing to do with your unfortunate conduct.

The utterly preposterous Blagojevich said on Friday, "Afford me the same rights that you and your children have – the presumption of innocence." As any self-serving politician knows, it's always good to work "children" into the conversation. Okay, if a child-governor was saying and doing the things Blagojevich has been saying and doing, that child's parents would insist that he or she resign from office and go to his or her room. Blagojevich may be legally exonerated someday, perhaps on a technicality. Who knows? But his ethical and moral breaches coupled with his sociopathy means that he must leave the public arena, now and forever. It has nothing to do with legal guilt. Otherwise governor, speaking of children, what lessons are they to learn from your conduct? And what costs will Illinois incur over the coming days and weeks as a result of your foolishness?

Thursday, October 30, 2008
Turkish Temperament
Readers know of my affection for Turkey. Unfortunately, that high regard always seems coupled with astonishment over Turkish governments' penchant for engaging in self-defeating activities. In a page ripped from Beijing's playbook, the government announced last week that it had banned 850 websites, including Blogger and YouTube. This is yet another setback for those of us who support Turkey's accession to the European Union.

If Ankara can't take the heat of today's technology, they risk removing themselves from the kitchen of modernity. It is hard to understand such overreactions to the occasional and even unwise mockeries of Ataturk or other forms of political opposition. Mustafa Akgul summed up the heavy handedness best when he told the *Christian Science Monitor* today, "It's like having a huge library and finding an error on a page in one book and closing down the entire library." Whether it's burning books or shutting down websites, those who fear the free flow of information always fail in the end. Closed systems naturally devolve to entropy – as they should.

Friday, October 3, 2008
Stop and Think
The Slovenian philosopher Slavoj Zizek is a piece of work. He would be the first to admit it, too. However, Zizek is one of the few polymaths who talks about the need for a new grand theory of everything and yet may actually deliver one. I disagree with him on so many matters, but strongly support his contention that we as a society risk losing a sense of what is happening amidst so much complexity, who we are and where we are going. He is right to say that journalistic shorthand labels such as post-modernism simply don't work. They not only fail to explain current realities; they actually make discussion about them more difficult.

Zizek says that the West needs to withdraw and think. Let's simply call it stop and think, since we Americans would have a difficult time dealing with the word withdraw. Nonetheless, we need to sort out the unprecedented events happening around us these days, why they are happening, and what to do about them. Yet we know in everyday organizational life how painfully difficult it is to get people to take a moment to stop and think. The US Congress comes to mind, right? Why is that? Have we forgotten how to think, or at least how to think well?

The best leaders create opportunities for their people to think and then to build plans based on the products of that mindfulness. Regrettably, too many folks in leadership positions are as caught up as the rest of us in the unrelenting pace of *doing* to create new, thoughtful narratives that better explain what we are doing and to help us do it better – or not at all.

Zizek calls for greater development of cognitive-mapping skills to help us achieve these new and better ways. Otherwise, we are getting near the time when some imaginary global parent of ours should pick us up by the scruff of our collective neck, issue a "time out," and send us to our room to think about what we have just done. If not, we're going to keep doing it, right?

Wednesday, August 20, 2008
John, Kwame and Monica, Meet Ted
Ted Sorensen's book, *Counselor: A Life at the Edge of History* (2008), is as delightful as the man himself. Yes, it is possible that Sorensen gave too much of his life to one politician. However, his 11 years with Jack Kennedy serve as testament to decency and thoughtfulness in what in his case truly was public service. Sorensen's approach to public life stands in sharp contrast to the now disgraced former Senator John Edwards (D-SC), indicted Detroit Mayor Kwame Kilpatrick, and former Justice Department political operative Monica Goodling. We are all human beings and we all make mistakes that warrant forgiveness. Yet it is the arrogance, narcissism and duplicity of these three individuals that set them apart from natural human frailty.

Sorensen is a pacifist and was once a conscientious objector. This is a difficult and even courageous position that repeatedly haunted him throughout his career. I'm sure Sorensen would support those of us who believe that two-year national service should be mandatory for all young men and women, including non-military options such as the Peace Corps and City Year. Just as he registered with the military medical service – and those guys are on the front lines without weapons – Sorensen would likely have readily enlisted in one of the civilian service options had they existed at the time.

Still, he makes a powerful point that is too often missed by folks who only think of the military in one, stereotypical way – war. No organization has done more to create economic opportunity, train and educate, develop leadership skills, and send young men and women into the mainstream than the US military. Besides, the last people who want to wage war are those who actually risk losing their lives or limbs. Sorensen's stated regard for Generals Dwight D. Eisenhower, Maxwell Taylor and Wes Clark as well as Admiral Elmo Zumwalt was that they knew the folly of war and sought first to exercise all options short of outright war to achieve peaceful resolution. How about that, "Five-Deferment Dick Cheney"?

It is arguably true that we would simply not be here today had Jack Kennedy listened to General Curtis "Bombs Away" LeMay's advice to bomb Cuba during the Cuban Missile Crisis. Yes, LeMay was a *Dr. Strangelove* (1964) character of those times who, thankfully, was the exception rather than the rule among most military leaders.

Monday, June 16, 2008
Tim Russert's Preparation
Tim Russert's death is a staggering blow to any citizen who demands truth from his or her elected officials. It would be difficult to find a better prepared, better read and more analytically insightful interviewer than Russert, who excelled at penetrating the flim-flam too often regurgitated by politicians and their handlers. Of Russert's many formidable assets, the greatest may have been the intensity of his professional preparation.

In his latest book, *The Post-American World* (2008), Fareed Zakaria writes that US national politics has become little more than "ceaseless, virulent debates about trivia – a politics of theater." He contends that a "can-do country" is losing competitive advantage at the hands of "doing-nothing politics," although like many of us he does remain bullish about America's future. His point is lamentably accurate and no better evidenced than during the Congressional leadership tenures of Messrs. Gingrich, Hastert and Lott.

Russert saw through this nonsense and held Republicans and Democrats alike accountable and within reach of informed public scrutiny. His loss in this and so many other contexts is almost unimaginable, given the dreadful state of contemporary journalism.

Russert's passing reminds me of an evening at the Ritz Carlton Hotel in Atlanta's Buckhead neighborhood a night or two before the 1994 Super Bowl. Russert's beloved Buffalo Bills were to meet the eventual champion Dallas Cowboys and earn infamy with their fourth straight Super Bowl defeat. Russert charmed a group of us at the bar with great stories of politics and sports drawn from a very deep reservoir and generous demeanor. So sad.

Thursday, June 5, 2008
Now That's a Leader: Iran's Million Signature Campaign
The world is experiencing food and oil shortages, but one commodity seems in full supply – fear-mongering, hate-filled ignorance. And it's hardly inexpensive, costing us dearly all around the globe.

A President of the United States inappropriately and incorrectly invokes the name of Hitler in the Knesset, Sharon Stone blames China's tragic earthquake on "bad karma" stemming from Beijing's Tibet policy and a right-wing commentator sets off a firestorm of protest among the crazies over a Dunkin' Donuts commercial where pitchwoman Rachel Ray wears what pundit Michelle Malkin conveniently but incorrectly believes is a keffiyeh.

This last item is so stupefying that it is even difficult to discuss. Malkin excels at playing to the lowest common denominator, generating self-serving heat with very little light. She claims the scarf resembles a keffiyeh, and that keffiyeh are symbols of terrorism. Oh really? In whose mind? Malkin certainly knows that Ray's all-too-trendy scarf is not a keffiyeh, which is worn around the head by Arab men. Scarves like Ray's are worn by women all over the world from New York and Paris to Stockholm and Tokyo – and yes, in the Middle East, too.

Are we unraveling to such an extent that this kind of nonsense is allowed to occur let alone be effective? Apparently, yes. Dunkin' Donuts has pulled the ads, and who's to blame them? What they don't need is 20 or 30 far-right bloviators with too much time on their hands making trouble.

Yet how does Dunkin' explain their actions to customers, employees, suppliers, investors and business partners around the world, some of whom likely wear the keffiyeh?

What's the remedy? Through the stench of ignorance, it really is possible to find some needed air freshener. It's the opposite of ignorance. It's smart, respectful, open-minded, thoughtful and courageous. It tries hard to place the interests of the many over the selfish ambitions of the few. It's the very best of leadership.

Today's example is the Iranian *One Million Signature Campaign.* Imagine the bravery of women (and some men) in Iran risking their lives right now to collect signatures to call for an end to discriminatory laws against women ingrained in the so-called Iranian system of justice. Malkin and countless others seek expedient political or economic benefits and worry little about the scorched earth they leave behind. The Iranian campaign organizers, on the other hand, look at the scorched earth around them and insist that we can and must do better. So, for a moment at least, try not think of these usual suspects. Consider instead heroic Iranian signature-campaign leaders such as Jelve Javaheri, Amir Yaghoub Ali and Maryam Hosseinkhah.

Sunday, May 4, 2008
Our Man: The Dangers of Simplistic Narrative
Washington, DC

There is a longstanding practice among US officials to invest great faith – not to mention money, weapons and unrealistic hopes – in "our man" in whatever hot spots arise. We historically buy into dubious personal narratives and even manufacture some of them ourselves to position somebody as our trusted pit bull.

We have cast our lot over the years with Chiang Kai-shek in Taipei, Ferdinand Marcos in Manila, Shah Reza Pahlavi in Tehran, Saddam Hussein in Baghdad, Pervez Musharraf in Islamabad, Ngo Dinh Diem in Saigon and Syngman Rhee in Seoul, in addition to enough heavily braided Latin American generals throughout the 19th and 20th Centuries to populate a Gilbert and Sullivan production. Sometimes these alliances are necessary, however, as was FDR's choice to work with Stalin during World War Two. He once explained the uneasy relationship with the unspeakable evil of a man he lightly called "Uncle Joe" as holding hands with the devil in order to cross the bridge.

In his account of The Korean War, *The Coldest Winter* (2007), the late David Halberstam suggests that the American-educated Syngman Rhee was a manipulator of the highest order. Like all the characters above, he knew when to play the anti-Communism card or, as others do more recently, the anti-terrorism card to induce the reflex on our part to pour weapons, money and political support into his cause – and his pockets.

One painful example of the risks associated with simplistic narratives is that of Ahmed Chalabi. He reinvented himself many times and, together, we reinvented him yet again as the purported embodiment of a free and democratic Iraq. Remember that in 2002 and 2003 some neoconservatives dubbed Chalabi "the George Washington of Iraq." We both bought and sold a personal narrative that bore little relationship to reality, using it as a key storyline in our run-up to the war in Iraq. For more on this history, read Aram Roston's book, *The Man Who Pushed America to War: The Extraordinary Life, Adventures and Obsessions of Ahmad Chalabi* (2008).

The trouble in all these cases is that we exhibit what *The Black Swan* (2010) author Nassim Taleb calls "the dangerous compression of narrative." After all, it is much easier to buy into a simple "good versus evil" story line with readily identifiable good guys and evildoers. "Our men" are always the good guys, of course, until they almost always prove otherwise. The problem with creating and enabling simplistic narratives that align our short-term interests with the wrong guy, however, is that we miss the long-term strategic benefits of playing it straight and right. Perhaps limited by our own ontologies and ideologies, we fail to work with the complexity that actually defines reality, unable to see embryonic democratic movements stirring beneath most any dictatorship. Eventually we find ourselves on the wrong side of history, which is precisely our dilemma in Pakistan right now as it will be in Saudi Arabia someday perilously soon.

Complexity leadership theorists tell us that nations, organizations and individuals exist in complex adaptive systems. These systems are marked by dynamism, interactivity, non-linearity and unpredictability, carrying with them the potential for small, unforeseen events to manifest out of proportion to their scale and in ways that obliterate the large-scale narratives otherwise intended. Indeed, it is difficult to achieve a simple, linear story arc in highly complex environments and trying to do so can actually make matters worse. The complexity folks tell us that these systems are less dependent on the one leader, per se, and much more engaged in constantly shifting patterns of leadership and followership undertaken by many actors – a much tougher story to understand, package and convey. Yes, politicians and the media generally want simple, reductionist stories with clear beginnings and endings, identifiable antagonists and protagonists, and grand, compelling plots. Sure, we love these stories. They're often called fiction.

Sunday, February 10, 2008
Why is John Nagl Leaving?
Washington, DC
Why is John Nagl leaving the US Army? Here is the quintessential scholar-warrior retiring from service at the age of 41, just when we need him most. Lt. Colonel Nagl is not to blame, of course, as he heads to the Center for a New American Security. Nonetheless, his sudden departure continues to raise questions about the Army's ability and willingness to retain its best and brightest. Scholars with combat experience are too valuable for a nation at war to lose.

Nagl holds a doctorate from Oxford and has been a key player in General David Petraeus' Iraq counterinsurgency planning and execution. Still, one always wonders how well scholars exist within the cultural parameters of military or even corporate life. I find the military to be more welcoming to scholars than the corporate community, but not that much more. I find the scholarly community to be more open to military men and women, but not much more than they are to the corporate community. I find the corporate community barely open to either one of them.

We are wasting so much time with our personal uneasiness over people from different tribes. There was a time when we seemed more comfortable as a society with citizens who were warriors, scholars and business people. For the good of the nation, isn't it time to get over it? Now more than ever, isn't it time we elevate to leadership positions people who can walk these different paths?

Saturday, September 1, 2007
Where Do Clouds Hang?
Much has been said about the sad tale of Senator Larry Craig (R-ID). After all, cruising airport restrooms is hardly a good idea for anyone, let alone a US Senator. What the hell was he thinking? Of course, it is a profoundly hypocritical act coming from a man who otherwise shows such politically convenient contempt for his gay and lesbian constituents and fellow citizens.

Aldous Huxley once wrote, "there is no such thing as a conscious hypocrite," so one must understand that Craig can't admit his hypocrisy because he simply can't allow himself to see it. In their new book, *Mistakes Were Made (But Not By Me)* (2007), the social psychologists Carol Tavris and Elliot Aronson write that cognitive dissonance occurs when our perception of ourselves is contradicted by the reality of our actions. That's why, according to Tavris and Aronson, we work overtime to bury dissonance as "an engine of self-justification."

I will let others psychoanalyze Craig's emotional and mental state and offer just two observations. First, megalomania is a crippling disease. When Craig first went public with news of his arrest for engaging in a mysterious set of restroom protocols with an undercover cop in an adjacent stall, he said that, "a cloud hangs over Idaho."

Excuse me? No sir, a cloud hangs over you and only you. Politicians-in-trouble need to understand that we don't buy their megalomaniacal, self-centered and completely fictional us-against-them fictions. I am sure that most of the people of Idaho want no part of that nonsense, Senator.

Next, Craig also makes the classic error of referring to himself in the third person all the time, as if to distance Senator Craig from, well, Senator Craig. Finally, he blamed everyone but himself, including the *Idaho Statesmen* newspaper that exercised extraordinary restraint. He would have found greater sympathy from Americans had he accepted his guilt, owned it in first-person terms and blamed only himself.

Thursday, August 16, 2007
Gaussian Bias in a Paretian World
We spent last Saturday with UCLA scholar Bill McKelvey. Currently Professor of Strategic Organizing at the Anderson School, Bill ranks

among the nation's foremost authorities in complexity leadership theory. He makes a compelling case about the dangers of the longstanding social science bias for normal distributions in which most scholars "manage the averages" and "ignore the extremes."

Carl Friedrich Gauss's Hanover experiments in the early 19th Century gave birth to normal or Gaussian distributions, the well-known bell-curve shapes in which the vast majority of statistical elements exist within the customary two or three standard deviations from the mean. McKelvey reminds us that most social science has been engineered to organize around normal averages and avoid the extremes, valuing statistical tidiness over inconvenient but potentially monumental variances.

He suggests that we actually live in a Paretian world, underscoring the value of Power Law distributions, for example – sometimes thought of as the "80-20 Rule" – conceived by Vilfredo Pareto. McKelvey believes there is so much to learn from exploration of extremes found in the statistical tails of quantitative research that can otherwise be so difficult to explain.

To understand our increasingly complex world, McKelvey underscores the utility of scale-free dynamics that can cope with the fact that emergence may not occur in homogeneous, linear ways and that some extreme events are well worth researching. He quips that upon discovering a talking pig most social scientists would wait to find a large "n" size so as to have enough talking pigs to study, inevitably leading to some kind of normal distribution used to describe an abnormal event. McKelvey says that the lone talking pig is worth studying now, right now, as the extreme event it is and that researchers don't need a large "n" size to gain legitimacy. Besides, they'll never achieve legitimacy anyway if there is only one talking pig. The moral of the story, you see, is never to ignore the talking pig.

McKelvey uses a 2006 Malcolm Gladwell *New Yorker* article on homelessness to demonstrate the value of studying extremes. He uses Gladwell's data to show that over a defined period 50 percent of homeless people in New York City use a shelter for one night at an administrative cost of $62 each, 30 percent use a shelter for two nights at a cost of $132 each, and 10 percent use shelters for several three-week periods at a cost of $5,179 each. The vast majority of the city's attention is paid to this 90 percent portion of homeless people. Yet, say, given 10,000 homeless people over the period my math shows a public cost of $310,000 for the 50 percent, $396,000 for the 30 percent, and $5,179,000 for the 10 percent.

In Paretian terms, of course, it's not surprising to learn that the remaining 10 percent of the "chronic homeless" actually cost $24,800 each or $24,800,000. So, while most public policy and operational activities are invested in the 90 percent that comprise $5,885,000 in expense, a small fraction (that final 10 percent) of the overall total actually comprises four times that annual cost. By ignoring the 10 percent so-called outliers, we forfeit our ability to effect real savings and make real changes to people's lives.

A Guassian approach to homelessness dwells on the 90 percent while, in McKelvey's terms, a Paretian approach addresses the needs of the vastly more expensive and chronic 10 percent. The City of Denver embraced the extreme, provided city-paid apartments for the chronic homeless and has already reduced costs from $45,000 per chronic case to $15,000 per year. Bill McKelvey has a point. Extremes matter.

Tuesday, January 9, 2007
On Francisco Varela
Santiago, Chile
It is the work of the late theoretical biologist and neuroscientist Francisco Varela that has taken us here to Santiago. Varela was a proponent of the "embodied mind" philosophy, building on the work of the cognitive linguist George Lakoff and others. He maintained that the mind can only be well understood in the context of understanding the body and the natural world surrounding it. Is it any wonder that we have started some of our days here with yoga and meditation, often to the mellifluous tones of Dr. John Kabat-Zinn of the UMass Medical School?

A serious practitioner of Tibetan Buddhism, Varela greatly advanced the science of consciousness by understanding that Western cognition and Eastern mindfulness have much to learn from one another. His integrative approaches serve as the foundation for the September 2005 *Journal of Management Inquiry* article by Karl Weick and Ted Putnam entitled, "Organizing for Mindfulness: Eastern Wisdom and Western

Knowledge," as well as the really terrific Mind & Life Institute book, *The Dalai Lama at MIT* (2006). Of course, the weakness with some of these prescriptions is in their very binarism, as if "we" Westerners only think and act one way while "they" Easterners are similarly mired in constrained stereotypes.

Varela believed in our own emergent qualities, arguing that the whole of ourselves appears only as a result of the dynamics of its component parts. Thus the importance of the mind-body symbiosis as well as the body-nature relationship. Of course, it is too easy for less creative, less romantic, less revolutionary and, yes, less brilliant observers than Varela to position his work as a flight of fancy. Far from it.

Yes, I have to admit a problem fully understanding what the mystic Varela and his mentor Humberto Maturana are teaching us. As with the entry below from Cuncumen, however, I understand that language quite simply eludes a full understanding – at least at present. Yet, just because language may seem obscurantist, or something may seem beyond our current capacity to understand, does not make it wrong.

Friday, January 5, 2007
The Insufficiency of Language
Cuncumen, Chile
Patricia May Urzúa and Sergio Saguez are extraordinary human beings. We have much to learn from them about leadership, language and life. They represent the very best of the Chilean approach to practical wisdom – what Aristotle called phronesis – and the purposeful, creative soulfulness of the examined life.

Pat says that language can elude the essential, complex conversations we have – or should be having – about self-knowledge, mindfulness and our universal connectedness. Maybe this is why we increasingly use the language of complexity theory and quantum dynamics to explore such realms.

A professor of Anthropology at the University of Chile and a leading author, Pat readily integrates the scientific with the philosophical and spiritual and believes that we think of these two forces as mutually exclusive at our own peril. "Poets speak to these truths in very different ways," Pat told us today. Perhaps it is not language, per se, but prose that eludes powerful, seemingly unspeakable concepts where science and spirituality comfortably intersect. Heidegger spoke to the power of poetry in this context, seeing it as a force for understanding meaning, being and the true nature of man. So too, Wittgenstein spoke of "language games" used to construct and convey seemingly impenetrable philosophical concepts and to reveal truths long hidden by society's need for institutions and boundaries that restrict the difficult yet essential conversations about who we are and where we are going.

In his book *The Heart Aroused: Poetry and the Preservation of the Soul in Corporate America* (1994), the poet David Whyte echoes Pat May and builds on the work of Heidegger, Wittgenstein, and others. Whyte brilliantly explores the growing restlessness of American executives who yearn for greater creativity in their jobs and meaning in their lives, trapped as too many of them are in political and inauthentic settings that painfully limit their potential contributions.

Whyte says that, "This split between our work life and that part of our soul life forced underground seems to be at the root of much of our current unhappiness." Whyte offers hope that some enlightened corporations are now starting to understand the real potential of liberating the total person at work.

Sure, the United States can retain its superpower status and our businesses their record of innovation. However, this will require engaging in difficult conversations about what really matters, understanding that each of us is merely a momentary occurrence in an infinite scheme of things, speaking from true humility and humanity and freeing our colleagues and ourselves to achieve the awesome creative powers that can be found in each of us. We won't read much about the likes of Pat May, Sergio Saguez and David Whyte in the *Harvard Business Review* today, but it is just a matter of time. As Pat said, "We need to evolve beyond our illusions."

Monday, November 20, 2006
Grounds for Termination?
It just doesn't seem like a very good idea. Yet, several times this year I have been an unavoidable passive participant in an employee's annual performance review at, yes, your friendly neighborhood Starbucks.

Given the company's welcome propensity for engaging in multiple lines of business these days, "America's third place" may want to create a more formal line of Human Resources services.

"This isn't coming from me, but some people don't think you're a team player," said one young technology guy across the table from his bemused employee. I really don't want to hear these highly personal conversations, as I am right now just two tables away, but how can this be avoided when they are broadcast throughout the store as if on the XM Radio Starbucks' Channel?

"John took a bullet for the team," said another guy who was likely never in a position to take a bullet in reality. "I don't understand these stupid forms," said another boss as he attempted to fill out a performance review that he was obviously reading for the first time.

Given the inappropriateness of conducting such personal affairs in public, it's no surprise that the quality of language and content is so equally appalling. I have never in my professional life heard so many empty clichés, meaningless sports and war metaphors and thoroughly inaccessible acronyms and initializations. My only hope is that the bosses civilized enough to hold such meetings privately and as part of serious performance management systems are doing so in truly informative, insightful, firm and mutually respectful ways.

Friday, October 20, 2006
Poll Bearers
Why are partisan pollsters on Democrat and Republican payrolls allowed to serve as media pundits? How did that happen? After all, they can make no claim of impartiality based on credible research. They are campaign or party spokespeople, nothing more, and they should be introduced by the media as such. Imagine using separate Bear and Bull analysts paid by outside interests to report the daily stock market results. Well, that actually kinda happens, too.

Yes, of course, candidates need their own pollsters who, it can be assumed, actually tell them the truth about the numbers in private. And yes, campaigns need to dissect the numbers to make their best arguments and deliver their best defenses. However, there was a day when pollsters from Gallup, Harris, Roper or Yankelovich appeared on the media to provide us with objective, unvarnished news that we were allowed to interpret for ourselves.

"Oh sure, Lou," the confident campaign pollster jumps in, "some of the numbers show us down by 25 percent. It was actually 26 points last week, however, so that's not really the way to look at it. It's very clear we're closing the gap. For example, there was five percent growth in turn-out among young women during the last election cycle. Our numbers now show that single, white, vegetarian women between the ages of 20 and 21 who are lapsed Lutherans are now crossing over to our side – in droves, Lou! To be totally honest, we're very encouraged by these trends. This is a campaign about jobs, education and the future and it seems that our message is starting to resonate with the American people."

Time for a commercial break.

Thursday, October 12, 2006
Organizational Learning: Knight Ridder
Dr. Dave Schwandt and Dr. Mike Marquardt of The George Washington University Executive Leadership Doctoral Program wrote a marvelous book entitled *Organizational Learning* (2000). For those who doubt whether organizations can learn, misinterpret and misapply learning, or simply forget what they learned, consider as the authors do, infamous case studies such as the flawed fabrication of the Hubble Space Telescope mirror in the late 1970s and '80s that came despite repeated warnings of problems. Everything that Perkin Elmer and NASA had learned all along the way was discounted by politics, poor communication, time pressures and low-trust levels.

On the other hand, the authors highlight an excellent eight-point learning code adopted by employees at the Knight-Ridder newspaper media company (now the McClatchy Company) in the late 1990s. KR asked its employees in *Organizational Learning* to "ask for and hear feedback and data from others that challenges assumptions and behaviors."

It's rare that journalists embrace such corporate formulations, but it's also worth noting that Knight Ridder was the only major media organization to suspend belief and question the premise for the Iraq war right from the start. While *The New York Times, Washington Post* and the major media were sourcing high-level Administration officials and drinking their Kool-Aid by the gallon, KR was asking the right people the right questions as to actual proof of alleged Weapons of Mass Destruction and the supposed Iraq-Al Qaeda links. And this from an organization with newspapers in cities with large military bases such as Lexington, KY and Forth Worth, TX.

The link between a media corporation that seems to encourage learning and the journalists who get things right may be pressing a point too far. After all, KR's Washington bureau was just doing its job. Still, one wonders if the war in Iraq might have been scuttled if enough media followed KR's thoughtful, diligent leadership and did their jobs instead of cheerleading us into war.

Monday, October 9, 2006
Doctorow, Doctorow, Give Me the News
E.L. Doctorow reminds us of the immense power of storytelling. Long before Guttenberg, oral storytelling was the universal media for passing knowledge and norms between generations.

Of course, stories are used by leaders to achieve outcomes that are both good and bad. In his latest book, *Creationists* (2006), Doctorow helps us understand how and why narrative, plot and character development are used to inform, motivate, persuade, control, unify and, yes, too often deceive us.

Doctorow suggests that we, as citizens and employees, have an excruciating job discerning between the fiction and nonfiction found in our leaders' stories. He said to Tom Ashbrook on NPR's September 20th *On Point* broadcast, "It's the people who tell the stories who claim that they are nonfiction who do the most damage. If I write a bad story, there are no great consequences. The book won't sell. It'll be reviewed, criticized and thrown out. But if the President tells a bad story, it'll resound around the world and have enormous consequences, usually bad."

February 11, 2005
It Really Happened: Charge Account
KwaZulu-Natal, South Africa
Our guide Sebastian suggested we take the jeep up to the Tembe Elephant Park near the Mozambique border, and so we did. Pat and I

have been on safari in the Hluhluwe-Imfolozi Game Reserve in South Africa and we were eager to see yet another side of this wondrous country. Tembe was teeming with elephants, especially at the large watering holes shared with countless zebra and wildebeests. We ventured down a sandy path enveloped by a rich, leafy canopy when we were confronted by a big old bull who was in no mood to let us pass. We waited in place, since Sebastian assured us that this gigantic specimen would eventually move on. He did not.

Every time we continued down the path, he snorted and feigned a charge. That is, until he actually charged us. Three times! The lane was too narrow to enact a quick turnaround, and Sebastian assured us that trying to exit the other side of the jeep or even attempting to turn around might encourage the beast to do more than simply scare us. On his last charge, the bull trumpeted loud, approached my window and blew a rather sizeable portion of sand at us from just yards away. As he backed off, and yet continued to stand his ground, we slowly turned around and got the hell out of there.

This big old bull was in an ornery mood. Tembe is home to 250 elephants and some of the largest in the world.

CHAPTER 3

JUSTICE

Saturday, January 28, 2017
Our Tortured Path

There are four compelling reasons why any serious, sane and knowledgeable leader opposes torture:

1. It is an abhorrence in violation of all moral, ethical and religious standards.
2. It is illegal both in terms of US law and international protocols such as the Geneva Convention and the UN Universal Declaration of Human Rights.
3. It will subject our own men and women in uniform to torture. Is waterboarding torture? Well, we hung Japanese soldiers as war criminals for waterboarding our POWs during World War II. We were right then and we are correct today to classify waterboarding as torture.

    Most real warriors who served our nation such as General Jim Mattis get this point and oppose torture. Much to our continued horror, however, we had in VP Dick Cheney and now, again, in the new occupant of the Oval Office, deferment-seeking, pseudo-macho, armchair-warrior pretenders who think that torture is plausible.

    Remember it was Jim Mattis who told his new boss that he can get more out of a prisoner with a cigarette and Coke than he can with waterboarding.

4. Besides, torture doesn't work. Not even remotely. Just ask the Israelis. There is vast research and scientific proof of torture's gross inadequacy. Put simply, enemy subjects will say anything to stop the torture. Tough interrogation? Yes, absolutely, and as required. Blatant torture including waterboarding? No.

As we travel through this darkness together, we must always remind ourselves that this great nation is better than this.

January 16, 2017

Now That's a Leader: John Lewis

Congressman John Lewis (D-GA) is a true American hero and authentic national treasure. Anyone with any sense would know this to be true. His exquisite "talk" over many decades is only surpassed by his profoundly courageous "action." On this day honoring Martin Luther King and other brave civil rights warriors such as John Lewis, it's useful to recall Dr. King's insight that, "Darkness cannot drive out darkness; only light can do that. Hate cannot drive out hate; only love can do that." These sentiments – and John Lewis' enormous legacy – are readily understood by any sane, serious leader.

Congressman John Lewis has seen it all before, so the uninformed attack on him by President-Elect Trump in January 2017 certainly came as no surprise.

August 4, 2016

Now That's a Leader: Stacy Bannerman

Atlanta

Stacy Bannerman's husband tried to kill her. She survived to tell the story. It's an all-too-common narrative of rage, domestic abuse, suicide and murder in families today with PTSD-afflicted veterans. We're very good at sending our sons and daughters into harm's way – too good at it, actually – and shamefully ill-equipped to help returning and often psychologically damaged service members re-enter civilian society. The toll this takes on military families is horrendous.

Bannerman's husband was a two-time Iraq War veteran who was prone to considerable violence. She chose to end their marriage, justifiably fearing that remaining married would have ended her life. She also chose to advocate powerfully for military families in a society that likes to salute our men and women in uniform at sporting events and then forget about them, their families and our nation's permanent-war condition. Bannerman's new book, *Homefront 911: How Families of Veterans are Wounded by Our Wars* (2015) places a necessary, harsh spotlight on this issue and gives families specific tools to cope with the situation at home, to advocate for more enlightened policies and, ultimately, to heal.

Saturday, November 15, 2014

Food For Thought

Ho Chi Minh City, Vietnam

I've been fortunate to sample interesting foods all over the world. There was the camel roast one evening in Dubai's Margham Desert, the reindeer in Thule at the top of Greenland, fresh-killed elk on a working elk ranch near the Franz Josef Glacier in New Zealand, the crocodile at Mama Africa's in Cape Town, the conger eel at Santiago, Chile's Liguria, a goat tajine in a friend's New Jersey apartment, unpasteurized camembert from Montreal's Jean-Talon Market and, well, an assortment of flowers, fungi and a few insects, too. Pat and I are expecting some culinary adventures here in the former Saigon, too, including dinner in a few nights at the highly regarded Cuc Gach Quon.

These forays occasionally, though perhaps not as often as they should, raise questions for me about humankind's relationship to all other animal species. What are our rights and responsibilities as consumers of animal flesh? I'm not a vegan or vegetarian, so I obviously believe we have the right, if not the need, to kill animals to survive and thrive as a species. I certainly respect vegetarians who disagree with this assertion, but only if they don't wear that choice militantly on their sleeves.

Still, it's reasonable to ask where the bright line of justice for animals should be drawn. How much torture of cattle, pigs and chickens in factory production of food is too much? How can we really know the precise provenance of much of our food, anyway? Am I to ask our hosts in a family-run pho shop here the origins of their ingredients, question the sushi masters near Tokyo's fabled Tsukiji Fish Market on the nature of their tuna suppliers' fishing methods or, for that matter, ask the counter person at the BBQ joint in Dallas' Deep Ellum neighborhood how much gasoline it took to produce that one ear of corn and deliver it to my plate? I don't think so.

Many of us should care enough to consider some of these questions, when appropriate. We should try to choose meals that both demonstrate a reasonable commitment to hunting, housing and processing meat in humane ways and using the entire animal from nose to tail. I'll never answer these questions well or conclusively, and the entire subject matter is a luxury for those who go to bed hungry, but we're better off thinking about it.

Ha Long Bay in Vietnam's Gulf of Tonkin is a UNESCO World Heritage Site. Sailing it in a traditional "junk" was another welcome addition to life's bottomless bucket list.

Sunday, May 4, 2014
Party Like it's 1399
Philadelphia
Prince once told us to "party like it's 1999." Now it's a Sultan who's frolicking like it's 1399. The Sultan of Brunei announced this week that his nation is adopting his version of Sharia Law, condemning his 400,000 citizens to medievalism – and worse. Bruneians will now be subject to public flogging, dismemberment and death-by-stoning for a host of "crimes" that no doubt will include being gay and lesbian or out of step with his edition of reactionary dogma. Yes, even Brunei's Christian and Buddhist minorities are now subject to this time-warp fantasy.

You might remember the Sultan Hassani Bolkiah for paying Michael Jackson $17 million to sing at his 50th birthday party in 1996. Here's Mark Seal writing about the "orgiastic wealth" of the Sultan and brother Jefri in the July 2011 *Vanity Fair*:

> *"They raced their Ferraris through the streets of Bandar Seri Begawan, the capital, at midnight, sailed the oceans on their fleet of yachts (Jefri named one of his Tits, its tenders Nipple 1 and Nipple 2). The brothers routinely traveled with 100-member entourages and emptied entire inventories of stores such as Armani and Versace, buying 100 suits of the same color at a time. When they partied, they indulged in just about everything forbidden in a Muslim country."*

Yes, hypocrisy knows no bounds. So read it and creep. There ought to be a law.

Wednesday, March 26, 2014
Now That's a Leader: Oral Lee Brown
Too many people in leadership positions are merely pretending to be leaders while most real leaders go unheralded. Oral Lee Brown deserves our recognition and respect. One of 12 children born into poverty in Mississippi, Brown relocated to Oakland, earned a college degree and started a career as a real estate agent. One day in 1987, she visited a first-grade class in Oakland. In the spur of the moment, and consumed by emotion, she told those 23 students from extremely challenging

backgrounds that she would somehow find a way to pay for their college educations if they got good grades and stayed out of trouble. Well, thanks to Oral Lee, almost all of these students have now graduated from college.

Friday, August 16, 2013
Oprah's Handbag and the National Purse
Zurich
The United States is hardly alone in struggling with its immigration demons. Even Switzerland with its fabled multicultural, multilingual social structure is dealing with nativist fears of the "other." Oprah might have been told at a pricey boutique here recently that she could not afford an expensive handbag, but that clerk's reported ignorance underscores a larger threat to the national purse, too.

The simple truth is that Switzerland cannot compete and succeed in today's global economy without the workforce and entrepreneurial contributions of immigrants. The same can be emphatically said of the United States or Sweden, for example, which experienced its own share of destructiveness around racially and religiously charged immigration issues earlier this year.

What's so concerning in Switzerland, however, where 1.8 million of eight million inhabitants are "foreigners," is that the view of outsiders is not what it used to be. Even in this highly civilized and welcoming nation, superficially not unlike Sweden in that sense, small but vocal pockets of far-right fringe groups exert disproportionate influence over the national dialogue on immigration. Sound familiar? They stoke primal fears of immigrants – chiefly those with dark skins and non-Christian faiths – that work directly against their own economic self-interests and wreak havoc with their national brands.

The successful effort by the populist, right-wing Swiss People's Party in 2009 to ban the construction of minarets in Switzerland is one case in point. Another is to be found in Bremgarten, a town 20 kilometers west of here, where legitimate asylum seekers have been banned from public accommodations such as swimming pools. The Swiss Refugee Council told *The Financial Times* that the law is intolerable in both legal and humanitarian terms.

An online poll by the Zurich-based, German-language tabloid *Blick* reports that 43 percent of respondents in this nation believe the Swiss are racist, though it's likely these results are inflated by the immediacy of Oprah's news. Still, this appears to be a different Switzerland than the 19th and 20th Century idyll we once knew – or thought we knew. Minimally, the tensions about immigration that have long simmered below the surface here have now percolated into the mainstream, abetted by voracious social media and an around-the-clock appetite for what passes as news.

The vast majority of cooler heads here know the facts, thankfully. The OECD's 2013 *International Migration Outlook*, for example, estimated that immigrants to Switzerland contributed net gains of nearly eight billion dollars to the national economy, almost two percent of Gross National Product. Yes, many of these immigrant workers are from EU nations, but the data nonetheless put a lie to claims by the Swiss People's Party and other xenophobes here and around the world that immigrants take more from the social welfare system than they contribute.

Furthermore, changing demographics find nations such as Italy, Russia, Japan and, yes, Switzerland getting older and in desperate need of young workers and consumers, as life expectancies grow and birth rates decline. Many nations have elevated concerns about aging populations to the level of national strategy, for who is going to fill technology jobs, build start-up companies and purchase what they make?

Sure, the United States is getting older as the Baby Boomers enter their retirement years, however partial and delayed these retirements have become. What has separated us from these other nations economically threatened by aging populations, however, is that we have, until recently, accommodated if not invited younger, more diverse immigrant populations to build their lives and careers within our borders.

Competitive advantage will accrue to nations with immigration policies that purposefully balance the irrefutable economic and demographic benefits of immigration with reasonable, focused efforts to modulate the number of immigrants and curb abuses. Societies that surrender to the forces of fear will sow the seeds of their own economic demise. So next time you hear such unfounded blather coming from anti-immigrant nativists and isolationists, take that $38,000 handbag Oprah wasn't allowed to buy and swing it over their heads.

Zurich's idyllic charm belies Switzerland's mounting tensions with immigrants and refugees.

It Really Happened: Andrei Codrescu

It was 1999 and I was reading Andrei Codrescu's latest book, *Messiah*. I was ensconced at the bar at Tipitina's in New Orleans, the original location that has played home over many years to the likes of Dr. John, The Meters and Allen Toussaint. Tipitina's remains a cradle for New Orleans music, slightly and thankfully outside tourism's gaze.

A fellow sitting next to me at the bar leaned over and asked, "Why are you reading that crap?" I remember that his treatment of the word "crap" took such disdainful, scurrilous form splayed as it was in a thick, gravelly Eastern European accent. I turned to this stranger and slowly realized that he was, indeed, author, editor and NPR commentator Andrei Codrescu. We ordered a round of drinks and spoke for 20 minutes on many subjects including his NPR commentaries, about which he raised his voice at one point and said, "Screw NPR." The network had just reduced his role there. He graciously signed my copy of his book. I later read his inscription that hilariously included the line, "Screw NPR."

Bringing it at the Maison Bourbon in New Orleans.

Tuesday, June 25, 2013
Polar Opposites
Woods Hole, MA
Nelson Mandela lays dying in a Pretoria hospital on the day Silvio Berlusconi is sentenced to seven years in prison for having sex with a minor. His tax-evasion trial will soon start. In a world desperate for

effective leadership at all levels, the former is among the best leaders in modern history while the latter is a fool. The former did 27 years in prison for his greatness while the latter will likely never serve a day in prison, despite being a crooked, buffoon-in-chief.

Thursday, May 23, 2013
Burning Isolation
My Swedish friends called it "invandrare ghetto" – immigrant's ghetto. I found myself living in a distant Stockholm "suburb" called Rinkeby years ago as I started a fellowship in Sweden. My new friends were appalled that the Stockholm School of Economics located me where no Swedes lived and so far away from the school. Truth is, they held Rinkeby in great disdain. Three weeks into my experience, they found a downtown apartment for me.

What I saw in Rinkeby – and what exists today in nearby Husby, the focal point of the Stockholm riots – was an interesting, restless pastiche of Turkish, Moroccan, Syrian, Croatian and Ethiopian guest workers and their families. Like many of Europe's northern economies, then and now, Sweden encouraged people from the "south" to take low-level manufacturing, restaurant, hospital and service jobs. And the immigrants came, attracted no doubt to Sweden's social-welfare amenities.

There was and remains a clear though unspoken problem, however. Insufficient efforts have been made to assimilate guest workers into Swedish society. They are treated as outcasts and, indeed, subjected to racial abuse by a tiny but attention-getting number of Swedes – especially late at night on Stockholm's subway and buses, for example.

Nations cannot invite others to join them, treat them poorly, keep them isolated and somehow expect to maintain peace. Of course, the immigrants themselves must do a much better job of not defaulting to their own enclaves and turning inward, though this is easier said than done. Expect more cars to burn, and worse. This problem is not going away.

Tuesday, May 21, 2013
Heaven Help Us
We live at a time when Orthodox priests lead thousands of fellow haters in beating and stoning peaceful gay and lesbian marchers in Tbilisi, Georgia last Friday. If these former Soviet nations expect to join the

civilized world – let alone achieve their dream of EU accession – they had better wake up. Bishop Iakobashvili, the apparent leader of this rogue gang of marauding clerics, told his flock on Sunday that he was not able to condemn or justify the attacks. Oh really?

Tuesday, March 12, 2013
A Lot of Sharp Lawyers
South by Southwest in Austin
Pulitzer Prize winner and *New York Times* reporter Michael Moss is here at SXSW with his important book, *Salt, Sugar and Fat: How the Food Giants Hooked Us* (2013). Given how much more complex the bad-food battle is than the tobacco fight, I asked him how society will ever make major progress. "It's going to take a lot of sharp lawyers," he told me.

Monday, February 18, 2013
Bart, Barbie and the Buddha
No, it's not the title of some zany 1970s chase film. Instead, here are three things – a Simpsons' cartoon character, a doll and a religious icon – that are banned by the Government of Iran. The BBC reminds us this morning of what insecure little men do to retain power and, thankfully, look utterly ridiculous in the process. Ayatollah Khamenei, Mahmoud Ahmadinejad and their crowd are afraid of so many things. Fear oozes from their every pore. They need a closed system to maintain power. It's just too bad that in banning Bart, Barbie and Buddha, they've not outlawed Bozos, too.

It Really Happened: Jesse Helms
Washington, DC
I was dining at Morton's in the late-1990s with my friend John Culver, the wonderful former US Senator from Iowa. John noticed somebody behind me and motioned him to our table, whereupon then-Senator Jesse Helms (R-NC) appeared. There wasn't a utensil on the table to prevent my skin from crawling. The ultra-conservative firebrand greeted John like a dear friend, however, portraying a civility across political perspectives that has vanished today. John asked Senator Helms to join us for a drink.

Helms' politics were loathsome. He never flinched in derailing and ultimately voting against, for example, support for mental health reform.

He was brutally wrong to oppose such measures over many decades. To be fair, however, Joe Biden told Tom Ashbrook's *On Point* show last week that many years ago Helms and his wife adopted a severely mentally ill girl confined to a wheelchair and that he had been personally generous on mental health issues. My opinion of Helms certainly does not change – he was a world-class, reactionary bastard – but Senator Biden's story reinforces the need to try to be open-minded about people who are otherwise far too easy to caricature.

Wednesday, February 13, 2013
An Illusion
Plenty of media coverage in Los Angeles last week of Archbishop Jose Gomez's decision to relieve Cardinal Roger Mahony of all duties. This censure stems from Mahony's role in covering-up sexual abuse scandals for years as Gomez's predecessor. Except, it was all an illusion. The LA Diocese has been forced to admit that Mahony "remains a bishop in good standing with full rights to celebrate the Sacraments and to minister to the faithful without restrictions." So that's always the trick, right? Huff and puff to look tough. Then hope that nobody discovers how weak you really are.

Thursday, August 28, 2008
Now That's a Leader: Ambassador James McGee
Monterey, CA
In an age of shallow tough talk, truly courageous leaders such as US Ambassador James McGee can and do emerge. A career foreign-service officer with four previous African postings as well as a Vietnam War hero, our envoy to the failed state of Zimbabwe presents a portrait of real courage under fire.

Zimbabwe's President Robert Mugabe is a first-class scoundrel; an embarrassment to all that is civil and civilized in our world. He has banned most media from his rotting country, once an agricultural and economic powerhouse regionally, so as not to reveal to the world his ruinous tenure since the decolonization of the former Rhodesia. We must increasingly rely, therefore, on heroic renegade reporters, NGO employees and others such as Ambassador McGee to protect innocent lives and shine a bright, hot spotlight on Mugabe's many atrocities.

In the recent issue of *Vanity Fair*, Peter Godwin tells us that against Harare's wishes, McGee assembled a team of diplomats and employees from several embassies and set out to locate and interview victims of Mugabe's abuses. During the investigatory field trip, a plainclothes police officer, supported by shotgun-wielding hacks, stopped McGee, inspected his credentials, blocked his convoy's passage and ordered him to report to a local police station for questioning. Godwin writes that McGee then walked to the gates blocking his way, opened them against the police officers' threats and asked, "What are you going to do, shoot me?" He stared them down and waved the convoy through to freedom. As the late Bernie Mac exclaimed in *Ocean's 13* (2007), "'nuff said!"

Sunday, April 1, 2007
Walking in Memphis
It's that time of year again and all is well. While some of us still prefer that baseball debut on an Opening Day, it will be Opening Night this evening in a Cardinals-Mets rematch of last year's NL Championship Series. The Cards played the Indians last night in the first-ever Civil Rights Game, an end-to-Spring Training affair held at the delightful AutoZone Park in downtown Memphis.

Why a Civil Rights Game? It is astonishing to learn that only 8.5 percent of major league ballplayers today are African American, according to the Associated Press. It seems that the sport has lost its appeal with African-American boys, who now prefer football and basketball, according to Richard Lapchick, director of the University of Central Florida's Institute for Diversity and Ethics in Sports, which conducted the study. Incredibly, 19 percent of players were African American as recently as 1995 and the number was well over 50 percent in the 1970s.

Memphis' central role in the Civil Rights Movement made it an obvious site for last night's game. Several years ago, my son Jackson and I stood next to the Lorraine Hotel balcony where Dr. King was assassinated and astride the hotel room where he spent his last restless night after delivering the hauntingly beautiful "Mountaintop" speech. These are all components of The Civil Rights Museum housed in the old Lorraine, which was also a hangout for Stax Records sidemen of the time such as Booker T., Steve Cropper, Duck Dunn and Al Jackson.

Just as these members of Booker T. & The MGs broke the color barrier with an integrated band in the Mid-South, last night's Civil Rights Game underscores the truly heroic leadership of Jackie Robinson, Larry Doby and others. What is less known is that Cardinals' great Stan Musial refused to sign a locker-room petition circulated by teammates who did not want to play against Jackie, signaling the end to that nonsense in at least one clubhouse. Dodger shortstop and Robinson teammate Pee Wee Reese refused to sign a similar petition and when, in 1947, Cincinnati fans were hurling verbal racist abuse at Jackie, Pee Wee visibly put his arm around the isolated 2nd baseman and made history. Musial and Reese responded to the leadership moment that often rises suddenly and unexpectedly.

Yes, there were heroic leaders between the chalked lines. Maybe they still exist today, somewhere. Our beloved David Ortiz here in Boston is a good man who makes many contributions to the community. Another Cardinal, Curt Flood, comes to mind. He single-handedly challenged the reserve clause that kept players in contractual bondage to team owners. There's Hank Greenburg, who refused to play a game on Yom Kippur, not wanting to disparage the Jewish holy day. And there's Roberto Clemente, who died trying to help earthquake victims in Nicaragua. (You can only really understand Clemente's heroic stature in his native Puerto Rico by visiting the Roberto Clemente Sports & Education Center in Carolina. It's wonderful and just a 30-minute drive from San Juan.)

MLB Commissioner Bud Selig did something right for a change with last night's Civil Rights Game. He reminded us of the essential role sport can play in leading social change.

Sunday, April 16, 2006
Bridges and Walls
Ensenada, Mexico
Globalization is inevitable. Making globalization serve the interests of the many and not just the few is the real challenge.

Very little can, will or should stop globalization over the long term. Those calling for building social, economic or even physical walls between the US and Mexico or, say, France and its burgeoning immigrant populations must understand that nothing will ever stop poor people searching for better lives.

Yes, much needs to be done to improve US border security and to enforce legal immigration. Yet the hypocrisy on all sides of the immigration issue is breathtaking. Consider the hardliners who call for all manner of condemnation and punishment for "illegals," some of which borders on racism. It's notable that these same folks are nonetheless willing to accept campaign contributions from businesses that rely on cheap labor made possible by undocumented Mexicans, Brazilians and others. Many of these same politicians claim that illegal immigrants are depressing wages.

We cannot stop globalization. However, we can reduce illegal immigration from Mexico by seriously collaborating with that country to help build a more robust Mexican economy. Illegal immigration is only the symptom. The real problem is the hopeless state of the Mexican economy, which gives its people little reason to remain. Build the equivalent of the Berlin Wall and illegal immigration will persist. Build real economic incentives for Mexicans in their own country and illegal immigration will abate.

When will our elected officials ever accept that true leadership means addressing complex problems at their root and over the long term? The hollow rhetoric and so-called "reforms" remain window dressing that in the retail business, come to think of it, is usually assembled by undocumented workers making $5.00 an hour.

A mariachi player on the streets of Ensenada, Mexico.

It Really Happened: Bass Instincts

Ron Carter is a world-class jazz bassist, cellist and educator. I once told my friend, the late Gene McDaniels that I was planning to see Carter perform at Cambridge's Regattabar. My dear friend Alex introduced me to Gene who was himself an extraordinary talent. Gene made it big with 1960s hits such as "A Hundred Pounds of Clay," "Point of No Return" and the protest song, "Compared to What." Oh yes, he also wrote the 1974 Grammy-winning, Roberta Flack hit, "Feel Like Makin' Love." Gene's instructions to me were something like, "Tell Ron that you and I are good friends and that he's a really terrific guy." So, as the club was clearing out, I approached Carter and said, "Mr. Carter, Gene McDaniels and I are good friends. He wanted me to say hello to you and added that you're a really great guy." Carter walked right past me as he said, "Yes, I am." I could only laugh.

Ron Carter is the best traditional jazz bassist alive, but nobody tops Marcus Miller (pictured here at the Dakota Jazz Club in Minneapolis) on the electric bass. Listen to "Detroit' or "Redemption" from his Renaissance CD and try not to move or be moved. Miller played with Miles, Herbie Hancock and, well, you name it.

Saturday, January 21, 2006
Writing off Turkish Liberty
The Boston Herald
The trial lasted only minutes. The long-awaited courtroom ordeal of Turkey's most famous author, Orhan Pamuk, was abruptly postponed last month until February. Pamuk dared tell a Swiss newspaper that Turkey had indeed massacred one million Armenians in 1915 and 30,000 Kurds since the start of that civil war in 1984. For these statements, he is accused of the "public denigration" of Turkish identity and faces three years in prison.

The actions taken by Turkey's angry, right-wing judiciary could not come at a worse time for that nation. As Turkey emerges from its post-Ottoman malaise and eagerly asserts its legitimate desire to enter the European Union, it continues to wrestle with the ghosts of its darker past. The Pamuk case and other public defamation actions against those who dare to speak truth are predicated on the notorious Article 301 of the Turkish Penal Code. These cases are once again – needlessly and recklessly – placing Turkey itself on trial in the court of world opinion.

Turkey is a land of extraordinary contrast and contradiction – a European nation bordering Iran, Iraq and Syria, a largely Islamic culture housed in a secular state, and a NATO member astride the Middle East that enjoys a reasonable, long-term relationship with Israel.

Turkey is expected to jump through many hoops as part of the 10-year EU accession process, now under way. It is also expected to continue undertaking needed economic and political reforms to achieve membership. It's clear that the country is on the move, however, opening wider to outside influences while justifiably refusing to sell its rather remarkable soul.

Turkey's real growth rate exceeded eight percent last year, making it the economic envy of EU nations such as France and Italy, whose economies have been growing at a one or two percent clip annually.

Still, it is the Pamuk trial and other reactionary tendencies that have the potential to undermine Turkey's EU application. The government of Prime Minister Recep Tayyip Erdogan says it is helpless to stop the judiciary's actions against Pamuk and others. It must realize, however, that growing numbers of politicians in Britain, France, Germany and elsewhere will cravenly use these cases to declare that Turkey has not changed its prison stripes.

The Erdogan government must certainly understand that these judicial actions provide Turkey's legion of critics in nationalist parties across Europe with a convenient cover to sell the fear, xenophobia, racism and religious intolerance that constitute their real opposition to Turkey's membership in the European Union.

Turkey must understand that fear, not economic growth rates, will determine the outcome of its EU bid. Only 40 percent of Europeans now support Turkish EU membership, down from 45 percent earlier this year. A meager one-third of French and German citizens support Turkey's EU accession at a time when fear of crime, job loss and terrorism are so high.

Just watch the jockeying now underway between Nicolas Sarkozy and Dominique de Villepin to become France's next prime minister, and you will see how fear of racial, ethnic and religious differences is being used to divide and conquer, whether it's in a Paris suburb or an EU bargaining table. The same can be said about the ways in which the new Merkel government in Germany, a weak coalition from the start, will pander to racist elements on its right flank to retain power. Listen to those who talk about preserving Judeo-Christian traditions in Europe and ask what they really mean.

The "us vs. them" politics of fear will work well in Paris, Berlin and elsewhere to frustrate Turkey's ambitions. So instead of labeling Pamuk and others who speak truth to power as traitors and unpatriotic, Ankara should simply rise above it and deny fear merchants more ammunition than they deserve. Indeed, it is the brittleness and pettiness of some of Turkey's top politicians and judges that may well be the undoing of its EU bid. Turkey is a great nation that can make a substantive case for becoming part of the European Union. However, it must first make the case that the ghosts of its past are gone but not forgotten.

Thursday, August 19, 2004
Cost of Success in Sweden
Boston Globe
I love Sweden. So I read with delight Jonathan Power's *Boston Globe* op-ed, "Sweden's quiet success" a few days ago. It is important to recognize,

however, that Sweden's experiment has been undertaken in a nation with a homogenous population of just nine million. Sure, America should look closely at the Swedish model of enlightened capitalism. Yet we should recognize that the Swedish approach would not survive in our extraordinarily diverse population of 290 million. I lived and studied in Sweden, at first in a bleak Stockholm suburb that my friends called "the immigrants' ghetto." Power says that, "immigrants have been welcomed generously." One has only to ride the Stockholm subway on a Saturday night to witness slurs hurled at Turks, Serbs and Africans from drunken, restless teenagers to understand that Sweden might get it more than most nations, but it is far from a paragon of virtue.

Sunday, July 20, 2003
S Marks the Spot
Boston Herald (with Martha Fields)
Seneca, Selma, Stonewall and San Francisco. Civil rights history comes alive with the mere mention of their names. It seems that "S" words consistently mark the spot when it comes to civil rights history in this country.

Recent Supreme Court decisions on affirmative action and gay rights have, once again, thrust civil rights issues back onto the American agenda. That was certainly the case in 1965, when the March on Selma forced the nation to confront an appalling lack of civil rights for its African-American citizens. Four years later, the 1969 riots at the Stonewall Bar in Manhattan catalyzed the civil rights movement for gays and lesbians. In 1977, the occupation of a government building in San Francisco finally compelled political officials to get serious about the rights of people with disabilities. In each case, progress took gut-wrenching, lapel-grabbing media moments to focus attention, demand results and force change.

Imagine, then, what it was like 155 years ago this week in Seneca Falls, New York. The groundbreaking 1848 Seneca Falls Convention on women's rights marked the emergence of women as a political force. In a year when abolitionists were heartened by the end to slavery on several Caribbean islands, social reformers like Lucretia Mott and Elizabeth Cady Stanton insisted that women should start asserting their rights, too. They had asked a handful of friends to join them in Seneca Falls on July 19th to organize a new political movement. Instead, some 300 women, dubbed by the local newspaper as a bunch of unhappy spinsters, heard their call, descended upon the tiny New York hamlet and forever changed the course of women's rights in this country.

So what do Seneca, Selma, Stonewall and San Francisco tell us about the state of civil rights in America today? For one thing, we should recognize and celebrate the fact that great progress has been made. At the same time, however, we must accept the painful truth that we have an equally great distance to travel before overcoming the fear of change and the fear of difference that continue to divide us. Sure, we should find purpose and inspiration in the courage and leadership demonstrated at Seneca, Selma, Stonewall and San Francisco, but we need to be realistic in acknowledging that the road to justice is never fast enough, never straightforward and predictable, and never without its opposition and reversals.

However, something very important happened during the recent Supreme Court deliberations on affirmative action and gay rights. A newfound maturity was evident that rose above the din of fear and hatred and powerfully underscored that we are slowly but inexorably evolving as a society. In the University of Michigan case, affirmative-action advocates were joined by hundreds of organizations supporting the school's admissions policies, including dozens of Fortune 500 corporations that have grown to understand the powerful and necessary role diversity plays in their own competitiveness. Gay-rights advocates also enjoyed increasing support from business, political and religious groups who were simply nowhere to be found when Stonewall erupted in 1977.

That's just the point. It's obviously important to celebrate Seneca, Selma, Stonewall and San Francisco as hard-earned civil-rights milestones, just as we recognize Black History Month in February, Women's History Month in March and so on. Each of these occasions holds special symbolic and substantive appeal. However, we'll never realize the full promise of civil rights as a nation until we stop narrowly interpreting these events and occasions as victories only for one disenfranchised group or another.

Isn't it time to start viewing Seneca Falls and the others as sacred ground for us all, not just for some of us? Isn't it time to celebrate the contributions of women, African-Americans, and all diverse peoples every day, not just during designated and increasingly commercialized periods? Isn't it time to reject fear-based, zero-sum logic that suggests programs like affirmative action benefit one group at the expense of another?

What's the best way this week to celebrate the 115th anniversary of the 1848 Seneca Falls Convention? Let's start by recognizing that women who are the beneficiaries of the progress initiated in Seneca Falls are of all races, sexualities and abilities, as they are the mothers, daughters, sisters, friends or colleagues of diverse men and women of every kind. Let's accept that the march toward freedom and justice for each diverse group is actually a march toward freedom and justice for everyone. By doing so, only then will we embrace the true lesson of Selma, Seneca, Stonewall and San Francisco – that "S" marks the spot for us all.

Tuesday, December 25, 2001
Pressuring Vietnam on Human Rights
Boston Globe (with Nam Pham)
Christmas bombing. That's a term loaded with paradox. Twenty-nine years ago this week, the United States bombed North Vietnam. The Nixon administration was frustrated over what it saw as North Vietnamese obstinance at the Paris Peace Talks. The administration believed that bombing would force Hanoi back to the table. It was a highly disputed strategy, but it seemed to work. Talks resumed, and a peace pact was reached in January 1973.

It is useful to examine where democracy stands today in Vietnam, almost 30 years later. A national obsession for decades, Vietnam has virtually disappeared from the scope of our war on terrorism.

Yes, Vietnam has made some tangible and laudable reforms, chiefly in normalization of diplomatic and trade relations. American business leaders and elected officials understand the value of doing business with Vietnam.

Expansion of trade relations, however, does not mask the tortured path to democracy. As is the case with China today, some will argue that effective trade relations are a precursor to actual democratization. They will say, "Take it one step at a time," and they are not entirely wrong.

However, patience has its limitations. The Bush administration must ask how long it will take to build democracy. Indeed, when will we know that Vietnam is getting serious about it?

Just days before the events of 9/11, the House of Representatives passed the Vietnam Human Rights Act by a 410-1 vote. The act would make granting non-humanitarian aid conditioned upon Vietnam's human rights performance. It would also assist democratic forces in the country, while authorizing additional funding for Radio Free Asia to penetrate jamming by the Vietnamese government.

The bill has been bottled up in the Senate for more than three months. If we've learned anything since 9/11 it is that our ideals transcend commerce. Yes, open markets are integral to our system, but human rights are indispensable. And Vietnam's record, under an elderly and repressive regime, would not meet the standards of most Americans.

Let's look at the facts: Vietnam has yet to evolve beyond the tyranny of one-party rule. The Communist Party remains the official voice of some 80 million people. Before Russia, the Czech Republic and other reform-minded states got serious about democracy, they rejected one-party rule and opened their systems to the ballot box.

Vietnam's persecution of its Montagnard population also continues without hesitation. Earlier this fall, 14 Protestant Montagnards from the Central Highlands were sentenced for up to 12 years in prison for participating in protests calling for religious freedom. Their trials were closed and lasted one day. In October, Father Nguyen Van Ly was sentenced to 15 years in prison. His crime? He had advocated a brand of Catholicism not sanctioned by the government, assisted in flood relief measures not approved by the government and advanced democratic reforms not welcomed by the government.

Last month Vietnam deported two German nationals for attempting to preach political and religious freedom. This followed the deportation of a Belgian national earlier in the year for wanting to meet with a detained Buddhist dissident, as well as the removal of a Norwegian parliamentarian after he dared to meet with Father Ly and others. Shades of the Taliban?

What is Hanoi's reaction to those who oppose its repression of political, religious and press freedoms? It makes them very nervous. They tell us to mind our own business. They even placed blame for the events of 9/11 on what they call "isolationist US foreign policy."

Two days after the collapse of the World Trade Center towers, the official *People's Army Daily* condemned America's chauvinism and linked the 9/11 attacks directly to brazen interference by the United States in Vietnam's human rights performance.

OK, so let's not be isolationist. Let us take a firm stand wherever universal human rights are denied. That's why the US Senate must follow the lead of its House colleagues and pass the Vietnam Human Rights Act. That's why Senator John Kerry (D-MA) must act in his capacity as chairman of the Senate Subcommittee on East Asian and Pacific Affairs. With apologies to Calvin Coolidge, the business of America is not just business. Trade relations are a good place to start, but true progress must ultimately reflect the passions of people and not just the promise of profits. That's why human rights can never be just business as usual.

Lunch break on the Thu Bon River in Hoi An, Vietnam.

CHAPTER 4

GLOBAL

June 29, 2016
What's the Matter with Yorkshire?
Detroit

The Brexit vote provides yet another painful example of people voting against their economic interests and their children's future because of misplaced fear of "the other" – immigrants in this case. After all, many of the rural communities in England and Wales that voted for Brexit enjoy substantial trade with European Union nations that is now at risk. The Brexit voters' understandable anger over diminishing jobs will now, ironically, diminish their employment prospects even further.

Besides, shouldn't we believe in something greater than ourselves? The time is never right to crawl into a dimly lit room, draw the blinds tight and hide under the covers. History shows us time and again that isolationism never works – never! Sure, the EU is a mess and in need of serious structural reform. So reform it. Don't run away.

The abject failure of leadership in this debacle has been breathtaking. First, there's the arrogantly myopic and moronic choice by Prime Minister Cameron to farm this decision out to plebiscite without any leadership role on his part or that of Parliament. That's not democracy; it's chaos.

Then there's the clownish, light-on-policy and even lighter-on-details Boris Johnson who placed his own lust for power ahead of doing the right thing. Indeed, the former London Mayor decided late in the game which side to take and then used his hucksterism to scapegoat immigrants and portray the troubled EU as the worst kind of demon imaginable. Johnson's selfishness, arrogance, ignorance, values-free and fact-free approach place him very high on any Trumpian measure of low character. Imagine those two hair-do-wells running both sides of the "special relationship"?

And Johnson's Leave ally and UKIP leader Nigel Farage has always been daffy, but his absurdist, nativist sputterings over the past few months would shame anyone actually capable of feeling shame.

That leaves us with Labor and its crackpot leader, Jeremy Corbyn. He was a half-hearted Remain supporter and, as with so many of these poor excuses for leadership, manipulated his way through this hot mess solely in keeping with his political ambitions.

Brexit was the proverbial perfect storm of imbecilic behaviors by second raters at the worst possible moment. Now there's hardly a decent leader available to pick up the pieces. These four historically tragic figures almost make our American politicians look good. Nah!

January 24, 2016
Right to Vote? Aussies Require It
The Boston Herald
Sydney
Australian Prime Minister Malcolm Turnbull made his first official visit to the United States this week for talks with President Obama on trade, terrorism, China and cybersecurity.

It's far too easy to take the US-Australia partnership for granted, given decades of harmonious, productive relations between Canberra and Washington. When it comes to staunch, reliable US allies, they hardly come any better than Australia.

Still there are substantial differences between our two nations – especially when it comes to voting. Americans tend to see voting in federal and state elections largely as a right whereas Australians believe going to the polls is a responsibility – officially. Australia is one of more than 20 nations (others include Argentina, Brazil and Singapore) in which voting is compulsory. It has been against the law not to vote in Australia for over 80 years. In fact, it's illegal to not register to vote.

Critics abound on both sides of the compulsory-voting debate. On the one hand, Australia can point to a 90 percent participation rate in federal elections that puts to shame our persistent 50 percent to 60 percent turnout for presidential elections. On the other hand, some observers question the utility and even veracity of these reported participation rates. First, not everyone registers to vote, despite the fact that they are required to do so. Plus, many people simply "mark" their ballots without actually voting for any specific candidate, complying technically with the law while registering their own kind of protest vote.

While supporters of compulsory voting speak about greater and better-informed engagement within the electorate, critics contend that forced voting by its very nature is undemocratic. In the United States, especially, detractors believe that compulsory voting denies citizens' First Amendment rights. After all, they argue, the right to speech would seem to support the right not to speak, too.

Critics also point out that many of the nations with compulsory voting requirements do not actually enforce these laws, and those that do so offer only minimal penalties for failing to comply. Nonvoting Australians typically receive a letter with a token fine, which some people pay and others protest. Nonetheless, compulsory-voting advocates maintain that greater levels of engagement by larger numbers of voters can help prevent demagogues and other assorted madmen from snaring elections based on the turnout of a small but rabid few.

On balance, compulsory voting would not seem to make sense for the United States. It's simply not part of our national character, and serious questions exist about its efficacy and even its constitutionality. That said, US politics are broken. We would be well-served to engage in a vigorous national dialogue about rebalancing our rights and responsibilities as voters and citizens. In that light, Australia can teach us a few things.

A koala bear in a eucalyptus grove on Kangaroo Island, Australia.

Tools of Trade: Promoting Freedom
The Boston Herald
January 24, 2015
The Obama Administration continues to push hard for the Trans-Pacific Partnership "free trade" deal, which the US been negotiating with 11 other Pacific nations since 2008. The embattled deal is seen as a cornerstone of the President's "pivot to Asia" and a bulwark against China's restless economic and territorial ambitions, including Beijing's own proposed trade deal for the region. Long-shot passage of the TPP would give

the President a desperately needed political win that, ironically, could come with the support of some Republicans in Congress who rarely see a free trade deal they don't like.

The still-developing pact has produced no shortage of controversies, however, such as the criticisms leveled by US Senator Elizabeth Warren (D-MA) and other politicians about the lack of transparency in TPP negotiations, the 20th round of which occurred in Ottawa in July. Add to these concerns over secrecy other contentious negotiations on currency manipulation, intellectual property, market access, agriculture and financial services and it would be difficult to imagine the successful completion of TPP any time soon.

The TPP represents much more than trade negotiations, however. The US, Australia, Canada and the other participating democracies are wasting a rare, once-in-a-generation opportunity to ensure that admission to the kind of club TPP represents brings with it minimum expectations for how member nations treat their own citizens. Vietnam is a critical case in point.

Vietnam entered the TPP negotiating framework in 2008 and hosted the 7th round of negotiations in 2011. In a perfect world, Vietnam deserves entry into all forums designed to integrate it into the global community. However, and this is a big "however," the human rights violations of the administrations of President Truong Tan Sang, Prime Minister Nguyen Tan Dung, Secretary General of the Communist Party Nguyen Phu Trong and their predecessors must be addressed prior to Vietnam's participation in any finalized TPP. Sure, we can hear it now. TPP advocates will insist that trade waters not be muddied with inconvenient truths about political prisoners, human trafficking, freedom of the press and other messy subjects. Really? Shouldn't we expect better of Vietnam and of ourselves?

After all, Hanoi promised to improve its human rights record as part of restoration of diplomatic relations with the US in 1995. They doubled down on these commitments after the US approved Permanent Normal Trade Relations for Vietnam and granted the country Most Favored Nation status in 2007. Yes, our policy of constructive engagement has delivered economic and other benefits to both countries – Ho Chi

Minh City's downtown is booming with construction sites and filled with Europeans and Americans eager to invest in Vietnam's future – but our approach is seriously lacking when it comes to protecting basic human dignity. Indeed, commercial progress was supposed to have come with reciprocal human rights improvements, but the Venerable Thich Quang Do, leader of the banned United Buddhist Church of Vietnam, is still under house arrest for daring to advocate for human and religious rights. So too, the gravely ill Roman Catholic priest Thadeus Nguyen Van Ly, a longtime advocate for democracy and religious freedom, remains a political prisoner of conscience. Regrettably, and ironically, Hanoi refuses to accept the relationship between freedom of trade and freedom of ideas.

Vietnam continues in vain to control the media, too, which should otherwise be taking up the causes of Reverend Do, Father Ly and other political prisoners. Yes, some quasi-private media outlets have started to appear in Vietnam, but that has more to do with the growing impossibility these days of trying to suppress citizens' interest in and access to objective news and opinion. Many young Vietnamese have grown tired of state propaganda and are turning in droves to foreign and social media for relief. Too much media in Vietnam remains state-controlled. Here too, Hanoi fails to understand the relationship between free trade and free media.

Vietnam's record in human trafficking is highly problematic as well, though Hanoi is not without some improvement in recent years. The nation receives a Tier 2 ranking from the US State Department, meaning that Vietnam does not yet fully comply with the minimum standards of the Trafficking Victims Protection Act. Indeed, the open trafficking of women and children to Russia, the Middle East, China and even the United States continues in large scale. And here, too, Hanoi does not connect freedom of trade to freedom of movement.

Freedom takes many forms. It's not just about free trade. While Hanoi is stubbornly demonstrating improvement in some of these domains, if only for show, it remains perilously far from the minimum standards one should expect from a full-fledged TPP member. Vietnam is a great nation; its people are on the move and on the rise. Plus, it can be an ally of the United States in helping to counter Chinese aggression in the region. That is why it is imperative that the Obama Administration and the other negotiating parties link Vietnam's role in TPP to clear any unambiguous expectations about human rights performance. Otherwise, we will have surrendered among the very few forums in which the US and fellow TPP democracies have any leverage to do so.

It Really Happened: One Night in Vladivostok
I had the great fortune of sailing on the *USS Princeton* into Vladivostok, Soviet Union in 1990. It was the first US goodwill visit to this "forbidden city" on the Russian Pacific in over five decades.

As Navy public affairs officers and soon-to-be the first Americans most of these people had ever seen, the men and women on my team were briefed on many things. We were instructed to be aware that a senior Greenpeace official was reported to be in Vladivostok at the time of our globally publicized visit, which was intentionally scheduled in parallel with a summit meeting between then-Presidents Bush and Gorbachev. Apparently, he was protesting the US visit while also attempting to call attention to the extraordinary environmental damage done to Vlad by the Soviet Pacific Fleet. Of course, how he was allowed to enter Vlad in the first place was the subject of much speculation.

After the pomp and circumstance of the arrival ceremonies, we ventured to a restaurant in town run by North Koreans. In fact, we were escorted there by an overzealous Russian guy who wanted us to think that he was KGB. We were treated like celebrities and could not buy a drink. That's when a man came over to our table and said, "Well, I don't see too many fellow Americans around here." It was the Greenpeace guy. We had a drink with him, too.

December 3, 2014
More Gas from the Middle East
Secretary of State John Kerry used the Arabic reference to ISIL yesterday, Da'ish. ISIL, ISIS, IS, Islamic State? Enough with all the names and initializations for these criminal terrorists. Let's choose one name – an appropriate acronym in this case – that positions them best. How about Fanatical Anarchists Reigning Terror, or FART?

September 27, 2014
Tunisia Seems an Oasis Amid Chaos
The Boston Herald
New York

Amongst so much bleak news from the Arab world this week, Tunisian President Mohamed Moncef Marzouki tried to paint a picture of his nation and the North African Maghreb as bright spots in a region otherwise descending into darkness. He actually succeeded in doing so, at least occasionally.

A medical doctor and human rights advocate, Marzouki was once held in solitary confinement by the previous president, criminal dictator Ben Ali. Now, Marzouki is cautiously but firmly moving Tunisia toward a more democratic future — maybe. He took great pride in the fact that the preamble to Tunisia's constitution now codifies equal rights for women. Translating this into reality on the street, however, will be quite a different proposition.

"We still have a problem with violence against women," he said. Now that's an understatement.

He was asked why, despite high-profile political assassinations in 2013 and other major troubles, Tunisia seems to be avoiding most of the calamities and turmoil to its east. He offered at least three reasons:

First, as he candidly put it, "We have no oil." This means the West is simply less interested in Tunisia.

Next, he asserted that "the Maghreb is stable and peaceful," although one has to be skeptical about Algeria in this regard. Marzouki insisted, "Our Algerian brothers are stable. We have good relations with them, and we need that." Adding that the Maghreb, the area west of Egypt, is "the most stable part of the Arab world," provides only cold comfort. To his east, however, Marzouki said that "Libya is a heavy burden on our shoulders," with two million Libyan refugees flooding a nation of only 11 million people.

Finally, he said Tunisia has higher education levels than most Arab nations and a reasonable middle class eager to avoid sectarian violence.

A reporter asked him whether the relative absence of US military and commercial interests also helps Tunis avoid political complications, both with internal populations and other Arab nations. He reluctantly agreed, while nonetheless reinforcing his ongoing desire for US business investments in Tunisia's energy, finance and agriculture sectors.

It was interesting to observe the president's practice of letting his senior officials — including one female minister — answer some questions, too.

Regrettably, too many people in leadership positions enjoy the sound of their own, often out-of-touch voices. One minister accepted the delicacy of Marzouki's deference by noting, "The president knows these answers, he just likes to showcase us." How rare! It's called leadership. Marzouki's leadership may itself provide a rare oasis of hope in the troubled desert of today's Arab world. Let's hope it's not just another mirage.

September 25, 2014
I Told You So
New York

Turkey's President Recep Tayyip Erdogan displayed petulance and even defiance in his remarks to the Council on Foreign Relations on Monday. He was prickly, to say the least. There can be a price for life at the crossroads of so many cultures, causes and contretemps, as Turkey now finds itself in the difficult center of an arc of conflict from the Ukraine and Russia across the Black Sea to the north, Iran to the east, and Iraq, Syria and ISIL to the south – among others. These only seemed like presenting symptoms in watching Erdogan, however, so it was easy to wonder what was really bothering him.

Maybe it's nothing more than the Rodney Dangerfield Syndrome at work. Numerous times during his remarks and in fielding our questions, Erdogan lamented – bristled, really – at getting no respect from Washington, London and Brussels and not being heard when he offers what he believes to be sound advice. "We warned about Egypt (Arab Spring) and elsewhere, but our views were not taken into consideration," he said. He talked about having sounded "warning bells" about Libya, too, only to be ignored. He added that, "I have to speak the plain truth. If we had worked together in Syria from the start, we would not be where we are now." Erdogan also attacked a prominent critic of his, living in Pennsylvania, though not by name. He was undoubtedly referring the cleric Fethullah Gulen. Erdogan lamented that he has been unable to coax the Obama Administration into extraditing Gulen to Turkey for prosecution – and persecution.

Despite his "mad as hell" Peter Finch moment, Erdogan makes an important point. The truth is, we don't listen well. We don't synthesize and integrate useful insights and advice made by allies and others into our policy prescriptions often enough because, well, we know it all, right? The inevitable result of this deadly combination of ignorance and arrogance is failure, and we're certainly listening to a great deal of that lately. This is an important lesson for anyone who finds himself or herself in a leadership position, and it underscores why some of our very best leaders believe so strongly in the power of listening and the humility that comes with it.

Fareed Zakaria pushed Erdogan on the subject of last weekend's ISIL hostage release, asking what Ankara gave up in the process to achieve that outcome. The President said, "There was no monetary relationship," which is an awkward way of indicating that they did not pay a ransom. Zakaria kept at it, however, and asked Erdogan whether they exchanged prisoners and other ISIL cronies in return for the hostages. The President was cagey but did add that, "These things are possible." I guess we know the answer to that question.

It Really Happened: Love, Polynesian Style
I count meeting my extraordinary husband Walt among the happiest and luckiest moments of my life. Here is a man as sweet as he is brilliant and as humble as he is confident. Thanks to our friends at SEA Education Association, where I serve as a trustee, we sailed the brigantine *SSV Robert C. Seamans* among Tahiti and other French Polynesian islands in 2011 as working crew members. One glorious day at anchor in a cove off Fare, Huahine, we were married by the captain on the ship's quarterdeck with all hands decked out in "aloha wear." We all subsequently boarded zodiacs below and made our way to a rustic, French beach club where geckos and tropical birds joined ship's company and complete strangers to celebrate our wedding. It almost seems too cinematic to have been true.

The only thing better than marrying a guy like Walt is doing so in the cinematically tropical paradise of Huahine, French Polynesia.

September 24, 2014
How Much Ambition?
New York
Mexico's President Enrique Pena Nieto described his country's vigorous reforms in a polished but all-too-scripted manner at a Council on Foreign Relations luncheon yesterday. There can be little doubt that he is determined to implement and integrate many deep and desperately needed structural reforms across virtually every major economic and legal domain such as banking and energy. The real question is whether his laudable ambitions are too vast and even remotely achievable.

Pena Nieto is certainly an ambitious guy. As governor of the State of Mexico, he advanced a mind-boggling platform of "608 Promises" in 2005. Only 150 or so initiatives were reportedly completed under his watch. Critics in the rival PAN Party say that the number is actually closer to 50. A question for leaders in this context is whether one is better off launching a high volume of high energy into the atmosphere to see what sticks, coheres and connects? Or, alternatively, does one lose credibility in suggesting such impossibilities and remain better served by setting more conservative, realizable initiatives? This conundrum is at the core of Pena Nieto's vast challenges as well as his personal reputation. For example, his claim to have cut the murder rate in his state by 50 percent during his gubernatorial tenure had to be retracted after *The Economist* proved it was untrue.

The meeting was hosted by Robert Rubin who expressed both admiration for Pena Nieto's reach as well as understandable skepticism about his ultimate grasp. He asked the president whether Mexico's meager economic growth rates since the reforms were initiated can possibly provide "enough confidence to spur future growth." Pena Nieto seemed to understand that last year's 1.4 percent growth rate will hardly do the trick so, as these leaders are often want to do, he promised much higher growth rates in the future. Hockey sticks, anyone? We won't hold our breath but, in general, one has to admire Pena Nieto's ambition, which the US needs to support in no uncertain terms.

Wednesday, September 17, 2014
Open the Door
Iran's Foreign Minister Mohammad Javad Zarif just concluded remarks to us at the Council on Foreign Relations. He's smart and savvy, for sure,

with a doctorate from the University of Denver. Please know at the outset that I share the view of Stephen Kinzer and others that the Persians are a great people and that Iran was, should be and will again be a friend of the United States, but for the maliciousness of its current leadership and our own ineptitude in managing relations with Tehran since the manufactured Mosaddegh coup in 1953.

It's hard to get past Dr. Zarif's initial claim that, "Iran has been a responsible partner in the region." Oh really? Does he expect us to swallow this nakedly false assertion in the face of Iran's ongoing sale of weaponry to Hezbollah terrorists and the Assad regime in Syria? He said, "Hezbollah is acting responsibly." Such statements only serve to undermine everything else he says.

On the subject of ISIL, the Foreign Minister said that, "many of those now opposing ISIL helped create it in the first place." He didn't name names but, of course, he was taking a swipe at Saudi Arabia, the UAE and the United States. He called these nations a "coalition of the repentant." His anger at being "disinvited" from last week's ISIL talks in Paris flared up several times during the session. Truth be told, it's ludicrous not to have Iran at the table. They're fighting ISIL – supplying intelligence, troops, equipment and money – and Iraq is their proxy state over which they have tremendous influence. Leaving them out because US and European politicians fear being seen as doing business with Iran – as we already are on the nuclear issue, anyway – weakens the coalition and creates myriad additional problems.

It seems to me that the key to solving messy foreign policy problems is to not create too many new ones in the process. We have been very clumsy in the Middle East over the past 14 years and it is coming back to haunt us. The mutuality of interests we share with Tehran on ISIL should be used to open doors and not close them.

Sunday, July 20, 2014
Hapless, Helpless, Hopeless
This is the problem with Nigeria. As with too many nations these days, it is run – certainly not led – by indifferent incompetents and scandalous scoundrels. The Nigerian people are more cursed than blessed by oil wealth that continues to buy them nothing but injustice and agony.

The National Assembly just chose to adjourn for a two-month recess in the midst of the nation's existential crisis with the bloodthirsty gangsters, Boko Haram. Assembly members brazenly turned their backs on President Goodluck Jonathan's urgent, albeit fumbled and late-filed, request to borrow $1 billion to equip and train the military and police to fight these ruthless terrorists. The Assembly tabled the request and went on vacation, as 250 schoolgirls continue to be held hostage by Boko "Moron" and their nation slips further into the abyss. This is precisely why Nigeria proves the old saw true – it is a country of the future and always will be.

Thursday, May 22, 2014
Now That's a Leader: Bob Gates
He has always struck me as a straight shooter – a tough guy, but a good and fair man. I first met Secretary Gates when he was deputy director of the CIA in the late 1980s. Here's a man who's served under eight US presidents for over 40 years. He spoke to us yesterday at the Council on Foreign Relations as part of HBO's *History Makers* series and, to nobody's surprise, he was deeply insightful.

Gates told us that President Putin sees the restoration of Russia as an "historic calling." He said Putin is "playing the long game," however, which is problematic for the US because, "Washington DC thinks the long game is a week from Thursday." Putin is not to be trusted, of course, but Gates detailed US complicity in its souring relationship with Russia since the end of the Cold War. Fareed Zakaria asked him whether Russia was told by the US in the early 1990s that NATO would not move east to Poland and the Baltics, indicating that then-Secretary of State Baker made such a commitment. Gates said this was possible, but that he's never seen any document proving it. Interestingly, he said NATO's eastward expansion to Poland and the Baltics was actually "not a big deal" for Putin. Our mistake came in pushing the alliance even further toward flirtations with Georgia and the Ukraine that, in Gates' words, "was a bridge too far" for Putin. I agree.

He subtly chastised some US presidents and top policymakers – without naming names – for celebrating the demise of the Soviet Union too overtly and without circumspection. "We underestimated the degree of humiliation on Russia's part," Gates said, adding that President George H.W. Bush had the wisdom to "refuse to dance on the Berlin Wall." If Bush had won a second term, Gates speculated that "things might have been different." Theorizing aside, Gates was emphatic in reminding us that "Putin really does believe that the collapse of the Soviet Union was the greatest catastrophe of the 20th Century." For a people whose forbearers fought and died in the Siege of Stalingrad, that's really saying something. Or worse, how about for a people whose supreme leader saw fit to annihilate millions of his fellow citizens, as Stalin did over a brutal 30-year reign of terror? That sounds slightly more catastrophic to me.

Gates understands that the Russian bear continues to be a legitimate threat, though not as threatening as it once was. Of course, therein lies the problem. Putin's bellicosity has as much to do with his need for respect and a desired return to a greatness in the wake of so many real and perceived humiliations. It's the rare leader such as Bob Gates, however, who understands these subtleties, knows that Russia suffers vast structural problems that will ultimately limit its bluster, and can act and react with wisdom in the appropriate use of economic, diplomatic and military levers to neutralize Putin over time. Those armchair warriors who otherwise want to fight Putin by being even more like Putin should pay close attention to Bob Gates.

Wednesday, December 4, 2013
Minding Our Business
The Pew Research Center just released its quadrennial survey of US public opinion on global engagement. Sadly, the largest percentage of respondents in 50 years (54 percent) believes "the United States should mind its own business internationally." Sure, it's essential these days to know when, where and how best to engage or, more important, not to engage. We would benefit from greater discernment and dexterity in all our international involvements, since we can no longer try to do it all.

Still, it's simply not possible for the US to mind its own business – whatever that means – in today's interdependent global economy. The world is our business (and vice versa) and we must continue to resist these isolationist instincts and be more curious about the world around us. The once-rigid lines between foreign and domestic policy have blurred almost beyond the point of distinction, a claim that would frustrate the 80 percent of survey respondents who believe the US should address domestic challenges ahead of international ones. I'm no longer sure how to demarcate the differences between domestic and foreign policies in today's globalized world, anyway.

The public offers some hope here, in seemingly contradictory fashion, since 56 percent of them also reject the idea that "the United States should go its own way in the world." We couldn't go our own way in the world even if it was possible to do so. Indeed, the best way to protect ourselves against terrorism and other threats is to achieve the right balance of soft and hard power when and where it matters most and, yes, to mind our own business when it comes to other, less vital interests.

Saturday, November 30, 2013
I Am A Rock. I Am An Island.
We find ourselves rattling sabers again over territorial disputes in the China Sea. This time, it concerns mutual claims among Japan, China, Taiwan and others such as Vietnam and The Philippines of sovereignty over islands and, more importantly, their ocean and air rights. Anybody remember the misguided obsession with Quemoy and Matsu during the 1960 presidential election? (Yes, I read about it in the history books.)

President Obama is right to ask US commercial airlines to notify Chinese authorities of their intention to cross this disputed air space. After all, the 1983 Soviet shoot down of that South Korean commercial flight underscores the disastrous consequences of heightened sensitivity over territory, real or alleged. Would China do such a thing? Not likely, but the history of warfare is littered with the results of accidents and other unintended actions. So, let US air forces continue to test and impede these false sovereignty claims while keeping civilians out of harm's way.

The president missed an opportunity, however, in not asking US commercial carriers to notify Japanese and Taiwanese authorities, too. This one-sided notification arrangement favors China unnecessarily at this point and overplays our hand.

Of course, the more troubling issue here is the way in which these territorial disputes are used by China to distract public opinion – at home and abroad – from more substantive human rights and economic issues. Let's resolve this one, boys, so we can refocus on the most important issues in US-Sino relations. These territorial disputes represent symptoms and not the underlying problems.

Wednesday, October 09, 2013
The Toll of Endless War
Aboard The World in Split, Croatia
The toll of endless war is reflected in the darkness of many works of art here at the Galerija Umjetnina Split.

The powder keg that is the Balkans has found Croatians, Serbs, Bosnians, other former "Yugoslavs" and their historic predecessors warring with one another and against external adversaries for much of human history.

The last 20 years of peace here seem the exception and not the rule. This is especially poignant in light of the many new books emerging now commemorating the start of the World War One Centenary next year.

It was in this context that a comment made by a resident of Dubrovnik the other day really hit home. He said that centuries ago the Catholic Kingdom of Dubrovnik adopted a self-preservation strategy of diplomacy over militancy. It really had no choice.

They negotiated a treaty with the Ottomans wherein Constantinople would protect them against an attack by the Hapsburgs. They reached the same accord with the Hapsburgs to protect them against the Ottomans. Then, they struck a deal with both these empires to protect them against the Venetians.

They had a knack for competing well on the "enemy of my enemy is my friend" chessboard – of necessity. Too bad such cunning was not available to the Croatians in the more recent 20th Century history of needless bloodshed.

Wednesday, July 13, 2013
Now That's a Leader: Lee Yoon-hye
People reveal their true selves in a crisis. Leading is relatively easy in good times; the true test comes when things are breaking bad. The crash of Asiana Airlines Flight 214 displayed the true heroism of flight

attendants, such as Lee Yoon-hye, who was the last person to leave the burning plane after leading the evacuations. People in Lee's business are well-trained professionals who put themselves in harm's way to save our lives. Tell that to the next Alec Baldwin wannabe creep who snarls at a flight attendant because he's been asked to put away his smart phone. Thank you for the good, Ms. Lee.

Friday, May 31, 2013
BRICS is Broke
The BRICS notion advanced by Goldman Sachs' Jim O'Neill in 2001 has always been an illusion. Cute acronym aside, Brazil, Russia, India, China and (later) South Africa have little to do with one another in terms of their stages of economic development or growth trajectories. In fact, the Russian economy is substantially slowing down. Forecasters anticipate annual growth at two-to-three percent in coming years, a major decline from Moscow's previous oil-and-gas infused growth of seven-to-eight percent.

This does not auger well for Russian social order, and President Putin knows it. He needs oil-price continuity at $120/barrel to deter civic unrest. Well, today's WTI Crude Oil price is $93/barrel. Watch for Putin to become even more ruthless in these circumstances as, almost unimaginably, he now needs to focus on consolidating power. Just say nyet, anyone? Thus, Russia's top economist Sergey Guriev has fled to Paris under mysterious circumstances. Prime minister (and former president and Putin crony) Medvedev is clearly on the "outs" with the boss, too.

Putin's behavior on Syria is especially telling. Yes, he's arming the Assad regime to protect the Russian naval base in Tartus there. However, the bigger ploy is to keep Qatar out of Syria. Qatar, a substantial supporter of the anti-Assad rebellion, rivals Russia in natural gas. Should the rebels win, Qatar would box-out Russian interests in Syria and build its own pipeline. Putin likely doesn't care if Assad remains in power, if an Assad-like regime replaces him, or if civil war continues in perpetuity. He just can't afford a Qatar-fueled rebel victory and the Qatari pipeline that will follow. It's in this harsh reality that all-too-neat postulations like BRICS become very untidy. There is no BRICS and never has been.

Sunday, April 07, 2013
Golden Farces
Monocle Radio's Andrew Miller described Greece's far-right Golden Dawn movement – an emphatically ignorant and decidedly dangerous bunch – as a "deeply unpleasant gaggle of bone-headed goose-steppers of the sort that tends to flourish in European countries struggling to pay their bills." You got it!

Tuesday, February 12, 2013
Syria and History's Harsh Judgment
I participated in a conference call last night that Christiane Amanpour facilitated with UN Secretary General Ban Ki-Moon. Ban came out swinging on Syria, calling it a "self-destructing catastrophe" rife with "war crimes" and "sexual violence." Syria is being "torn apart limb by limb," he added, stressing with justifiable frustration that the international community – and especially his own Security Council – will receive the "harsh judgment of history" for not taking action. Of course, taking serious action is highly unlikely and, besides, it's all in the details anyway. Nothing will happen without Russian and Chinese leadership on the Security Council, so don't hold your breath.

Friday, May 11, 2012
Gerry Adams at it Again
Dublin, Ireland
Gerry Adams and Sinn Fein can be interesting to watch, though never to trust. Adams is using the "anti-austerity" victory of Francois Hollande in France and the results of Greece's economic and political carnage last week to voice deep-throated opposition to the pending EU fiscal stability treaty. A national referendum on the treaty will be held here on May 31st. Reasonable people can agree that Europe tilted too far in the direction of severe, no-growth policies over the past four years. Yet the grandstanding of Adams and Greece's Far-Left EU rejectionists are sobering reminders that there are few credible ways out of this mess than as one moderately integrated European Union with a far more robust growth agenda.

Pat and I happened upon a Sunday afternoon "session" at McGann's Pub in Doolin, County Clare, Ireland. The small coastal village is internationally recognized as the heart of traditional Irish music.

Friday, September 16, 2011
Connecting Dots, Incorrectly
It was a surprise, to say the least. I was almost through a September 8th Fouad Ajami column in *The Wall Street Journal* and found myself in agreement with it. And then it happened. What had been a surprisingly reasonable piece by the likes of Ajami concluded – as the "From 9/11 to the Arab Spring" headline promised – by making dubious connections between the US invasion of Iraq and this year's Arab Spring.

Ajami writes, "The spectacle of the Iraqi despot (Saddam Hussein) flushed out of his spider hole by American soldiers was a lesson to the Arabs as to the falseness and futility of radicalism." He continued, "America held the line in the aftermath of 9/11. It wasn't brilliant at everything it attempted in Arab lands. But a chance was given the Arabs to come face to face, and truly for the first time, with the harvest of their own history."

This is a dangerous, post-facto rationalization. It's also a patronizing attempt to suggest that we Americans are the chosen ones, somehow destined in this context to give other peoples their "chance." To the contrary, our choice to enter Iraq in 2003 continues to embitter the Arab Street. To act as if that decision somehow empowered if not mobilized people to rise up against dictators is delusional revisionism. Qaddafi aside, most of these dictators were or are our "friends" anyway, and nobody knows that better than the Arab people. It is not clear what the Arab Spring will ultimately look like through the long lens of history. One thing is clear right now, however; it occurred in Egypt, Libya and Tunisia – and perhaps Syria – in spite of and not because of the Iraq War.

So what is said of people who jump off the deep end in, for example, continuing to rationalize the Iraq War? They're all wet! As next year's 10th anniversary of the war approaches, we'll need much greater scrutiny of these kinds of claims if we are to separate fact from self-justifying fiction and learn from our bitterly tragic mistakes. We were faulted once for not connecting the dots. Claims like Ajami's, however, connect them dishonestly, incorrectly and dangerously.

Thursday, May 26, 2011
Gypsies, Tramps and Thieves
Detroit
This is the problem with Berlusconi. Well, actually, there are many problems with Italian Prime Minister Silvio Berlusconi. But here's one very big one. His fear of an unprecedented Center-Right defeat in Milan's mayoral elections, fueled by a stunning loss in the first round last week, finds Berlusconi and his henchmen resorting to predictable scare tactics and – guess what? – attacking immigrants and less-than-pure Italians. Sound familiar?

With breathless claims of "Zingaropoli," suggesting that Milan will become a sinister "Gypsy City" should the Center-Left win the mayoralty, Berlusconi is once again playing the petty hatred card to stoke fear and scare the vote his way. Right wingers in Europe frequently fiddle the "blame the Gypsies" tune when made insecure by economic or political misfortune or its prospect. The Le Pens in France would gladly make the

Roma people the primary focus of their scorn and ridicule, too, except they have more convenient targets for their selfish, xenophobic scare tactics in the form of North Africans.

Here's the point that Berlusconi and anti-immigrant crowds everywhere completely miss. Nations such as Italy, Japan and Russia, for example, are confronting huge demographic time bombs. Simply put, they're not producing enough babies to fuel future economic productivity and consumption and, just as alarming, taking care of all the old people. It's the opposite problem facing Egypt, Iran and Saudi Arabia, which have staggeringly large populations of restless and unemployed young people. Without immigrants and people of mixed heritage, Italy risks suffocating its own economic growth and regional clout. This point is conveniently lost on some US tub-thumping politicians, too, who cannot dare to imagine where this nation would be economically and in other ways without the energy, creativity, labor and innovation of immigrant communities.

There is good news from Milan, though. *The Financial Times* and other European media are suggesting that Berlusconi's fear-mongering may be backfiring. Despite serving as Berlusconi's power base, Milan is obviously a sophisticated place. And now even the conservative Catholic Church there is debunking "Zingaropoli" and, in doing so, perhaps thwarting Berlusconi's efforts to steal an election by blaming "the other." Wouldn't it be nice to send a message to Russian nationalists, Islamic fundamentalists, Japanese arch-conservatives, right-wing Hindu extremists and ignorant, vein-popping haters in this country that this garbage isn't going to work anymore?

To those of us hoping we can grow beyond self-serving politicians pandering to primordial base instincts, this weekend's run-off election in Milan may provide some comfort. There's reason to hope.

Saturday, May 7, 2011
Mr. Y and Sacred Cows
The Woodrow Wilson Center has just published *A National Strategic Narrative*, which should be required reading for any serious contender for national public office. Published under the pseudonym "Mr. Y," evoking George Kennan's 1947 "Mr. X" essay *The Sources of Soviet Conduct*, the

piece argues that in our new interconnected global system the United States must invest less in defense and more in sustainable prosperity and renewed global engagement.

No kidding, right? Except Mr. Y is actually two of Joint Chiefs Chairman Admiral Mike Mullen's top strategic thinkers, Captain Wayne Porter, USN and Colonel Mark Mykleby, USMC. This really shouldn't be a surprise. Many of the Pentagon's best thinkers have long maintained that old systems of fear-based containment – be they focused on Communism or terrorism – are calcifying in the face of today's Internet-accelerated, asynchronous and often unpredictable open systems. Indeed, both Mullen and Defense Secretary Gates have delivered major speeches on the need to demilitarize US foreign policy. The problem is politicians and defense contractors who insist on consuming their greasy slabs of pork in the form of expensive and even needless weapons systems designed to fight the last war; platforms that Gates, Mullen and many of our top warriors say they don't need and don't want.

Porter and Mykleby urge Americans to compete on innovation and trade with a renewed willingness to invest in education, infrastructure and alternative energy sources. Yes, they fully understand that our deficit and debt addiction ranks among our greatest national security threats. They realize, however, that reducing the deficit has much to do with appropriately calibrated withdrawals from the $3 trillion Afghanistan and Iraq forays, reductions in gold-plated weapons platforms that are unneeded and unwanted by so many people in uniform, and wise, serious restructuring of entitlements.

What they and most thinking people "get," but that otherwise eludes too many ideologues, is that deficit and debt reduction cannot come at the expense of addressing our other top national security challenges such as energy and education. We do need to walk and chew gum at the same time here. Seriously, can there be any doubt that finding alternative sources of energy for a post-oil world and ridding ourselves of reliance on Persian Gulf oil is a more serious existential issue than terrorism? Can there be any questioning that our broken K-12 mediocrity is more of a clear and present long-term danger than terrorism?

Besides, how should a proud and patriotic American feel about this country spending more on defense – in what has become something of a national security state – than the rest of the world combined and at a time of untenable deficits and urgent requirements to invest in education and infrastructure? Something is very wrong. Mullen, Porter and Mykleby are real leaders – citizen-warrior-scholars of the highest order – and they are showing us the way. Will we listen?

As an aside, my friend Dennis and I served for a week with Admiral Mullen in the mid-1990s. You'd be hard pressed to find a better leader and Naval officer, whose well-deserved retirement from service later this year is making me squeamish. We concluded our assignment aboard the carrier USS *George Washington* off Cape Hatteras, observing 24/7 flight operations with a flotilla of opinion leaders. Just prior to catapulting off the deck, then two-star Admiral Mullen motioned me over and said, "So nice of you to come out to play with the Navy, Commander McWade." Yikes! He then smiled broadly and added, "Great job. Thank you." Admiral, thank you. I'd follow you anywhere.

Tuesday, October 5, 2010
Beware Sudden Embraces of Democracy
One has to laugh at the pronouncement yesterday by former Moscow Mayor Yuri Luzhkov that he plans to form a new democracy movement. It's always fascinating to watch desperate political strongmen, such as the 18-year veteran of the Moscow mayoralty just dumped by Russian President Dmitry Medvedev, suddenly and conveniently discover the joys of democracy.

Luzhkov has been tarred by claims of corruption, some undoubtedly true and others likely not so true. What is known is that he has been notorious over two decades for helping his billionaire wife, construction mogul Yelena Baturina, secure lucrative contracts for the reconstruction of Moscow. Friends tell me that Moscow is today a high-energy city on the move, thanks in part to the Luzhkov-Baturina vision. Nobody should kid themselves, however, that this "new Moscow" emerged from anything remotely resembling democracy.

Luzhkov's cynical embrace of democracy now has to be seen in the context of the strong-armed, anti-democratic impulses that built both his city and his fortune.

Wednesday, June 17, 2009
Frightened Little Men
New York

This is what frightened little men do. At the sign of people exercising their right to live, work, love and vote in freedom, they shut down the system. The pathetic cabal of "holy men" who run Iran must be apoplectic at the thought that their hand-picked stooge – Mahmoud Ahmadinejad – may have lost last week's presidential election to the so-called moderate Mir-Hossein Mousavi. As a result, they rigged the election in favor of their boy and denied what is likely to have been a majority of Iranians – a great Persian people who are as naturally westward leaning as any in the Middle East – their choice of leader. In quintessential Ahmadinejad fashion, however, their vote-rigging was done so clumsily and awkwardly so as to have blown their cover.

These characters are now predictably resorting to the totalitarian playbook, expelling western journalists and cutting access to websites and cellular networks. People like these in leadership positions – one cannot seriously call them leaders – who fear the freedom to think and communicate openly and seek to block the unrelenting advance of technology are doomed. The only question becomes; how long will they cling to power? No country today can turn a deaf ear much longer to the aspirations of its young people, and 70 percent of Iran's population is under age 30. No country today can deny much longer the rights of women who comprise more than 50 percent of its population and over 60 percent of its college graduates.

The events now unfolding in Tehran will prove truly historic. Either these frightened little men will be forced to cede power and relax their holy dictatorship in coming years or, more likely, they will become more brutal and isolated enroute to relinquishing power a decade or two from now. Either way, the deed is done and the deal is sealed. For Iran, quite simply, there is no turning back.

Monday, March 23, 2009
Say Wa
Santa Monica

Well, it's their loss. Baseball fans and those passionate about international, cross-cultural exchanges had every reason for joy last night at Dodger Stadium. The championship finale in the World Baseball Classic between Japan and Korea was worth witnessing. Those who spurn this still-awkward tournament with all its growth pains are missing a point. This is larger than traditional American baseball. It's an emergent phenomenon that one should treat with unfolding, patient delight.

The Los Angeles Times' Bill Shaikin, a wonderful baseball scribe, writes today that fans of both sides "exuded passion and spirit for 10 of the most memorable innings ever played at Dodger Stadium, a weirdly wonderful mix of baseball game, rock concert and pep rally." You bet, although this is not a new thing for those of us who have enjoyed béisbol in the Caribbean (I once attended the Caribbean World Series in Puerto Rico) and besuboru in Japan (and was able to enjoy games at the Tokyo Dome and Jingu Stadium). The games evoke the joyous feeling and colorful sensibility of a world-class soccer match without most of the hooliganism, drunken self-indulgence and angry nationalism we find in world futbol.

Tonight's game took place against the backdrop of the painful history of the brutal Japanese occupations of the Korean Peninsula on and off for centuries. One can only imagine from Chavez Ravine, adjacent as it is to LA's Chinatown, what emotions were stirring in Little Tokyo and Koreatown here as well as in Tokyo and Seoul. After all, Japan won the inaugural 2006 WBC in San Diego, which I was also fortunate to attend, although the Koreans had twice beaten the Japanese in this tournament and served up starting pitcher Jungkeun Bong – dubbed "the Japan killer" – in the finale.

Still, many of the young Korean and Japanese fans at Dodger Stadium tonight seemed far more interested in baseball rivalry than political revenge. With Korea's loss, we will never know whether the team would have planted their flag on the mound with a certain self-righteous albeit understandable indignation, as they had in previous victories over Japan. For tonight at least, the Japanese side successfully displayed great "wa," the uniquely Japanese term for team harmony and chemistry.

Monday, February 23, 2009
Shipping News and Other Fears
Singapore
The number of heavy cargo ships idling here in Singapore's harbor bears brutal witness to the depths of this recession. So little merchandise is shipping through the Straits of Malacca that efforts are being made to rent cargo carriers for one-tenth the going rate. One reads in *The Straits Times* and elsewhere that citizens here cannot recall a time when the shipping industry was so dormant.

And speaking of scary, one can only grimace at the dangerous rightward shift of the Israeli government. Yes, tough times, coupled with perceptions of insecurity, generally reward those who sell fear, anger and hatred. As if a return to Bibi Netanyahu is not bad enough, however, his re-emergence is being made possible with support from ultranationalist Avigdor Lieberman, head of the far-right Yisrael Beiteinu and a dangerous guy. There is hardly any doubt that this rightward shift will deepen the current crisis there and result in a failed government. The question in these reactionary thrusts is always how many more lives will be sacrificed and how much more precious time wasted before more rational, centrist adjustments are made?

The news in the fear-mongering department is not much better in Moscow, either. What a profound tragedy it is that the two Chechen accessories to the October 2006 murder of Russian journalist Anna Politkovskaya were acquitted this week. Everyone knows these clowns were accessories before, during, and after the fact, but that they are not Politkovskaya's real murderers. Unhappily, it seems, nobody will ever face justice for actually killing this brave PEN and Amnesty award-winning woman who dared to write truth to power about then-President Vladimir Putin. The result? Well, such political witch-hunts will continue, with Putin allies and other crazies feeling completely empowered to keep killing anyone who threatens them. Just witness last month's assassinations of human rights attorney Stanislav Markelov and young journalist Anastasia Baburova. Few could have imagined the extent of murderous neo-totalitarian rule as is the case today in Mother Russia, but maybe we should have.

The intensity of checkers in Singapore's Chinatown.

Tuesday, January 13, 2009
Reinvest In the Foreign Service
Palm Beach
J. Anthony Holmes writes in the current issue of *Foreign Affairs* what we already know to be painfully true. The Department of State and the US Agency for International Development have been thoroughly gutted over the last decade. In essence, the greatest country on the planet has very little capacity to carry out sustained diplomacy everywhere it is needed. Far too many national security, intelligence, diplomatic, peacekeeping and nation-building requirements have been deposited in a Defense Department that is both operationally inappropriate and philosophically ill-suited to handle some of them. Just ask the best colonels when their armchair-warrior politician bosses are not in the room, and they'll validate this contention.

Holmes writes that the number of lawyers at Defense exceeds the entire US diplomatic corps, and that there are more musicians in military bands than there are US diplomats. I have worked with some of those wonderful military bands, by the way, so this is no knock on them.

It is simply a matter of proportion. Holmes also notes that the 2008 DOD budget was over 24 times as large as the combined State and USAID budgets. No serious analyst would argue for anything less than a robust defense budget in these treacherous times, but the imbalance here borders on lunacy.

If the United States stands any shot at rebuilding its position in the world, we will need to reinvest mightily in the Foreign Service and place it on a somewhat more equitable status with the military. The only major weakness in Holmes' argument is that he predictably places 100 percent of the blame for this situation on the Bush Administration. To be fair, the disinvestment in diplomacy long preceded George Bush and Condi Rice. They complicated and magnified the dilemma, as they did most things, but they didn't start it.

Sunday, September 28, 2008
What an Aso
It is not easy to decipher the meaning of Taro Aso's election as Japanese prime minister last week, though one thing is virtually certain. The former foreign minister and first-ever Catholic to lead Japan will soon call for snap elections. It will be a high-stakes gamble, however, since fatigue with Aso's Liberal Democratic Party could favor the Democratic Party of Japan led by Ichiro Ozawa.

In the long run, however, Aso's election may mean very little on the world or regional stage as Japan continues through a less muscular period under the weight of a greatly enfeebled economy. It will be a weak coalition government with relatively few policy innovations. Still, there are some downside concerns worth watching. First, Aso is widely thought to have a big mouth. His fiery conservative rhetoric can be as "colorful" as it is unpredictable, especially when directed at China. As with a United States weighed down these days by financial crises, loose lips can and will sink economic ships of state.

Furthermore, Japan suffers from a mounting demographic challenge that could fuel acrimony over the nation's single biggest taboo subject – immigration. Japan has a seriously declining birth rate, so it grows increasingly reliant on immigration to deliver the services its people demand and won't perform for themselves. Most of these immigrants are Chinese. So the combination of the rhetoric of anti-Chinese posturing and the reality of Chinese immigrant-dependency could make for a disturbing and even destabilizing road ahead for Tokyo.

Thursday, September 25, 2008
Now That's a Leader: Michelle Bachelet
New York
We were privileged to hear Chilean President Michelle Bachelet speak today about world and hemispheric matters. She is a truly remarkable person whose life story is the stuff of movies. She has demonstrated the courage that too many other politicians portray only in rhetorical terms.

Chile lived through its own 9/11 in 1973 when strongman General Augusto Pinochet overthrew the democratically elected government of Salvador Allende – complete with US support. Bachelet's father, General Alberto Bachelet, remained loyal to the democratically elected government, opposing Pinochet's coup and refusing to go into political exile. He was tortured and killed by Pinochet operatives in the Santiago Public Prison. The future president and her mother were subsequently detained, imprisoned and tortured at the infamous Villa Grimaldi detention center in Santiago.

So here is a surgeon, pediatrician and epidemiologist who speaks five languages, has training in military and defense matters, served as her nation's Minister of Defense, and knows the horror of torture firsthand. It's a curious, albeit, wonderful thing, but some people such as Bachelet are actually experienced, trained and ready to lead their nations. This brilliant, honorable and proven woman is certainly one of them.

She was diplomatic in discussing the United States. And why not? Our two nations enjoy reasonably productive relations. What a Monroe Doctrine blast from the past she delivered, however, when asked how she could help the next US president take Latin America more seriously. She said, "You can't see us as children. We're adults and we've been behaving well." Indeed, she cited 21 free and fair elections in Latin American in the recent past; none of them doubted or disputed. Those of us watching Latin America for many decades remember all too well the interchangeable line-up of thuggish juntas that led most of these nations for much of their post-colonial periods, largely with US support.

She urged the US to rediscover the benefits of multilateralism as the only platform from which to address three immediate global crises she identified: food, fuel and finances.

In defense of democracy, Bachelet said that Brazilian President Lula told her yesterday that over 20 million Brazilians have been lifted out of poverty and into the middle class. These trends are encouraging, although they have as much to do with changes in global commodity markets, improvements in the Brazilian economy and infrastructure and Lula's somewhat effective tenure as president. After all, China is also lifting tens of millions out of poverty without any pretense of democracy. Still, the region is blessed to have an effective, stable leader like Bachelet.

She was passionate about conditions on the ground in Haiti where 600 Chileans serve as United Nations peacekeepers, reminding us of what four devastating recent storms can do to an already-destitute land. She was also entertainingly canny in dodging anything to do with Venezuelan President Hugo Chavez. That's always a good idea.

Wednesday, September 24, 2008
Testy Lavrov, Testy Relationship
We just concluded a conference call with Russian Foreign Minister Sergey Lavrov and, well, he was rather testy. He assured us that it wasn't because he had just left a meeting with Secretary of State Rice. Perhaps it had something to do with being on the receiving end of repeated questions about Russian imperialism, hegemonic intentions and otherwise atrocious conduct in Georgia last month.

Lavrov made points both insightful and inciteful, once clearing past the usual empty rhetoric about acting in Georgia in accordance with international law. He called Russian actions – provoked by Georgian actions that had been, in turn, precipitated by Russian actions – the right to "exercise the human security maxim" (whatever that means). When asked by *The New Yorker's* David Remnick about a reported quote from President Medvedev claiming that Russia was surrounded by enemies, Lavrov denied the president ever said this. However, he later added the elusive comment that, "We are not enemies with anyone, but the military planners must take this into account." You decide.

When asked about the various "color" revolutions bringing grudging democracy to some former Soviet states – rose in Georgia, orange in Ukraine and tulip in Kyrgyzstan – he oddly claimed that, "It was not right for democracies to make revolution in the name of democracy." Excuse me? He said that Russia's own 1917 Revolution was red and didn't quite work out. Remnick reminded Lavrov that Soviet Leninism was hardly a democratic movement, a point that did not seem to amuse Lavrov (as best one could tell on a phone line).

Lavrov said that Russia welcomed a more "practical" Bush Administration, which he perceives to be moving away from holding Russia "hostage" to the raw emotions of Georgia. Yet he tartly added that President Bush needs to produce a list of the areas in which the United States will and will not now cooperate with Russia, suggesting that Moscow never really knows where and when we will choose to play ball with them. He chastised the Bush Administration for offering condolences for loss of life in Georgia without doing similarly over loss of Russian lives, adding the dig that such one-sidedness is "not consistent with Christianity." Ultimately, he urged us to accept, in his words, that the time when "the US is always right is absolutely at a dead end."

The US-Russia relationship is not merely troubled; it is deeply troubled. Foreign Minister Lavrov's comments tonight were tough in both substance and tone. They suggest just how much work a new US president needs to undertake to rebalance this vitally important relationship and, in doing so, to make desperately needed progress on Iran, North Korea and nuclear non-proliferation to name just a few pressing matters.

Saturday, August 23, 2008
Folly and the Failure to Learn
San Francisco
Why is it that we keep making the same mistakes? The belligerence between Russia and Georgia demonstrates once again humankind's collective inability – often, it's really our politically convenient unwillingness – to learn from our mistakes. Yes, Russia is the much-larger aggressor here. Moscow has far more blood on its hands than Tbilisi and it has earned our strong condemnation.

Yet it was Georgia that naively succumbed to Moscow's constant school-yard provocations by choosing to attack South Ossetia in the first place. It was just the excuse Russia craved to help "liberate" its "citizens" and occupy two breakaway territories, lest we forget Abkhazia, too. Russia's espoused concern for human rights in South Ossetia and Abkhazia is ludicrous in the face of its own historic atrocities stifling breakaway territories in Chechnya, Dagestan, Ingushetia and elsewhere throughout the Caucuses.

Behind Georgia's patently stupid move, however, are some American hawks eager to revive the traditional Russian menace. Blaming ambiguous terrorists for everything has stretched pretty thin in recent years, so some armchair warriors welcome the return of a tangible, familiar enemy that you can actually locate on a map. Sure, the Georgians are to be commended for choosing democracy and Western integration, irrespective of President Saakashvili's imprudence and impetuousness. We are right to support Tbilisi in this regard for there is little that Putin's Russian fears more than real democracy. As is too often the case, however, we have overplayed our hand.

First, we have been relentless in taunting the Russian bear from its post-Cold War sleep. Hasn't much of 20th Century history underscored the intensity of Russian nationalism that we so brazenly helped reignite during the Clinton Administration and fanned furiously during the Bush years? One look at Versailles in the rearview mirror shows the limits of bullying a bully when he is down. Our support for Kosovar independence and Georgian, Ukrainian and Baltic integration into NATO have been implemented with incompetence by consistently creating new opportunities to rub the Russian nose in our Cold War "victory." Add to this the painful decision to place American missile defense assets in Poland and the Czech Republic and, well, can Dr. Strangelove be far away? Poland had been thoughtful in its considered nervousness about this new conceit, which Russian aggression in Georgia ironically eviscerated.

Next, we undoubtedly helped create expectations in Tbilisi that the United States would somehow come to Georgia's rescue when Russia repelled its clumsy invasion, fueled as it was by US arms and logistics. Did President Saakashvili actually expect US forces to confront Russian troops on the Russian border? Some observers have likened this to our supposed promise to support Hungarian revolutionaries in 1956. Yet there was truly nothing we could have done to support the Budapest revolutionaries in direct military terms then, and that's true now in Georgia, too. If hindsight in that rearview mirror is so perfect, why do we remain blind to the mismatch between theoretical expectations and practical capabilities in these scenarios? The Georgians should have understood we could not have – and should not have – saved their bacon with any direct military action. The mere thought of it is dangerously preposterous.

Finally, we have no direct military card to play, anyway. Our Army and Marine Corps forces are spread too thin in Afghanistan and Iraq to give any bite to our barking rhetoric. History repeatedly shows that Russia will pounce when it understands that an adversary is too weak to act on its rhetoric. That rearview mirror makes vivid a post-Vietnam America embroiled in the Iran hostage crisis with neither the might nor the will to respond militarily to the Soviet invasion of Afghanistan in 1979. Moscow understood this fact, although its ill-conceived, unjust invasion of Afghanistan was a major contributor to its eventual unraveling. Still, one price of the war in Iraq is that it robs our capacity to wage an effective war in Afghanistan and respond to other real contingencies around the world. This only weakens our ability to deal credibly with Russia.

Friday, July 25, 2008
Behind Bars, Finally
How coincidental that Radovan Karadzic was finally captured just as Serbia strives for ascension to the European Union. It certainly underscores the situational power of economic leverage. Still, it seems that the BBC and others had a good sense of where Karadzic had been hiding – when he was not otherwise visibly working and living among the citizenry – over these past 13 years. Yet the Serbs chose not to apprehend him, until now. Nonetheless, his capture is well worth celebrating. This man is a butcher, as was his enabler, former Yugoslav President Slobodan Milosevic. So it is right and just that he now faces the most severe penalties administered by the International Criminal Tribunal for Yugoslavia. It is also damn well about time.

Separately: Happy birthday, Nelson Mandela. Your goodness reminds us why evil like Karadzic must be relentlessly ostracized, vilified, pursued and put away for good. The fact that you spent even one day in prison while this guy walked free for 13 years is an affront to humankind. I recall standing with my sister Pat in your tiny, Robben Island cell in 2005 and feeling consumed by the injustice of it all.

Sunday, June 29, 2008
Fear Need Not Apply
Galway, Ireland
This is an important moment in Ireland's remarkable economic renaissance. Even from the Republic's fastest-growing city, Galway, one regularly hears the Irish use the phrase "the 'R' word" to refer to the possibility of the first recession here in recent times. One newspaper headline yesterday featured a front-page quote from a Limerick teenager who asked his parents, "What's a recession?"

Ireland's challenge over the next year or two is to avoid turning inward and blaming others for what, at worst, will be a short-term setback. GDP forecasts for 2008 peg economic growth at a reasonably healthy 4 percent, albeit down from 4.5 percent in 2007. There is a young generation of Irish here that knows nothing but economic growth approximating that of the Asian tigers. There is also an older generation here that says "never again" for a return to the darkness of much of Ireland's economic history.

A provision in the Irish Constitution required that a public referendum be held to ratify the European Union reform measures packaged as the Treaty of Lisbon. The Irish electorate rejected "Lisbon" on June 12th by a vote of 53 to 47 percent. The Treaty of Lisbon is a seriously flawed instrument, but it has already been ratified by 18 EU member nations. By turning its back on Europe and the very EU mechanisms that helped give rise to the "Irish Miracle," Ireland actually risks pushing itself away from prosperity and back to older, insular ways. The knee-jerk reaction of blaming "bureaucrats in Brussels" is hardly the answer to Ireland's momentary concerns about recession. Indeed, fear is almost always the handmaiden of even greater economic decline.

Thursday, June 26, 2008
Rwanda Rebirth?
It is almost unimaginable. Rwanda as an economic role model for Africa and beyond? Rwanda as a finance and high-technology entrepôt in the fashion of the Asian tigers and Dubai? This from a country racked by a monstrously bloody civil war between Hutus and Tutsis resulting in the near-genocidal death of a million people only 15 years ago?

Veteran journalist Stephen Kinzer asks us to consider these possibilities in his book, *A Thousand Hills: Rwanda's Rebirth and the Man Who Dreamed It* (2008). It seems quite a stretch, but Kinzer is a serious thinker and terrific journalist who merits our momentarily suspending judgment on the matter. For those of us who so greatly admire Canadian General and 1990s Rwanda peacekeeper Romeo Dallaire and his painful book, *Shake Hands with the Devil: The Failure of Humanity in Rwanda* (2003), it is hard to see Rwanda through anything but blood-colored glasses.

Still, in producing what *Publishers Weekly* calls a "hagiographic account" of Rwandan President Paul Kagame, Kinzer believes that this one man – no innocent himself – is, in his own autocratic way, moving Rwanda toward unprecedented single-generation change. In a video plugging the book, he says that Rwanda has "riveted the development community" and that Kigali is "on the way to becoming one of the great stars of Africa." Hmmm. Let's hope so.

In light of the brutal incompetence and Stalinesque thuggery of Zimbabwe President Robert Mugabe, coupled with the continued dismal performance of his "quiet diplomacy" enabler, South African President Thabo Mbeki, the continent could use a dash of hope these days. Kinzer certainly has us looking for it in a most unusual place.

Wednesday, February 20, 2008
On Qatar
Doha, Qatar
Qatar has the unbridled energy and singular focus of a place on the move – and on the make. There seems no limit to what can be bought here and no subtlety about building or buying the world's biggest "that" or tallest "this." It is an adolescent growth stage with considerable

exuberance and exorbitance. Of course, who wouldn't have such brash ambitions with one of the largest reserves of natural gas in the world?

Of the nation's 800,000 residents, only 20 percent are Qatari. The rest are "guest workers" from India, Pakistan, Nepal, Kenya, Tanzania and elsewhere. Our driver here is from Manila, for example. One can live and work here for many hours a day and never actually see one of the 160,000 or so Qatari who cannot possibly build and run this nation without imported labor. They would not be winning medals in the Asian Games or elsewhere either, without buying distance runners and other world-class athletes from Tanzania, Kenya and Morocco.

Still, the Qatari are smart in how they are going about their development. Taking a page from the Dubai playbook – and the competition between these two states is intense, so the Qatari would not appreciate the comparison – government officials understand the need to move well beyond the energy sector. As the prime minister told *The Weekend FT* in September 2007, "Our hydrocarbons won't last forever. We need to secure the same standard of living for our children." That is why the Al-Jazeera media empire is based here as well as the Education City project whose tenants include Carnegie Mellon, Cornell, Georgetown, Northwestern, Texas A&M and Virginia Commonwealth. That is also why Qatar is becoming a global investment and financial services powerhouse, almost overnight. And that is why the new Doha International Airport will feature the longest runways and most military-friendly facilities found nearly anywhere. For better and worse, the long shadow of US foreign policy as well as economic and national security interests is never far from Qatar's remarkable development.

One looks at the skyline under development here in Doha, already larger and taller than Boston's, and shudders at the notion that Qatar was nearly bankrupt just 15 years ago. What will they do for an encore? Well, don't be surprised when Doha makes a serious run at the 2016 Summer Olympics and actually wins it. The ruling al Thani family can make anything happen here; just witness the extraordinary athletics infrastructure already in place. Furthermore, Qatar can come as close as any other dictatorship to guaranteeing a peaceful Games that would also be free of debt. Besides, the Games have never come to this part of the world and what a statement that would make, despite the improbability of asking athletes and spectators to endure summer temperatures well in excess of 100 degrees.

My guide and friend after I enjoyed a brief camelback trek along the Persian Gulf shore of Mesaieed, Qatar. The camel saw fit to hiss at me, so I gave it right back to him.

Tuesday, February 19, 2008
Our Thoughts Turn To "Nothing"
Doha, Qatar
We heard from Georgetown University's John Esposito at the gorgeous Diplomatic Club here last night. Professor Esposito has written a new book with Dalia Mogahed entitled *Who Speaks for Islam?* (2007). The authors argue that we need to let the data drive discussions and opinions of what Muslims actually think, since so many politicians, pundits and reporters around the world speak for Islam incorrectly, incompletely and inappropriately.

Esposito and Mogahed worked with the Gallup World Poll, which conducted tens of thousands of interviews with Muslims in 35 nations. Esposito underscored the need to resist the painful, fear-mongering stereotypes of Arabs, Persians and Muslims perpetrated by some in the US and Europe who knowingly "choose to play the extremist card," he said tonight.

Esposito reports on many views Muslims have of America and Americans, some of them quite negative but more of them neutral to positive. When asked about what they like or do not like about the United States, respondents had much to say on both counts. What was profoundly disturbing, however, was that when Americans were asked what they knew about Muslims, 57 percent responded either "nothing" or "don't know." I thought we were supposed to learn the painful lessons of 9/11 about the damage done by our ignorance of the world and how it works.

Saturday, February 16, 2008
Open For Business
Doha, Qatar
Signs of the growing prosperity and resulting popularity of Qatar as a business destination immediately registered upon arrival here tonight, both at the Doha International Airport and the Ritz Carlton. Maria Sharapova, Venus Williams and the other stars of the women's tennis circuit were arriving at the same time in advance of this week's lucrative Total Qatar Open competition. While waiting for baggage, one was greeted by an enormous poster promoting Placido Domingo's arrival here in two weeks to open the astonishing development called The Pearl, an artificial island spanning nearly four million square meters. Arriving at the hotel amidst tight security, we learned that the Ritz was hosting the 3ʳᵈ annual US-Islamic Conference that opened today. Secretary Madeleine Albright, Afghan President Hamid Karzai, Ambassador Martin Indyk, *Newsweek's* Joe Klein, and Palestinian negotiator Saeb Erekat are all staying at our hotel to participate in the talkfest. Ah, the magnetism of money.

It Really Happened: Serendipity in Mayfair
London
Funny how life works. I read the *Vanity Fair* piece on the late Mark Birley as I was flying here today. Birley was the king of upscale Mayfair social life

for decades, opening the fabled members-only Annabel's in Berkeley Square in 1963. The Beatles, Stones, Sinatra, Jackie Onassis and a galaxy of celebrities, high-society types and posse members made the scene there, and it remains a relevant destination today. So tonight, Pat and I met a friend at our hotel who took us to dinner. As we left the restaurant and headed back to the Dorchester, our friend asked if we wanted to share a nightcap with him. He said, "Trust me; you'll like this place." It turns out that he was among the original founding members of a private club in Berkeley Square that was, of course, Annabel's. Be careful what you read or imagine, for it can quickly come into your life as if on cue.

Tuesday, November 13, 2007
Smart Power
San Diego
It seems abundantly obvious. The Center for Strategic and International Studies (CSIS) is nonetheless correct in stating in its November report on smart power that "to maintain a leading role in global affairs the United States must move from eliciting fear and anger to inspiring optimism and hope." Well, no kidding. Too few of our leaders were providing such wisdom on the eve of the Iraq War in 2003. It felt mighty lonely back then to caution that an unprovoked, unjust war was not in America's best interests and that true democracy is never imposed at gunpoint.

With maturity, even some loud-mouthed, schoolyard bullies start to learn the dangerous, counter-productive pitfalls of their behaviors. These lessons have been available to us at least since the Spanish-American War as the American experiment entered puberty.

It is ironic to see that one of the report's key architects and spokesmen is Richard Armitage, a respected soldier and diplomat who nonetheless danced to the drumbeat of the Iraq War and, later, revealed Valerie Plame's CIA identity to the media. The CSIS is right in asserting that we as a nation must get much smarter about the severe, disabling consequences of using power in dumb ways. Advancing smart power, however, will require smart people in office or people whose brainpower is not otherwise blunted by partisan politics or foolish ideology. This is precisely why "hard" power can be so soft and the smartness of "soft" power can be so hard.

Separately, kudos to Spain's King Juan Carlos who could take no more of Venezuelan President Hugo Chavez's constant interruptions at last weekend's summit of the leaders of Spanish-speaking countries. Your Highness, we are grateful to you for telling the typically out-of-control Chavez, "Por que no te callas." Translation? "Why don't you just shut up."

Tuesday, October 16, 2007
Ticking Off Turks
Readers know that I love Turkey. It is singularly situated at the strategic crossroads of east and west. It has long offered hope that secular modernity can coexist with Islam, as has been the case over many decades now of Kemalism. It is also a country filled with extraordinary cultural history, if we actually take time to understand and cherish it.

I recall sitting at a lovely sidewalk café with Pat outside Istanbul's Hippodrome, where 100,000 people once gathered for chariot races, wrestling and political rallies in what was then the ancient Byzantine capital, Constantinople. As I enjoyed the sight of the adjacent Blue Mosque there, sampled an Efes Pilsen beer and cautiously considered sampling a raki, I was impressed both by the beautiful scene and the high regard Turks seemed to have for Americans.

How painful it has been, therefore, to watch Turkish public opinion of the United States plunge over the last five years. The June 2007 Pew Global Attitudes Project showed only a 9 percent favorability rating against 30 percent in 2002 and, as others have written, well over 50 percent in the 1990s. The same poll showed that 83 percent of Turks hold an unfavorable view of the United States today, even before the latest Armenian genocide vote in Congress, against a 54 percent unfavorable rating in 2002.

It seems we have worked very hard to alienate the Turks, our longtime NATO ally and Iraq War logistical enabler. The war certainly plays a role behind this enmity, but there is much more to it, such as our lukewarm support of Turkey's ascension to the EU. Now the US Congress has decided to declare that the 1915 Armenian massacre at Turkish hands was, technically, a genocide. Nothing makes Turkish blood boil more than outsiders opining on this sore subject so many years later, as the Democrat-led Congress has seen fit to do. Yes, Turkey has Armenian blood on its hands. And yes, Ankara has refused to account for its ancestors' actions, akin to the Japanese failure to come to grips with its own World War Two atrocities. For this, the Turks are wrong. Yet how far should an outside government and purported ally go in condemning a nation for its history? Imagine Ankara somehow chastising our own atrocities against Native Americans or vicious history of slavery? How would we react?

Congress has no right to raise this issue; it is simply none of our business. The Democrats are pushing it, of course, because of the influence of the Armenian lobby and the many Armenian contributions to their coffers. Instead, Congress should focus on how to help Turkey join the EU, ward off Islamic extremism, deal with the growing PKK insurgency and re-engage with us in a mutually productive manner. Yes, somehow, Turkey must come to grips with its Armenian atrocities, but this is not the way to do it. The French were wrong to impose themselves in this issue last year, as the Democrats are today. The Bush Administration has created most of the Turkish ill-feeling toward the United States, but it is right in condemning these Democrat manipulations. The search for wisdom remains elusive.

The children of repressive regimes find their futures compromised, whether it's in Putin's Russia or Mugabe's Zimbabwe. These proud kids had just concluded a recital at the School of the Arts, Matanzas Cuba. Their future seems brighter these days.

Thursday, December 14, 2006

That Fascist Funk

It was breathtaking to learn that Louisiana bigot David Duke attended this week's Holocaust-deniers conference in Tehran. And how pathetically sad for the Persians, a truly great people, to be forced to play host to such an astonishing embarrassment. The scene in Tehran reminds us that fascism remains very much alive and well in our troubled world.

This was also the week that Chilean strongman Augusto Pinochet perished without ever being held accountable for his crimes of fascism. Yes, Chile has been a remarkable economic success story, born of Pinochet's embrace of the so-called "Chicago School of Economics." However, getting economics right never compensates for the almost unthinkable cruelties visited upon Chileans under Pinochet's rule. Adam Smith spoke of the "hidden hand" of the capitalist system, but in the case of Pinochet and his flirtations with capitalism that hand was long dripping with other people's blood.

We were told that at least Mussolini kept the trains running on time, but what if those sleek, punctual and profitable trains were loaded with innocent victims enroute to torture and death in Santiago's main football stadium, one of Rome's many piazzas or even places with names like Auschwitz and Buchenwald. Oh, that's right, whack jobs like David Duke and Mahmoud Ahmadinejad tell us the Holocaust never happened.

This was also the week in which the ugly memory of fascism fell once again over Ethiopia. Former dictator Mengistu Haile Mariam, hiding in Zimbabwe under the protective cloak of neo-fascist Robert Mugabe, was found guilty of genocide. Mengistu and 70 of his henchmen were called to account for the mass murder of tens of thousands of students, intellectuals, and innocents in a Red Terror campaign that Human Rights Watch labels "one of the most systematic uses of mass murder by a state ever witnessed in Africa." Mengistu is undoubtedly advising Mugabe right now on how to eliminate his political enemies just as he personally strangled Ethiopia's last emperor, Haile Selassie.

David Duke, Mahmoud Ahmadinejad, Augusto Pinochet, Mengistu Haile Mariam and Robert Mugabe all serve notice that fascism is a potent, brutal force against which all decent people must remain vigilant.

Thursday, November 30, 2006
Putin Redux
It is becoming increasingly clear the Vladimir Putin's Russia is on a frightening oligarchical if not fascist course. The poisoning-death of Putin-critic Alexander Litvinenko last week, coupled with yesterday's suspicious and sudden collapse of former Prime Minister Yegor Gaidar, another Putin critic, bring back memories of the still-unexplained attempted poisoning of Ukrainian President Victor Yushchenko.

These developments conjure up Ivan the Terrible's bloody reign in 16th Century Russia. Ivan IV Vasilyevich was Russia's first tsar and murder served as one of his primary tools of political control. This from a man who ultimately murdered his own son, too. So where are we in Russian toxicology these days? Well, keep in mind that there was a high level of mercury found in Ivan's remains when they were exhumed in the early 1960s. He appears to have been poisoned, too.

Saturday, January 21, 2006
Writing off Turkish Liberty
The Boston Herald
The trial lasted only minutes. The long-awaited courtroom ordeal of Turkey's most famous author, Orhan Pamuk, was abruptly postponed last month until February. Pamuk dared tell a Swiss newspaper that Turkey had indeed massacred 1 million Armenians in 1915 and 30,000 Kurds since the start of that civil war in 1984. For these statements, he is accused of the "public denigration" of Turkish identity and faces three years in prison.

The actions taken by Turkey's angry, right-wing judiciary could not come at a worse time for that nation. As Turkey emerges from a century of post-Ottoman malaise and eagerly asserts its legitimate desire to enter the European Union, it continues to wrestle with the ghosts of its darker past. The Pamuk case and other public defamation actions against those who dare to speak truth are predicated on the notorious Article 301 of the Turkish Penal Code. These cases are once again – needlessly and recklessly – placing Turkey itself on trial in the court of world opinion.

Turkey is a land of extraordinary contrast and contradiction – a European nation bordering Iran, Iraq and Syria, a largely Islamic culture housed in a secular state and a NATO member in the Middle East that has enjoyed a reasonable, long-term relationship with Israel.

Turkey is expected to jump through many hoops as part of the 10-year EU accession process, now under way. It is also expected to continue undertaking needed economic and political reforms to achieve membership. It's clear that the country is on the move, however, opening wider to outside influences while justifiably refusing to sell its rather remarkable soul.

Turkey's real growth rate exceeded eight percent last year, making it the economic envy of EU stalwarts France, Germany and Italy, whose economies have been growing at a one- or two-percent clip annually.

Still, it is the Pamuk trial and other reactionary tendencies that have the potential to undermine Turkey's EU application. The government of Prime Minister Recep Tayyip Erdogan says it is helpless to stop the judiciary's actions against Pamuk and others. It must realize, however, that growing numbers of politicians in Britain, France, Germany and elsewhere will cravenly use these cases to declare that Turkey has not changed its prison stripes.

The Erdogan government must certainly understand that these judicial actions provide Turkey's critics in nationalist parties across Europe with a convenient cover to sell the fear, xenophobia, racism and religious intolerance that constitute their real opposition to Turkey's membership in the European Union.

Turkey must also recognize that fear, not economic growth rates, will determine the outcome of its EU bid. Only 40 percent of Europeans now support Turkish EU membership, down from 45 percent earlier this year. A meager one-third of French and German citizens support Turkey's EU accession at a time when fear of crime, job loss and terrorism are so high.

Just watch the jockeying now under way between Nicolas Sarkozy and Dominique de Villepin to become France's next prime minister and you will see how fear of racial, ethnic and religious differences is being used to divide and conquer, whether it's in a Paris suburb or an EU bargaining table. The same can be said about the ways in which the new Merkel government in Germany, a weak coalition from the start, will pander to racist elements on its right flank to retain power. Listen to those who talk about preserving Judeo-Christian traditions in Europe and ask yourself what they too often really mean.

The "us vs. them" politics of fear will work well in Paris, Berlin and elsewhere to frustrate Turkey's ambitions. So instead of labeling Pamuk and others who speak truth to power as traitors and unpatriotic, Ankara should simply rise above it and deny fear merchants more ammunition than they deserve. Indeed, it is the brittleness and pettiness of some of Turkey's top politicians and judges that may well be the undoing of its EU bid. Turkey is a great nation that can make a substantive case for becoming part of the European Union. However, it must first make the case that the ghosts of its past are gone but not forgotten.

It Really Happened: Thule, Greenland
We were flying with American, Canadian, British and Dutch P-3 squadrons for a week over the North Pole region in 1994. Working from our headquarters at the US Air Force base in Thule, Greenland, we were producing print and broadcast pieces of NATO crews engaged in what was both a military and scientific exercise.

The Canadians established a raucous "officers' club" in one of the weather-fortified Quonset huts. Late one bright, sunny night, the four-inch-thick double doors to our little oasis opened with a howling, snow-carrying wind to reveal five individuals in hooded, military-issue snow parkas. The first arrival removed her hood and exclaimed, "Hi, we're the band. Where should we set up?" Indeed, the powers-that-be had hired a wonderful rock band from LA to provide well-deserved entertainment for folks working 15-20-hour shifts at the top of the world.

Wednesday, December 29, 2004
Sidelines of Tragedy
The Boston Herald
That song. It's been all over the radio during the Christmas season.

But 20 years after singer-activist Bob Geldof brought us the "feed the world" musical appeal for Africa, little has changed.

To their credit, Geldof and friends such as Paul McCartney and Bono recently re-recorded the holiday hit, "Do They Know It's Christmas?" It's now making the rounds on the airwaves and finding its way to store shelves, just as the original did in 1984 when Geldof was moved to action after watching a television show on the Ethiopian famine.

Natural disaster, inbred corruption and dreadful indifference had condemned over one million people to death. Relief agencies performed heroically back then, but too many government, institutional and corporate leaders did nothing. Well, not exactly. Once the bright spotlight of shame and guilt coaxed them from their protective shells, they did wring their hands and promise "never again." Until 1994, that is.

Ten years later, the world watched as 800,000 Hutus and Tutsis mindlessly slaughtered each other in Rwanda. In the words of the PBS *Frontline* series, it was a "triumph of evil." Not exactly our finest hour. So, what did we learn? Well, after the bloodshed subsided we got even better at calling press conferences, wringing our hands and promising "never again." It was the cruelest illusion of leadership.

Now, another ten-year cycle has passed and it's happening again. In fact, genocide has been occurring in Sudan for many years as the United Nations and the great powers serve as concerned spectators. Sure, the situation is complex, with at least two civil wars underway simultaneously in Africa's largest nation. But aren't the worst of times precisely when we require the best of leaders? Why is it when times get tough, so many of our purported leaders simply vanish?

Blame starts with the morally bankrupt regime in Sudan's capital, Khartoum. This Arab network of the north has systemically murdered, raped and tortured Christian and animist political opponents in the south, real and imagined. To date, experts estimate that two million people have perished. Some say that peace is at hand in this unyielding saga of north-south butchery. Don't believe it.

In more recent years, the Khartoum government and its cutthroat Janjaweed militia have driven one million people from their homes in southern Darfur and into ghastly refugee camps, some of which relief agencies can't even reach. The death count is already 70,000 in this bloodbath among nomadic, government-armed Arabs and black farmers – countrymen all. By most accounts, another one million Sudanese could starve to death in the coming years as a result of the conditions created by genocide, lawlessness and poor harvests.

One should never overlook the heroic work undertaken by Non-Governmental Organizations. They may talk little, but they walk directly into harm's way. Every day, they risk their lives to feed, heal and house people who otherwise serve only as backdrops on the nightly news. And yes, there's the occasional politician, such as former Bush-appointed envoy to Sudan and outgoing UN Ambassador John Danforth, who rises above the business-as-usual pretensions to find humanity and justice. One suspects that the Episcopal Reverend Danforth may have some greater spiritual insights than are available to the standard-issue politician. And yet, one can't help but think that this Ralston Purina heir knows that most American pets eat better than the people of Darfur.

So, sometime soon there will be yet another hand-wringing episode over Darfur filled with the customary "never-again" promises. Yes, life-saving initiatives are being attempted. Some are succeeding against all odds. Still, it's abundantly clear that the Sudanese genocide is simply not a priority for world leaders. There's just no short-term gain in it for them.

While the murderous bunch in Khartoum is the first to blame for this genocide, a secondary source for blame, and the primary source for solutions, belongs to nine men. Until George W. Bush, Tony Blair, Jacques Chirac, Gerhard Schroeder, Silvio Berlusconi, Vladimir Putin, Kofi Annan, South African President Thabo Mbeki, and African Union Chairman Alpha Oumar Konare get serious about Sudan, we will have no claim to living in a civilized world.

In fact, these men may want to consider spending more time on this crisis and less time on, say, ignoring HIV/AIDS, destroying same-sex marriages, breaking up world-class corporations for personal gain, preventing Muslim children from wearing religiously appropriate clothing, crushing efforts to use stem-cell research to save lives, waging needless wars and dodging varied allegations of political or criminal wrongdoing.

Instead, they may want to suspend their personal fears and confront really big issues, like genocide. As was the case with Ethiopia and Rwanda, Sudan is a tragedy of Shakespearean proportions. Indeed, the tendency to talk tough and do little may be best summarized by Constance in the Bard's *King John* who said, "Thou wear a lion's hide! Doff it for shame, and hang a calf's skin on those recreant limbs."

We'll witness true leadership when Bob Geldof won't have to issue a 30th anniversary edition of "Feed the Children." That'd be a very good thing, since Zimbabwe or the Ivory Coast is next on the genocide watch.

Monday, November 25, 2002
In the Time of Butterflies
The Boston Herald
Minerva, Maria Theresa and Patria. Forty-one years ago today, three Mirabel sisters were murdered by the Dominican Republic strongman, General Rafael Trujillo. These young moms were "freedom fighters" when that term actually meant fighting for freedom. They were known as Las Mariposas, or The Butterflies.

In helping to build an underground resistance movement, they gave powerful meaning to another term much later in vogue – ``working moms." The Mirabel sisters were beaten to death by thugs on the payroll of a dictator whose military medals were exceeded in size only by his cowardice. Trujillo feared Las Mariposas, and for very good reason. He was dead six months after disposing of them, assassinated by a growing, US-funded opposition.

Twenty years ago today a prominent group of Latin American women declared November 25th to be the International Day Against Violence Against Women in honor of the Mirabels. Who says that butterflies are free? The events of 9/11 have made this Thanksgiving just past all the more sobering. It is a time of reflection on American values and how we give voice to them throughout the world.

History will ultimately determine, for example, whether bombing Afghanistan actually achieved anything of value. However, history repeatedly demonstrates the extraordinary achievement of leaders like the Mirabel sisters who fight oppression in the name of a better world. Aung San Suu Kyi is another such overachiever. "The Lady," as she is called by her supporters, leads a political movement that in 1990 won Burma's first free election in more than 30 years. To this day, however, the ruling junta refuses to recognize the now-rotting fruits of Burmese democracy.

Like so many before them including Trujillo, the Burmese junta actually believes it is bigger than the people it purports to represent.

Well, nobody has had a more sizeable presence in Burma in recent years than the diminutive Aung San Suu Kyi. Like the Mirabels before her, Suu Kyi stands for ideals that are universally more powerful than all the bombs in all the world's arsenals. Truth, justice and liberty remain terrifying concepts to dictators. Ironically, Suu Kyi is still alive today because the Burmese thugs learned well the lessons of Trujillo – the only thing more powerful than a passionate, brilliant and beautiful woman resistance leader is a martyred one.

Closer to the front lines of America's "war on terrorism" is Iran. As with the Dominican Republic, Burma and other "sooner or later" democracies, Iran is moving slowly toward a more just and humane tomorrow. The streets that once echoed with familiar strains of "Death to America" remain filled with young voices. However, the oratory these days is not always political or religious. It's been about soccer lately. That's right, soccer. A recent photo in *The Financial Times* said it all. A young boy was pictured waving his nation's flag with patriotic resolve as his mother drove their car. They were celebrating Iran's victory over the United Arab Emirates in a World Cup qualifier. News reports poured out of Tehran of young people engaged in activities forbidden by the ruling mullahs, such as dancing, holding hands and kissing. The news of such momentary liberation was forever captured in the modest, uncertain smile of an Iranian soccer mom.

America is awash in a junk-media culture that is often criticized for ignoring international news. To be fair, however, Iran's soccer moment was widely reported. Burma's trials have also been well chronicled in our media. And there's a compelling 1995 movie on the subject, *Beyond Rangoon*. Even Showtime has been airing an original movie on the Mirabel sisters based on the Julia Alvarez book, *In the Time of Butterflies* (1994).

In these days when we are told that shopping is a patriotic duty, why not head to the local mall and find these stories for yourself. They're readily available in magazines, books and movies about real heroes like the Mirabel sisters, Aung San Suu Kyi and maybe even a new generation of Iranian soccer moms. It's also there in the stories of the women of Northern Ireland, who have resisted a profoundly stupid conflict, as well the Revolutionary Association of the Women of Afghanistan that seeks to earn for women minimal status as human beings. It's hard to imagine more patriotic purchases on a day when we honor such brave women.

Sunday, October 20, 2002
The NATO Club
The Boston Herald

The North Atlantic Treaty Organization will hold its annual summit meeting next month in Prague. Leaders from 19 member nations and 27 partner countries will review continued NATO expansion. In preparing for this meeting, it is essential that the Bush administration put aside the language of diplomatic generalities and ask tough questions about long-term American interests.

We worked with one Northern Alliance to unseat the Taliban and diminish al-Qaeda, but are we now giving birth to a very different Northern Alliance – a sort of NATO-on-steroids that is slowly encompassing much of the Northern Hemisphere? Is this good or bad for America? NATO comprised 12 nations when it was created in 1949. It grew to 16 members through the Cold War. In 1999, Hungary, Poland and the Czech Republic joined, followed by Russia's entry as a "junior partner" earlier this year. It's just a question of time before Estonia, Latvia, Lithuania, Slovakia and Slovenia join, with Bulgaria, Ukraine and others waiting in the wings. Some analysts suggest NATO eventually might have 50 members or more.

Who's to argue with success? NATO certainly played a key role in winning the Cold War and protecting our principles of market democracy. The alliance helped give us the time and security needed to let communism rot from within and ultimately collapse. It worked. That former enemies are now partners is obviously a very good thing, too. So what's the problem? In short, the rest of the world. On its current trajectory, NATO risks creating a "gated community" of the North, one that will deepen an already perilous divide between rich and poor nations.

Set aside for the moment that NATO, a mutual-defense treaty organization, has no traditional nation-state enemies. Never mind that an "Atlantic" alliance now encircles a huge chunk of northern Pacific geography. Forget that a security alliance designed to deter Soviet aggression now counts Mother Russia among its proud affiliates. It seems so long ago that we were anticipating potential Warsaw Pact tank movements through Germany's Fulda Gap or watching Soviet "fishing trawlers" watch us during naval exercises in the North Atlantic. Decades of East-West confrontation ended with the fall of the Berlin Wall, thanks in good measure to NATO.

Ironically, NATO now risks building a new North-South "wall" of sorts, with the increasingly isolated, poorer nations of the South becoming cauldrons for the politics of resentment, retribution and revenge that give birth to terrorism. Consider sub-Saharan Africa, where one in four soldiers tests HIV-positive. Not even the most formidable fortresses found in swanky gated communities can disarm AIDS, which respects no boundaries. It does make one ask whether NATO should spend less time on Turkish tank tactics or Portuguese port procedures and more time worrying about hundreds of thousands of HIV-positive soldiers running around Africa brandishing AK-47s. The same questions apply to Kashmir, the Middle East, Afghanistan, Iraq, Indonesia and the Philippines.

Will our new Northern Alliance soften or harden developing-world opinions of the United States? Answering these questions effectively will require the White House to overcome its penchant for simplistic "good guys and bad guys" notions of how the world works and carefully weigh the complex, long-term consequences of leading a members-only club of the North.

These men were grooming an ox near Tagaytay, Philippines when we happened upon them.

CHAPTER 5

COMMUNICATIONS & MEDIA

Wednesday, July 20, 2016
Good Night and God Help Us

National Review Senior Editor Jonah Goldberg described himself to NPR this morning as a "conservative journalist." You can be conservative, fine. You can be a journalist, of course. Being a "conservative" or "liberal" journalist, however, should be deemed ridiculous, given the standards of objectivity and fairness we're supposed to expect from so-called journalists. Yes, Fox News started this particular bastardization of journalism 20 years ago and MSNBC was eager to follow suit, but shouldn't we expect better? Call yourself an activist, columnist or commentator, but let's try to reserve for real journalists a special place as the Fourth Estate.

The more journalism bows to ideology, the greater the risk we end up with an ignorant, demagogic carnival-barker-in-chief as president of the United States. Let's save journalism for real journalists, which may help us save public service for real public servants. Wait a minute; what's that noise? I think it's Ed Murrow rolling in his grave.

Tuesday, December 8, 2015
Now That's a Leader: Mohannad Sabry
Cincinnati
"He saw things that could have saved Egypt from the ticking time bomb in the Sinai." That's what David Ignatius wrote about Egyptian freelance journalist Mohannad Sabry in the November 27th *Washington Post*.

At great risk to his life and livelihood, the Cairo-based Sabry, 32, has fought tenaciously to uncover the indifference, mismanagement and corruption that has produced lawlessness in the Sinai, created conditions for terrorists to thrive there and likely made possible the downing of that Russian airliner.

Sabry reported ominous "things," but nobody in a position to correct the Sinai's downward spiral over recent years paid any attention. Except, of course, those who wanted to harm him for embarrassing them by speaking truth to power.

We live at a moment when shameless, little politicians are merchandising ignorance and invective the world over. Here in stark contrast is a brave, young man – a recent cancer survivor, too – who is leading with determination, reason, narrative and data to make our world a better, safer place.

Friday, November 13, 2014
Nice Try
Austin
We're treated daily to celebrities, athletes and politicians who make racist, sexist and other outlandish comments only to repent insincerely the next day, usually through their PR handlers. Their shallow apologies are frequently joined by the "my comments were taken out of context" trope. Oh really? Why do the media never then ask these characters, "Okay, what conceivable context should we have taken your outrageous remarks?"

Saturday, October 11, 2014
Mad Ads
Tyler Brule makes an interesting point in today's *Weekend FT* about placing advertising in locations where consumers are frustrated and angry. He cites the Accenture ads plastered all over the misbegotten security-screening area at Heathrow's Terminal 2. I see examples of this every week. How does your product or service really fare when presented to people who are pissed off and want to be anywhere else in the world but there? He also points out the irony of Accenture promoting strategy-consulting services in a location seemingly devoid of any strategy. This

is a subtle but important point that bean counters likely miss, but that sharp advertising and media-buying minds hopefully do consider.

Saturday, August 2, 2014
Now that's a Leader: Dr. Warren Bennis, RIP
Or, WTF about Leadership Today?
Vail

Okay, I admit it. My eyes watered when Jon Lester departed Red Sox Nation. So too, I got a bit emotional enroute here with word that Professor Warren Bennis has died. I sometimes question myself for expecting a great deal from people in leadership positions. I have occasionally curbed my desire over the years for authentic leaders who are visionary, strategic, fair, creative, multidimensional, articulate, curious, nimble, nuanced, emotionally well adjusted, reasonably selfless and truly prepared to lead – and be led by – men and women in a shared quest. Do they even exist?

To paraphrase Nelson Mandela, however, shame on the person who lowers her ideals merely to accept and be accepted by the status quo. So, dammit, let it be said that the last thing any of us should do is accept the suffocating, stultifying mediocrity that too often passes for leadership in our world today.

That rant was inspired by the now late and always great Warren Bennis. Army Lieutenant Bennis, a Purple Heart and Bronze Star recipient in World War Two, felt this way – intensely. He inspired generations of us to be intentional about our own leadership development and try to move beyond the standard-issue corporate politicians, bean counters and cost cutters, just-say-no lawyers and Peter Principle pretenders who do little but get in the way, hold people back, stunt innovation and growth and ruin organizations.

Saturday's *New York Times* said it well in quoting from Dr. Bennis' 1989 book, *On Becoming a Leader*: "The leader who communicates passion gives hope and inspiration to other people," he wrote. Ah, "communicate." There's that word again. *The Times* added, "A dearth of visionary business leaders, he (Bennis) said, meant that companies were being led more by managers of the bottom line than by passionate independent thinkers who could steer an organization."

I recall my corporate peers and CEO bosses in the late 1980s and '90s ridiculing sentiments like these, largely because they were so incapable of understanding and delivering them. The boys would scoff at these so-called "soft skills" – they're the hardest skills of all, of course – while some of their best, most talented people chose to limit their productive engagement with the firm or go elsewhere for professional fulfillment. These sometimes reasonably well-performing firms often did not realize their potential. Of course, the problem is that it's impossible to know what these organizations could have been but for the lack of real leadership. Yes, one can minimize the importance of communication, emotional intelligence, human nature and the quest for potential, fulfillment and joy in the workplace. If that's the case, however, just make sure your organization doesn't need to employ any people to succeed and isn't currently operating in the 21st Century.

Slowly, albeit glacially, boards of directors and executive recruiters are realizing what employees understood a long time ago. To hell with the business-as-usual lowering-of-standards that still populates organizations with failed, tired leadership recipes of the past. Surely, over time, we are starting to understand that the theater of "tough guy" boorishness regrettably still found across the Global 2000 has nothing to do with the reality of driving effective performance and making difficult decisions while treating people with respect and dignity. I wrote too many leaders' speeches back in the day – and delivered some of them myself – that offered inclusive "talk" about valuing diverse opinions and creating open, sharing crucibles for creativity and change that we on our executive management teams had no intention to "walk." These words represented so many wasted molecules of breath deposited into an unreceptive atmosphere. Enough already! We need to do much, much better than this.

After all, we are privileged to have some leadership and organizational greatness in Wegmans, SAS, Nordstrom, Quicken Loans, the US Navy Seals and even the new Ford Motor Company. The people who lead these outfits understand – sometimes in lessons learned the hard way – that virtually all of their job must be devoted to inspiring, informing, developing, rewarding, connecting and cajoling people. In our region, folks like Eric Dawson, who heads Peace First; Rev. Kim Crawford, who leads the Arlington Street Church; Catherine D'Amato, who runs the Greater Boston Food Bank; and Mary Grant, the gifted leader of MCLA in North Adams, MA and newly named Chancellor of UNC Asheville show us the way, too. Yes, I'm proud to say they're all my friends.

The problem is that engaged, enlightened and effective leaders who know how to move a room let alone an organization are very hard to find. They are both born and made that way. I'm not talking about great professionals and managers, who are easier to find. We are already expert at developing successful doctors and dentists, lawyers and financiers, engineers and IT specialists – and we should be proud of doing so. The problem is that we put some of them in leadership positions for which they lack the experience, training and temperament to handle well. Too many of them are uncomfortable with the human touch that compels and propels organizations toward greatness. Often, the brilliant, narrowly-gauged skills that ambitiously drove them to the top can be antithetical to the more broadly-calibrated requirements of gifted leadership at the top – vision, wisdom, patience, inclusiveness, humility, subtlety, listening skills, not being threatened by smarter people and, indeed, relishing in the brilliance of hiring and retaining the best and brightest.

Now we can't possibly expect Renaissance men and women to lead us, right? Of course not. Well, upon second thought, why not? My military colleagues will affirm that more of these kind of well-rounded leaders – warrior-scholar-executives – seem to be available in the military, where it can sometimes be more difficult to succeed solely as a bullshitter. Lieutenant Bennis likely understood that point. Besides, unlike corporate and professional life, the military formally educates and trains people to serve in what Warren Bennis considered to be that highest calling – leadership. Yes, it really does matter with whom you find yourself in that proverbial foxhole while under fire. For your own good, she or he had better be a leader Warren Bennis would respect.

Tuesday, March 25, 2014
North Korea Would Be Proud
"We will root out Twitter," said Turkey's Prime Minister Recep Tayyip Erdogan. Imagine any sane head of state believing he can silence social media these days? The US State Department equated the move with

"book burning." Erdogan must be pretty desperate given the scandals that surround him, and we know that desperation often exposes these kind of charlatans. The only thing his ill-conceived move ensures is an enormous wave of well-deserved criticism on Twitter and other media platforms. Erdogan has certainly done Twitter a very big favor.

Friday, November 29, 2013
False Binarisms
Washington DC
Here's the problem with most policy debates today. One point of view is expressed as an extreme binarism by supporters, detractors and the media who portray them while the opposing opinion is positioned in equally extreme, foreboding terms. The problem is that the truth involving complex issues is rarely as simple as this "either-or," "my way or the highway" approach to argumentation.

The US Army finds itself in just such a debate these days. On the one hand, some analysts and pundits argue at one extreme, as quoted in today's *Washington Post,* "that new technology has rendered large ground forces increasingly irrelevant." In response, Army Chief of Staff General Ray Odierno says, "There are a lot of intellectuals who believe that land power is obsolete," which is a "naive" and "dangerous thought."

Too often, advocates such as Odierno take an opposing view and reduce it to ridiculousness. No serious observer thinks that land power is going away. On the other hand, no fair analyst can dismiss the role of technology in reducing land forces and substantially changing their composition. The difficult truth is often found in the serious work of understanding and optimizing relationships between two binarisms. In this case, that means identifying and applying the right mix of human and technological power to best meet each circumstance. The media and ideologues do us a great disservice by covering these debates in such cynical, binary terms.

Saturday, June 1, 2013
Two Words Instead of One
Word inflation is fascinating. Instead of "price," we now say "price point." "Skill set" has substituted for "skill." A cable TV reporter this

morning pointed to a trickle of water in Oklahoma and proclaimed the possibility of a major "flood event," borrowing no doubt from auto sales that are now heralded as "sales events." Enough with this major inflation expansion.

Wednesday, May 29, 2013
In Brief
Lydia Davis just won The Man Booker Prize for short-story fiction. Some of her works are a paragraph or even a sentence long. Lincoln summoned the pain of Gettysburg in 272 words and Pythagoras the magnitude of his theorem in a brief equation. Let's all give it a try.

Thursday, March 14, 2013
The Crowdfunding Comedian
Austin @ South by Southwest
The oatmeal.com comic-satire website is the brainchild of Matthew Inman, comedian, cartoonist and former web designer. Inman told an SXSW audience here that his ongoing search for a meaningful career brought him to the realization that, "I'm a stand-up comedian whose stage is the web." What an interesting synthesis of his many talents.

Like too many folks here, Inman has that studied, post-modern, ironic, hipster thing going on. It works, however, because of his considerable talent. Rare is the person who can speak, draw and write well. He's become a formidable crowd funder, too. He offered three keys to successful crowdfunding: 1. "Be wary of the perks; you can drown in them." Put the cause ahead of the stuff people get for giving. 2. "Keep your appeal short and sweet. No giant walls of text." 3. "Don't feel like you need the obligatory video." They're too long, too similar and people are getting bored with them. Of course, it helps if you can instead create comic-infographics of his quality. He told us that crowdfunding "is not about products or selling books; it's about righting a wrong."

Inman did not expect to become a national crowdfunding expert. Like so many things in life, it happened accidentally. He adroitly parlayed a "nuisance lawsuit" – and the lunacy of an angry lawyer who failed to understand the consequences of suing an online comedian and producer of comic art – into $250,000 for the American Cancer Society and

National Wildlife Fund. He also raised $1.4 million to reclaim Nikola Tesla's laboratory site in New York.

In worrying aloud about running out of creative ideas, Inman reinforced something Bobby McFerrin said at his Circle Song camp at the Omega Institute last year. "If you have nothing to say, don't say anything." Fortunately for us, Inman still has plenty to say – and do.

Wednesday, March 13, 2013
The "Bored at Work" Network
Austin @ South by Southwest
Jonah Peretti says the explosive growth of his BuzzFeed platform owes to capitalizing on what he calls the "Bored at Work" Network. BuzzFeed has 40 million unique visitors a month, so the graduate of MIT's famed Media Lab has substantial credibility on the subject of growth.

The BuzzFeed CEO and Founder told a SXSW audience here that more people around the world are getting news content from each other at work than from all the traditional television networks combined. Of course, as the driving force behind a platform made famous by photos of cute basset hounds and other Ed-Murrow-is-turning-in-his-grave nonsense, Peretti's definition of news could be called, well, "flexible." Still, he is unequivocally correct in asserting that BuzzFeed and similar digital platforms have forever changed the way we view journalism. Thus the title of his session here, "The Big Power Shift in Media."

Peretti has his sights set on the "Bored in Line" Network – or "on line" if you're a New Yorker – which is now relevant because of the growing sophistication of mobile devices. "Social and mobile have merged," he told this South by Southwest gathering, "and mobile no longer stops things because somebody says, 'I can't do that now because I'm on my Blackberry.'" Indeed, he says that mobile comprises 40 percent of BuzzFeed traffic.

He is guiding BuzzFeed's evolution from what David Letterman calls "stupid pet tricks" to something far more substantive – and complex. BuzzFeed has hired serious political journalists and is now breaking hard news. He says his organization was the first to reveal President Obama's secret trip to Afghanistan in 2012, if you remember that controversy.

Indeed, BuzzFeed now has an approved White House correspondent traveling with the "inside the Beltway" crowd.

Peretti remains unabashedly committed to delivering the fun stuff, too. And you know what; he should. He used a Paris Café analog to make his case, and it worked for me. "Publishing is a Paris Café today where you can read Sartre, check out business news in *Le Monde*, flirt, and pet the dog under the table." His point, though a bit overripe, was that a general news and feature platform today needs to appeal to all aspects of life and living. Hey, as I thought about it, haven't the world's great newspapers long earned Pulitzer Prizes for serious journalism while trafficking in gossip, astrology, comic strips and photos of babies and pets? "Be human," Peretti said. Ok, I'm sold.

It Really Happened: Luciano Pavarotti
Washington DC
The great one passed away last night. I never met Pavarotti and only saw him perform once, at the old Boston Garden in the 1990s. An acoustically less sensitive or sensible building would have been difficult to find.

He was singing the exquisite "Nessun Dorma" from Puccini's *Turandot* when, at the worst possible moment of perfected, painful silence between breaths, a pay telephone rang somewhere in the rafters of the old barn. He had a legendary temper, yes, but one almost imagined a slight grin on Pavarotti's face in recognition of the sheer absurdity of the moment.

Monday, February 11, 2013
Media? What Media?
The Pope had good reason not to tell anybody of his decision to resign ahead of today's staggering announcement. After all, the news would have been leaked to Italian media the moment somebody internally disclosed it to the Vatican's Press Office. Still, it was painful and rather ridiculous to see Father Frederico Lombardi, spokesman for the Holy See, stumbling around at this morning's press conference. "The pope took us by surprise," he said. We know the Pope cares little about the media and their reportage. Yet disclosing the news to Lombardi late last night and giving him the overnight to prepare, alone and sequestered, would have helped the Vatican avoid looking so foolish.

Tuesday, January 29, 2013
Talk Isn't Always Cheap
New York City
I wrote on Sunday of Maestro Daniel Barenboim's use of music to break down barriers and open communication. Now that's somebody who understands the communication imperative of leadership. Apparently, according to *The New York Times*, Maine Governor Paul LePage has a very different view. He's been refusing to speak with Democrats since last November's election. When will these characters understand that they are elected to communicate, negotiate and appreciate the value of respectful, two-way engagement – even with people they don't like. There may be other jobs where listening to and speaking with colleagues can be avoided, but governor is not one of them. Grow up, governor.

Tuesday, January 8, 2013
Let's Get Phygital
The Financial Times' Lucy Kellaway announced her *Golden Flannel Awards* yesterday for corporate BS and doublespeak. One category included exquisite word combinations, such as "solutioneering" from Yanmar, "innovalue" from the Government of Taiwan, "sustainagility" from Atos Origin and "phygital" from Momentum UK. Good grief! In other categories, she celebrated Lloyds Banking Group's statement that, "We have made substantial progress against our strategic objectives." Next year, let's hope they make substantial progress toward their objectives.

Wednesday, August 29, 2012
RIP Malcolm Browne
The legendary war correspondent and photojournalist Malcolm Browne passed away this week. How sad that these great chroniclers of the Vietnam War are all now leaving us, especially with the recent deaths of Horst Faas and others in that once-in-a-lifetime AP Saigon Bureau. You may recall the Pulitzer Prize-winning Browne's image of the Buddhist monk setting himself on fire to protest the regime. That photo ranks among the most strikingly honest images of that entire sad chapter. Our men and women in uniform performed heroically in a reckless, needless and unjust war. That's part of the greatness of our military. Let's not

forget, however, the heroism of the journalists who speak truth to power and expose the folly of such catastrophically ill-advised adventures.

Wednesday, May 4, 2011
Low Post
The Washington Post was once a great newspaper. Those days are long gone, for sure. Its dwindling size and relevance is now only surpassed by its lack of judgment and good taste. Imagine any serious organization hosting Donald Trump at a public event right now, as the *Post* did at Saturday's White House Correspondents' Association dinner?

Trump's asinine behavior, race-baiting, self-aggrandizement, appalling lack of knowledge about public, foreign and economic policy and flat-out lying are a shame to this nation. Worse, Trump's nonsense has been a costly strategic distraction at a time when we need serious people engaged in serious issues. It's one thing for TMZ, *The Hollywood Dish*, *The National Enquirer* or Fox News to cover, honor or host this guy, but not the once-fabled *Post.*

Memo to *Washington Post* heir and celebrity interviewer Lally Weymouth, or whomever concocted this beaut of an idea. Suggestions for next year's dinner could include Charlie Sheen, Lindsay Lohan and the ghosts of George Wallace and Father Coughlin.

Still, there are four welcome developments here. First, Osama Bin Laden's death has removed Trump and the birthers from the top of the news, let's hope permanently. Second, the *Post's* Dana Milbank did a fine job using his column to question his own management's thinking about Trump and the Correspondents' dinner. Third, President Obama and Seth Meyers humiliated Trump at the dinner in front of all of official Washington with humor that exposed him with his own words and deeds. And fourth, I have cancelled my e-subscription to *The Washington Post.* Adieu.

Saturday, October 9, 2010
Wooden Figures Behind Wooden Podiums
Why do they even bother? I'm referring to the countless CEOs and other so-called leaders who deliver speeches and say absolutely nothing or worse, sometimes collecting big fees to embarrass themselves and bore us. The phrase "mailing it in" comes to mind.

Here's an example of the "saying absolutely nothing" syndrome. I attended a 2008 Houston speech by Major League Baseball Commissioner Bud Selig that still irritates me today. Here's this guy, no Bart Giamatti for sure, speaking to higher education leaders about one of America's great institutions – baseball. It was clear that Selig spent not one second thinking about the many interesting issues shared by university leaders in the audience and professional sports such as recruiting Asians and Latinos, competition and growth, drug abuse, leadership training and such. All we got were the same tired stories and PR gloss he had delivered over the previous 50 speeches with not even an intern's hand present in trying to make some connection – anything, please – to his audience.

Here's the "worse" part. We at the Council on Foreign Relations heard earlier this week from Intel president and CEO Paul Otellini. Now don't get me wrong. I have the utmost respect for Intel and especially its longstanding visionary leader Andy Grove. I don't know anything else about Otellini other than his speech was indefensibly selfish, predictable and contradictory.

He called for a "culture of investment" in the US to "create the conditions" for entrepreneurial success. Well, who can argue with that? The key questions are always, what are the specifics and who's going to pay for it? In whining about businesses being overtaxed, it's clear that he doesn't see Corporate America as the source of such new funding. So, Mr. Otellini, where will the money come from to fund this new investment culture and what's not working with the billions of taxpayer dollars the US already invests in such initiatives? He complained that California has become a "third world nation" in terms of services and infrastructure. Fine, let's grant him that point for the sake of argument. Please tell us then how your incessant call for cutting taxes will help us find the taxpayer resources needed to repair California's infrastructure – and that of so many other cities and states?

This is the same narrow-interests fallacy underlying Tea Party calls for tax cuts, especially now amidst recession and unprecedented budget deficits and national debt. Until you tell us how you will find the money – in specific policy and financial details, please – to pay for your needs and expectations and those of your fellow countrymen, then, well, sit down, be quiet and let somebody else speak. And please, speakers, do your homework before asking us to invest our precious time in your thoughtless messages.

Friday, September 12, 2008
Now That's a Leader: Magomed Yevloev
Washington, DC
How many politicians or journalists could ever demonstrate the courage and leadership abilities of slain Ingush website owner Magomed Yevloev? It's not even close. As with so many journalists and opposition figures speaking truth to Kremlin power these days, Yevloev was assassinated because he operated a website that attempts to hold Russia accountable for its actions in Ingushetia and throughout the Caucuses.

Yevloev died on August 30th from a single bullet wound to the head while in custody of state police in Narzan. Ironically, Yevloev had recently stepped up criticism of the treatment of Ingush civilians by Moscow's police puppets. He had just landed at the Narzan airport on a flight also carrying Putin-buddy and Ingush President Murat Zyazikov, who upon disembarking from the flight immediately ordered police to apprehend Yevloev.

Monday, February 4, 2008
Carnac Does CarMax
Washington DC
We make too many assumptions about our language use in business meetings. I am told of a recent story in which a top executive told his management team that he was going "to do a Carnac" to find the answer to a particular question.

This official held a piece of paper to his head, simulating the way in which legendary *Tonight Show* host Johnny Carson imitated a psychic by holding an envelope to his head. Unfortunately, some of his staff had never heard of Carnac, did not quite hear what the boss was saying, and left the meeting thinking that their organization was about to do something with CarMax – the used-car giant. Once again, you just can't make this stuff up.

It is a lesson for us all to understand the dynamics of intergenerational and intercultural communication and to assume nothing.

Remember what legendary Boston Celtics coach Red Auerbach often said, "It's not what you say; it's what they hear."

And speaking of language, one had to marvel at the Democrats' use of the term "prebuttal" in their so-called response to the State of the Union Address ahead of its actual delivery. It is certainly an accurate reflection of the times that we look to respond to something before it even happens.

It Really Happened: Barbara Bush

We at the World Affairs Council were hosting First Lady Barbara Bush years ago upon the publication of her memoirs. My mother joined me at the head table for the breakfast event in Boston, whereupon she and Barbara took turns telling stories and bragging about their children. For every Jeb or George story, Doris had one about Pat and me. The Bushes and McWades could not be from more diametrically different socioeconomic origins, yet the joy of maternal pride united us that morning.

Monday, May 19, 2008
Zipf's Law
New York City

The Second Edition of *The Oxford English Dictionary* suggests the English language may possess a quarter of a million distinct words. Achieving an exact count is impossible, given the abundance of current use, obsolete use and derivative constructions. It is also likely that English contains more words than any other language. Sociolinguist John McWhorter tells us there have been 6,000 languages over time with another 10,000 dialects, most of which are dead or dying.

The linguist George Kingsley Zipf was credited with illustrating and proving what became known as Zipf's Law in which the frequency of any word is inversely proportional to its rank in frequency tables. That is to say, the more we use certain words, the more use they get. The Brown Corpus contains "only" 50,000 English-language words, but Zipf's mathematical formulations of the 1930s and '40s demonstrated that nearly 50 percent of the Corpus is comprised of the same 135 words.

Zipf's work is a classic case of Power Law. Its inverse logic and Pareto-like distribution underscore how "preferential attachment" works. As in the "the rich get richer" framework, use accumulates more use just as money accumulates more money. It makes sense that we should use such few words to be efficient and effective in daily conversation, conventions and commerce. How many times has somebody dropped a pretentious word in cocktail-party chatter only to silence the conversation? *"Who was that creep, anyway?"*

Nassim Taleb rightly tells us in *The Black Swan* (2006) that Zipf was not the first to understand this phenomenon, nor is Zipf's Law a "law" in any real sense of that word. Still, its implications for leaders and language are very clear. On the one hand, a leader must achieve concise, unambiguous meaning in language use. On the other hand, leaders seem to use the same words all the time, thus rendering those words relatively meaningless. Boring too. The key is to find the right word-use balance between what is direct and understandable and what is interesting, compelling and different enough from everyone else's tired business clichés.

With content analysis, CEOs and other leaders can actually determine how much they sound like everyone else in today's language risk-averse, "me-too" business environment. In doing so, they may decide to move fractionally out on Zipf's distribution and embrace a slightly more distinctive spoken and written vocabulary that will help them distinguish their organizations and themselves and extinguish the tired, lazy verbiage found too often with today's business jargon.

Saturday, September 29, 2007
That's Unhelpful
Politicians, diplomats, and business people often label particular actions, statements or developments that contravene or contradict their purposes as "unhelpful." Of course they're unhelpful; that's their intent. Saddam Hussein undoubtedly saw the US invasion and occupation of Iraq as unhelpful, as Enron surely believed that the government's prosecution of its endemic corruption was unhelpful, too.

A *Reuters India* report yesterday underscored the helplessness of being unhelpful. It may be the only authority with any clout over the diabolical leaders of the Burmese military junta, but China has predictably ruled out calling for sanctions against Burma or even the standard UN condemnation of Burmese officials for suffocating democracy and development and quashing the current uprising in its customary blood-thirsty manner. "We believe that sanctions (are) not helpful for the situation down there," China's UN Ambassador Wang Guangya told *Reuters*.

Unhelpful to whom and why? These are the questions we must ask when somebody opines in the conference room or on the editorial page that a certain action or statement is unhelpful. Yes, pushing the cruel and downright bizarre Burmese officialdom to do the right thing is absolutely unhelpful to China. Beijing wants unbridled access to Burma's extraordinary gas reserves and other natural resources, so it plays nice with Burma as it does with the criminal gangs running Sudan and Zimbabwe. However, the removal and punishment of Burma's junta would be helpful to the brave, beautiful monks whose skulls are literally being crushed as well as to the Burmese people, the region, the planet and every value an evolved humankind is supposed to hold dear.

The Allies were decidedly unhelpful to Hitler. Police are sometimes unhelpful to criminals. Hell, the Boston Red Sox seek to be unhelpful to the New York Yankees. So when people spout the "unhelpful" line, sometimes to quiet a reasonable and helpful question or comment in a staff meeting, ask them about their perspective and interests in the matter. The word can be otherwise too subjective, too political and too vague to be, well, helpful.

Wednesday, June 6, 2007
Hot Air
Lee, MA
Brian Lamb is something of an American hero. For many years he has helped us escape the detritus of commercial television. There is a notable exception to this well-deserved plaudit, however. C-SPAN's *Washington Journal* morning call-in show has become simply unwatchable and unlistenable. It's damaging, too.

The hosts, guests and subject matter generally work just fine. I am seeing the enemy, however, and it is we, the people. By actually encouraging viewers to call the show on Democratic, Republican or Independent phone lines, C-SPAN is contributing to the ugly, uninformed partisan bickering that comprises too much of today's political discourse.

One Republican caller this morning said the answer to illegal immigration is to "string-up these illegals at the border" as a deterrent to others considering a border crossing. One simply shudders. On the other hand, Democrats blame President Bush for absolutely everything, even though he is right on some issues such as immigration. Mr. Lamb, you have left an indelible mark on high-quality conversation. Inviting and channeling the participation of the angriest, most partisan callers is a profound exception. The practice should stop.

And speaking of hot air ... The shadow of our balloon as Walt and I made a final approach for landing in Quechee, Vermont.

Wednesday, April 25, 2007
Judgment Call
Some might consider this observation trivial, but they do so at their own risk. It's extraordinary to read in today's *Wall Street Journal* that Andrew Wiesenthal, a physician leading Kaiser Permanente's troubled HealthConnect project, participated in an important industry podcast on his cell phone while traveling in a cab. This is not a very good idea. Are you really that important, Dr. Wiesenthal?

Thoughtful and ultimately successful articulation requires taking control of your physical space and time. It requires that you show some respect, too. Besides, any good reporter, blogger or podcaster will know that you are approaching the moment in a half-assed manner. That reporter might even choose to make this awkward slight part of the story, which is why Dr. Wiesenthal's taxi tactics found their way into the lead item of today's *Journal.*

Friday, April 20, 2007
Now That's a Leader: Dr. Liviu Librescu
The relationship between mass murderers and the media is a long and controversial one. The decision by NBC to broadcast images supplied by the Virginia Tech assassin is considered by some (including me) to enable his horrific actions, understanding as he did that he would get a global forum for such egregious sociopathy.

In this sense, is NBC an accessory-after-the fact for these crimes or future ones of similar ghastly consequence? This regrettable symbiosis cannot be denied, but it begs that much greater wisdom, judgment and common sense be exercised by our media decision-makers. Running these images is bad enough, but NBC's decision to integrate them with its *Nightly News* musical score, endless promotion and Brian Williams' breathless intonation illustrate a media today that has truly lost its way.

Isn't it time for the broadcast and cable media to turn down the volume? Enough already! Let the Virginia Tech community grieve. Let the true heroes be honored. Let the true healers speak as credible experts and enough with uninformed pundits, politicians and advocates using the situation to cast blame and to advance their own interests.

One such hero is the remarkable Dr. Liviu Librescu. A Holocaust survivor, this professor of aeronautical engineering actually blocked the classroom door with his body when the gunman attempted to enter, giving his students time to escape. The madman killed Librescu by shooting through the door.

How would any one of us have reacted in the same split-second situation? Dr. Librescu served on Mahmood Tabaddor's dissertation committee. The latter describes him on a CNN blog as a "humble and gentle" man whose "courage was constant." Yes, the humble, gentle ones often emerge as heroes and leaders amidst the bluster and bombast of people merely pretending to be heroic.

Tuesday, December 26, 2006
Homelessness is no Genocide
National Public Radio's Ina Jaffe reported from Central Los Angeles recently, vividly underscoring the tragedy that is Skid Row. Those of us who have walked or driven by the area of South Central and Sixth Street know that hundreds of American men, women and children continue to live in woeful, wretched conditions associated more with Lagos or Sao Paulo.

LA City Councilwoman Jan Perry is to be commended for her advocacy of the homeless. We need more people in leadership positions who share her concern. This comes despite the fact that she and her estranged husband owe the Federal government nearly $300,000 in back taxes. However, Perry makes a troubling rhetorical error when she says that the mostly African-American homeless population in Skid Row are confronting "a form of genocide." Wrong.

Perry's sloppy, overinflated language hurts both the homeless she is trying to assist as well as the victims of real genocide. Yes, the situation in LA's Skid Row is tragic, deplorable and absolutely unacceptable. However, it cannot be presented as a deliberate and systematic attempt to exterminate a people. One need only to look at the Nazis and the Jews, the Tutsi and Hutu of Rwanda, as well as today's tragedy in Darfur to understand the true nature of a systematic eradication of a people undertaken for political purposes. Perry was trying to make a point, but her overreaching hyperbole only compels greater, dismissive indifference to victims of homelessness and genocide alike.

Friday, July 28, 2006
On "Staying the Course"
It is hard to imagine a more rhetorically vapid and painfully wrongheaded phrase than "staying the course" in the Iraq War. Imagine careening 100 miles per hour toward a very large brick wall. Would we look macho and resolute by insisting on staying the course? No, I'm afraid we would simply look foolish.

What made Alexander the Great, Napoleon, Grant and Patton such military marvels was their ability and willingness to see the entire map and to adjust course as conditions and contingencies warranted. Staying the course with a losing proposition is hardly ever the right approach, Mr. President.

It Really Happened: Hola, Big Papi
I attended the 2003 Caribbean World Series in Puerto Rico and saw the Dominican Republic team, Aguilas Cibaenas, win the championship. The name of the Series MVP was completely unknown to me that February, since David Ortiz was little known to fans and a brand new member of the Boston Red Sox. I returned from my "scouting trip" eager to tell everyone that this Ortiz guy, who went on to earn three World Series rings with the Sox and may well be the most clutch hitter in team history, might just amount to something.

Tuesday, October 28, 2003
Words Are Assets, Too
Business Forum Online
We are drowning in rhetorical clutter these days. In a society bloated with endless claims, clichés, jargon, hyperbole and ritualistic argument, it's no wonder why customers, investors, employees and voters are simply not listening anymore.

Blame it on human nature. Blame it on the explosion of marketing and communications media. Whatever the underlying cause, it's become far too easy these days to say a great deal without saying anything. In the process, too many businesses, governments and non-profit organizations seem like randomly changing kaleidoscopes that, in Shakespearean terms, are "full of sound and fury, signifying nothing."

We've cheapened our language and, by doing so, we've created an epidemic of what my old high school teacher crudely called "verbal diarrhea." There are many symptoms of an illness that has been more politely called "message du jour."

Some of these may seem painfully familiar to you:

- Finding safety in copying the competition. We want differentiation, but when in doubt we jump right back into that big pot of vanilla.
- Creating ad hoc messages for one-time situations, such as an event, speech or advertisement. How many of us have seen well-crafted, thoroughly tested messaging suddenly changed in the car while driving to a speech? Maybe we've done it ourselves.
- Using wholly unrelated (and sometimes contradictory) messages for different audiences. Do we really think that employees don't read newspapers or that analysts don't hear about an internal speech?
- Allowing dominant personalities to shape our messaging and lacking the research to support or refute them. These days, loud and wrong often wins over quiet and right.
- Outsourcing to vendors who change our messages. It isn't easy getting advertising, PR, direct mail, website and design agencies to work within a messaging system. That's why many organizations are moving more work to truly integrated shops, preserving message discipline while saving time, money and frustration.
- Acting in ways that contradict our messages. Executives whose actions contravene stated company values and customer-service behaviors that corrupt our marketing claims are two regular brand killers.

So, what's the solution? Let's start by developing and enforcing strategic expectations and quality control standards for our words. Words embody concepts. Where words fail, or where they are too easily shuffled and replaced, the underlying vision is also subject to failure. Let's treat our language assets strategically; applying the same precision we do to our financial, human, technological, and real estate assets.

Enter messaging systems. Creating a messaging system starts with a discipline-forcing challenge so simple that it renders brilliant executives speechless. Try placing your value proposition in one sentence. It's tough work, and that's why organizations make so many excuses to avoid it. Here's an excellent starting point. Just try filling in the following blanks: "We are something that does something that results in something." Easy, right?

Sure, it's the proverbial "elevator speech." The problem with most elevator speeches, however, is that they are, in fact, speeches, and not interesting or inviting insights. The typical elevator speech assumes we're traveling in a skyscraper with the benefit of several minutes or more to tell our story. In reality, given today's impatient and cluttered market, we're really on nothing more than a mere one-flight ride.

A brief, compelling few sentences can often break into three consistent, integrated messages supported by numerous proof points. An otherwise smart executive once declared, "Consistency is the hobgoblin of little minds," invoking Ralph Waldo Emerson to undercut the value of message consistency. Alas, poor Emerson is frequently misused in this manner. He actually wrote that, "A *foolish* consistency is the hobgoblin of little minds." I don't know about you, but I certainly want my doctors, mechanics, pilots, and bankers to be consistently good. There's nothing foolish in consistency that works. It's called discipline.

The best messaging systems are brief, simple, externally focused and enforceable. First, keep it short. Long, ponderous passages, complicated sentence structures, faulty logic and twisted syntax rob messaging of its power. We should find inspiration from Lincoln, whose Gettysburg Address was a mere 268 words. Or how about good old Pythagoras, whose 22-word theorem changed our view of the world.

Einstein said that, "Everything should be made as simple as possible, but not simpler." Thus the beauty of E=mc2. Think of Einstein the next time you hear somebody say their organization is too complicated to reduce to one sentence. In his book *Victory* (2002), management guru Brian Tracy says, "The natural tendency in all human activities is to increase complexity." He tells us to cherish simplicity and resist the inevitable slide toward diffusion and confusion that marks human endeavor.

Perhaps the single greatest impediment to effective messaging is forgetting that it's all about the customer, not about us. Organizations too often describe themselves, stressing how they're organized and when they were founded. The understandable impulse is to look internally, but these facts are of little interest to customers. Instead, we need to condition ourselves to look externally toward the market and prescribe interesting, appealing and memorable reasons why we're worth customers' time and money.

The process of developing a messaging system may seem daunting. It doesn't have to be so onerous. It should take a matter of weeks with good market research in hand, not months, and the product is always worth the wait. That's because a good messaging system gives any of us worrying about that next annual report, advertisement, press release, speech or website revision a healthy running start. Indeed, in the race for brand recognition and market share, it's always worth remembering that words are assets too.

CHAPTER 6

CREATIVITY & CULTURE

January 8, 2017
Foodie Fodder

Here are three good food reads we acquired over the Holidays. Anthony Bourdain's cookbook *Appetites* is fine. Still, it's a distant third to the *FT Weekend* Nicholas Lander's beautifully illustrated book on the history of restaurant menus, *On The Menu* and Ina Yalof's homage to New York City's many culinary scenes, *Food and the City*. Yalof takes us into many fascinating worlds, with stories about Bronx meat purveyors and fishmongers to baking geniuses, halal food truck operators, chefs at the highest-end restaurants and even a firefighter-cook on Staten Island.

Wednesday, June 29, 2016
Now That's a Leader: Girls Rock Detroit
Detroit

Melissa Coppola, Willa Rae Adamo and Rosalind Hartigan help girls build self-esteem in a world that continues to finds ways to destroy it. Participants in their Girls Rock Detroit initiative spend a week at camp taking music lessons, forming bands, writing songs and rehearsing for a live performance at venues such as the Detroit Institute of Music Education. The lessons are innumerable, but chief among them is that these girls learn with the help of mentors and in a safe environment that they can and should express themselves. As one 11-year-old participant told the University of Michigan recently, "We rocked the house," which can only help her rock our world someday, too.

Sunday, March 6, 2016
Go Ahead, Quit Your Day Job
Miami

I loathe when people toss out the distressingly trite line, "Don't quit your day job" to somebody else who is happily singing. One difference between pessimists and optimists may be that the former offers this clichéd put-down while the latter joins in the singing. If you want to sing no matter the quality of your voice, do it. And if somebody else is singing, jump in with them or just leave them alone. In today's angry, ignorant and bombastic Trumpscape, we could use less insult and more consult.

Sunday, December 27, 2015
Boundaries: Volume Two
Chatham, MA

It's only natural to get stuck in grooves, literally in the case of music. I enjoy classic rock as much as the next baby boomer and have seen most of the major acts of the late 1960s and '70s. Sometimes, I do agree with those who criticize much of today's music for the squeaky, homogenized middlebrow stuff that it is. Still, this is far too simplistic a formulation.

There's plenty of great music out there today with young artists who have something to say, and say it well. It takes intentionality, however, to leave your comfort zone and discover new performers. It's invigorating to see 24-year-old, Boston-born saxophonist, singer-songwriter and arranger Grace Kelly play in *The Late Show with Stephen Colbert* house band, for example, or to hear 27-year-old singer-songwriter Elle King belt out blues-rock tunes that conjure the best of Ruth Brown or Koko Taylor. So here's one "safe" way to discover that the kids are truly alright. Television shows such as the BBC's *Later with Jools Holland* or *Live from Daryl's House* on MTV Live present plenty of acts from the 1960s through 2000s, but they are spliced with new, up-and-coming artists that can open new worlds and help us stay young.

Sunday, November 15, 2015
Boundaries: Volume One
Chicago
Grant Achatz's restaurant Alinea challenges people. That's the whole idea. We loved the experience here last night, which included his green apple balloons. I lament the folks who automatically reject an experience such as this one because, well, they think it's pretentious, experimental, avant garde, precious, showy, expensive or confusing because it draws from too many creative disciplines. Sometimes, it's all of the above to people we meet in life who are automatic door closers.

Yes, Chef Grant has pushed molecular gastronomy to levels that are mystical and even over the top, infused as his thought-provoking work is with influences such as Miro paintings, jazz riffs and theater production. Why not? Can't we appreciate the statement he is making and how he draws it so brilliantly at the crossroads of art and science? Why does everything have to align with past patterns and single disciplines just to keep us safely tucked into our comfort zones? Maybe the world would be a better place if we left our comfort zones every now and then and learned something in the process – especially about ourselves.

Monday, June 2, 2014
Creativity Pit Stops
Hartford
Here's a terrific way to jump-start your day, creatively. Next time you see a highway sign for an interesting museum, gallery or library, stop. Yes, stop. Don't make excuses. Even if for 30 minutes, as was the case today for me at the Mark Twain Museum and Home, a brief creativity pit stop can work wonders.

I love the Twain line, emblazoned in the museum lobby, "I have sampled this life." Words to live by, indeed. Two other inspiring Twain quotes include, "My pen has been warmed up in hell" and, my favorite, "Travel is fatal to prejudice" from *Innocents Abroad* (1869). It would be difficult to find a better cure for bigotry and the self-certainty of narrow-mindedness than travel, though music and literature clearly rank high on this list, too.

Tuesday, March 12, 2013
Swoop and Poop
Austin @ South by Southwest

I was worried about Brian Sullivan's "Design like Da Vinci" presentation here at South by Southwest. After all, Michael Gelb covered the "Think like Leonardo" ground pretty well many years ago. I spent a long weekend with Gelb and others at an Omega Institute seminar on the subject in the late 1990s.

Happily, Sullivan provided useful reminders to those of us who enjoy the cottage industry that is Da Vinci for creatives. And just as happily, he credited Gelb for his work. Focusing on Da Vinci's sketches, which number in the thousands, Sullivan spoke to us from his vantage point as a web usability expert at the Sabre Human Factors Center in Dallas. He offered many tips including striving for quantity in creative development, a view some might challenge, and understanding that the search for perfection "will kill you."

I was most intrigued, however, by his discussion of what he called the "swoop and poop executive seagull maneuver." Sure, we all know this one. It's the infuriating habit that some busy and, yes, self-important executives have of ignoring a project and making no contribution to it until the moment it's revealed when, as if on cue, they crap all over the idea – usually in front of everyone. Scholars ask in these situations that we make room for "appreciative inquiry" and, in Sullivan's words, that we "defer judgment, both positive and negative." After all, as Da Vinci himself once said, "It's easier to resist in the beginning than in the end."

Sullivan said that we have 65,000 thoughts each day and that 65 percent of them are negative. He offered no citation, so he was likely pulling that data point from his hind reaches. He argues that it's important for creators and evaluators alike to resist the very human temptation to pick things apart immediately without asking productive questions and letting something marinate. Sullivan told of a situation in which Da Vinci's way-ahead-of-its-time design for a movable wall was rejected by the City of Venice, immediately and out of hand.

Sullivan's prescription here would intersect nicely with the work of Daniel Goleman and others in emotional intelligence. If self-awareness and self-regulation are key pillars of emotional intelligence, then we need more leader-evaluators who can control their emotional impulses and let creative work breathe before condemning or praising it.

Sunday, March 10, 2013
Labors of Love
Austin @ South by Southwest
South by Southwest is everything you've heard about it. The prevalent body piercings, tattoos and vague whiff of ganja in the air mix easily with executives from *The New York Times*, Chile's Creative Economy, IBM, Sony Pictures and scores of other firms working deals.

Tina Roth Eisenberg opened today's events paying homage to clean and elegant design and the joys of white space. The Swiss Miss, as she's called, runs a Brooklyn design studio and off-the-charts-popular blog with a million unique hits a month. She says she's found joy in living her own values and honoring her own standards, to which I say – you bet. Is there any other way?

She offered 11 principles for living well, personally and professionally. The most compelling advice was to "invest your life in what you love." She added that, "Happiness matters and the lack of it affects your creative work." She enthusiastically suggested that each of us "be a master in the art of living" where work and play are inseparable.

So, what's your level of creative joy and professional happiness? As Behance CEO Scott Belsky says, "A labor of love always pays off." I'm not sure this is always true, but the sentiment is wonderful.

It Really Happened: Woody Allen and the Romanian Twins
Tony was the longtime maître de at New York's celebrated Café Carlyle, one of my favorite spots on the planet along with Bemelmans Bar across the hall. On several occasions, he let me stand near the sound station next to the bar for sold-out shows. He'd say, "Get a drink (in Bemelmans) and come back at 8:30." I followed his orders one Monday night when Woody Allen was playing clarinet there with the Eddy Davis Band. Tony parked me with a producer from Sony Music, an excitable Russian dude and a pair of Romanian show-business sisters known as the Indiggo Twins.

As show time approached, somebody knocked on the back door against which I was leaning. I opened the door and, of course, it was

Woody Allen and his bodyguard. "Come right in Mr. Allen," I offered with faux authority, "we've been waiting for you." I didn't expect an acknowledgement, and I guess the lack of eye contact was only mildly surprising. His bodyguard joined us at the sound station and we all had a wonderful time, given our proximity right next to the bar. I opened the door for Woody upon his departure and that was that. Or so I thought.

There was another knock and, yes, it was Allen again. "I need to see the twins," he told me. It seems he had made a commitment to somebody that he would say hello to them. He met them out back for a few minutes, and then they rejoined us.

As we left the Carlyle, I turned to the producer, twins and Russian and asked jokingly, "When will we all be together again?" Next thing we knew, a taxi was dropping us at a wonderful West Village restaurant owned, as it turns out, by the Russian gentleman who was an exceptionally gracious host. We sang and danced, joined by an international cast of revelers and musicians until 3:00 in the morning – never to see one another again.

Sunday, January 27, 2013
Now that's a Leader: Daniel Barenboim
Maestro Daniel Barenboim started the West-Eastern Divan Orchestra (performing in Boston today) as, in his words, "an orchestra against ignorance." Comprised of Israeli, Palestinian, Lebanese, Syrian, and Iranian youth, the orchestra uses the language of music to break barriers made more rigid by the language of violence. Barenboim has just announced (with Frank Gehry and Brown University) a new conservatory based in Berlin that will also teach young people leadership, politics, humanities and required Arabic and Hebrew. So where can the rest of the world sign up for such an "awareness academy"?

Sunday, May 16, 2010
Now that's a Leader: Antonio Pappano
New York City
Antonio Pappano is an interesting guy with no shortage of useful opinions. He's the music director of London's Royal Opera House and Rome's Orchestra of the Accademia Nazionale di Santa Cecilia. When

asked by *The Financial Times* recently for his views on Italian culture and politics, his answer was instructive.

He claimed that Italy needs a new style of cultural leadership, capable of nurturing and coalescing talent, because, as Pappano explained, "one of the difficulties in Italy is how to create teams." Pappano has no franchise on wisdom on this subject, for too many of us have seen the consequences of failing to develop teams, organizations and even nations so that the whole is greater than the sum of their disparate pieces. Politics in the United States these days comes to mind.

Pappano builds and leads teams for a living. His job in two global capitals is to develop the whole so that it exceeds the sum of its parts, quite literally marking the difference between symphony and cacophony. Too many teams today are a muddle of conflicting visions and competing agendas, so often because they lack the cohering, synthesizing and unifying leadership of an Antonio Pappano.

Unlike so many conductors, especially bygone greats such as Bernstein and Solti, who could be dictatorial and sometimes put their ego needs ahead of their players, Pappano is in *FT*'s view, "the opposite of dictatorial. Colleagues talk of a hands-on, hard-working boss, more approachable than many other top-flight conductors who can be charismatic but aloof."

This is what is missing in so many leadership contexts now, where entities big and small seem atomized by the selfish needs of their loudest constituents. Let's take Italy for example. Under a photo caption of Italy's ridiculous President Silvio Berlusconi and two coalition partner-rivals dubbed, "The three stooges running Italy," *The Economist* reports that far too many Italians think the unification of their country 150 years ago was a mistake.

The truth is when leaders fail to understand their essential, cohering role in helping those they lead see beyond narrow, selfish interests, they generally fail. Berlusconi is clueless on this subject, since he's been focused solely on his own selfish ambitions. Plus, he's just not that smart.

I saw Judy Collins perform the other night at the Cafe Carlyle here. To paraphrase her, isn't it time to stop sending in the clowns? It seems that the wrong guy is running Italy.

Thursday, February 26, 2009
Rashomon, Encore Edition
Singapore

It has been over 30 years since I last saw the Kurosawa-Miyagawa classic film, *Rashomon* (1950). How can it be that people see the exact same events and interpret them so very differently, as is the case in the film of the rape of a woman and murder of her husband?

This question is certainly the scourge of courtroom lawyers and anyone else who tries to discern truth (or at least their version of it) from the same set of facts. Our personal ontologies blind us to reality and especially to the realities of other people's lives. We see what we want to see and hear what we want to hear to avoid the hard work of rising above ourselves. This is why fierce liberals and conservatives, each of whom derives so much self-identity from their chosen labels and the lockstep theologies they require, will use a political speech only to validate their own beliefs and discredit non-conforming ones. The cognitive dissonance that the truth produces must be otherwise too painful to bear.

For those of you who know the movie, the woodcutter's agreement at the end of the film to take the abandoned baby home to raise it as his own fills the priest with renewed hope for humanity. This provides a welcome metaphor for where we are today as a people. Getting to a better place, however, will require each of us to work that much harder to surrender clichéd views of the past and open wide to seeing and hearing the possibilities of some very different futures.

Tuesday, February 24, 2009
The Mozart of Madras
Singapore

How wonderful it is to see the Mozart of Madras, the incomparable A.R. Rahman win two Oscars for his musical score for *Slumdog Millionaire*. The soundtrack has completely sold out here just one day after Rahman's well-deserved recognition by Hollywood.

As an African-American President of the United States attempts a political, financial and moral recovery like few others, our nation now finds an appetite to award Oscars to three Muslims including Rahman, his lyricist Gulzar and soundman Resul Pookutty. It is a hopeful moment. Maybe we do have the power to move beyond ourselves.

Peter Gabriel's work provided my first introduction to the musical diaspora represented by Sufi-convert-from-Hinduism Rahman and others. The blend of Sufi mysticism, Afro-pop, Arab hip-hop, Tamil folk, western rock and much more conveys an energy that one readily feels in Singapore, Tokyo, Mumbai and Istanbul these days. Well, it sure beats the Gordon Lightfoot Muzak playing here at this hotel right now. Salamat.

And while not on the subject, Singapore is a haven for street food lovers. Try the murtabak (chicken, onion, garlic and spices in traditional Malay bread with curry sauce) at Zam Zam on Arab Street across from the Sultan Mosque here.

Wednesday, January 14, 2009
Creativity the Right Way
Delray Beach, FL
Nancy Schaffer of the Tribeca Film Festival recently told *The New York Times* that Qatar is a vastly more sophisticated haven for culture and arts than most other Persian Gulf nations. "Doha is much less flashy and more sophisticated than some of its Arab counterparts," she said.

Dubai should take notice of how they do things in Qatar, at least in this context. Money buys most anything, but credit for doing so with acumen and some minimal measure of class owes in large part to Qatar's Sheikha Mozah and her daughter Sheikha al Mayassa. It turns out that the Duke-educated Sheikha al Mayassa interned at Robert DeNiro's Tribeca Productions, without ever telling her Tribeca employers at the time that she was one of the wealthiest young women in the world. The Sheikhas' imprint is all over the nation, which we discovered there first-hand last year at Education City as well as in a raft of art galleries in Doha's Souk Waqif. Of course, the new I.M. Pei-designed Museum of Islamic Art is now the signature building on Doha's corniche and DeNiro expects to open a Tribeca Film Festival there soon. It sure beats Dubai's more garish displays of wealth for wealth's sake, such as its indoor ski slope housed inside a shopping mall – which I confess to have visited as well.

How interesting it is to learn that Roger Mandle, the former Rhode Island School of Design president, is now the executive director of the

Qatar Museums Authorities. Roger helped us develop and launch the Creative Economy Council in the late 1990s. I wondered what had happened to Roger after discovering the compelling new RISD president several weeks ago, the new-media guru John Maeda. Maeda's integrated background in computer science, graphic design and fine arts coupled with his most recent stint as an associate director at MIT's Media Lab will serve RISD well.

What I like so much about Maeda, and what we tried to communicate with the Creative Economy Council with only marginal results, is that there are no longer many lines between creative and commercial enterprise. Much to the detriment of our culture and economy, old stereotypes linger that place "the arts" in the non-profit sector somehow divorced from all the creative energies found in technology, new-media, publishing, advertising, music, cuisine and so much more. Maeda gets this point because he knows no other way. One suspects that Sheikha al Mayassa, Roger Mandle, and their colleagues in Doha get it, too. We need to do a much better job of "getting it" in New England.

It Really Happened: Robert Shaw
New York City

Boston University invited alumni to join in a large amateur chorus backing a practice session with the BU Chorus and Symphony Orchestra under the direction of visiting luminary Robert Shaw. Shaw is a magnificent, exacting figure who has stood at the pinnacle of leading choral composers and conductors in the world. Watching him rehearse such a large group was mesmerizing; acting like I was actually participating in it as a member of the chorus was ridiculous.

The point is that I can sing, but not particularly well. My sister Pat and I thought this would be an interesting afternoon's education and entertainment, however, so we took our mother with us. We didn't tell Doris that we'd be expected to sing. The first clue should have been an usher questioning us as to whether we wanted to sit in the soprano, mezzo, contralto sections or elsewhere. I don't recall what we chose, but I knew that my mother missed that entire exchange – thankfully. The next clue might have been another usher handing us a libretto for the Brahms' *German Requiem*. Yet it wasn't until we all started singing that my mother understood we were far more than just spectators. The look of shock and humorous dismay on her face when, at one point, Shaw turned toward our section and yelled at us, was worth the price of admission alone.

It reminds me of a story the late George Plimpton told a small group of us at Boston University many years ago. He had convinced Leonard Bernstein to let him play triangle in a piece to be performed on a Canadian tour of the New York Philharmonic. One night in Vancouver, however, he missed his sole triangle moment. He told us that Bernstein later excoriated him in a manner that was worse than anything he ever experienced with the Detroit Lions, playing goaltender for the Boston Bruins, in the ring with Sugar Ray Robinson or on the tennis court with Pancho Gonzalez.

I'm blessed to have great traveling buddies such as my husband Walt, sister Pat, son Zack and, of course, Mikey. Pat and I enjoyed obligatory Bellinis – say that fast three times – at Harry's Bar in Venice – with Mikey.

Wednesday, October 22, 2008

Imagine That

The 9-11 Commission suggested in its 2004 report that the terrorist attacks were not prevented, in part, because they were never imagined. The commissioners labeled the attack and our failure to identify and thwart it a distinct "failure of imagination" among US policymakers. Despite endless fictional portrayals of airplanes crashing into skyscrapers over many decades, few if anyone in senior government circles ever imagined its possibility. Creativity it seems is not especially valued in some national security settings, although it often makes the difference between success and failure in policymaking and governance.

There is little doubt the business-as-usual crowd thinks that one of Stephen Kinzer's imaginative ideas for Afghanistan is crazy, too. Quite the contrary. Kinzer is a creative thinker whose ideas often appeal, especially during tough times when people are open to new ways of doing things. He suggested in a *Boston Globe* column this month that instead of bombing villages in Afghanistan in search of Taliban, and earning the lifelong enmity of countless Afghans, we consider more constructive long-term approaches.

For example, the economy of Afghanistan relies immensely on poppies used for production of opium and other drugs. Kinzer writes that, "The country will not be stable as long as the poppy trade provides huge sums of money for violent militants." However, trying to eradicate poppies is an unachievable objective and what little we destroy in non-stop spray-and-burn campaigns once again works against us by needlessly creating enemies on the ground whose livelihoods depend solely on this crop. Instead, Kinzer suggests that the US "should allow planting to proceed unmolested, and then buy the entire crop and burn it." We are spending much more than the $4 billion annual value of the crop in spraying, burning, bombing and enemy-making. That's why Kinzer adds, "That sum would be better spent putting cash into the pockets of Afghan peasants than firing missiles into their villages."

So many bold, creative ideas seem politically untenable at first. This imaginative offering, suggested in different forms in the past, deserves study amidst the growing recognition that too many of the old ways are bankrupt and broken.

Tuesday, August 26, 2008
Steinbeck's Cannery Row
Cannery Row, Monterey, CA
Despite its obvious touristy sensibility, Cannery Row still lets even the casual observer hearken back to an earlier day when Monterey Bay was a global capital of sardine harvesting. Imagine that time in the 1930s and '40s described so vividly by John Steinbeck in *Cannery Row* (1945) when the purse seiners arrived loaded to capacity with fresh catch. What was then called Ocean View Avenue would come alive as townsfolk raced for spot employment cleaning, preparing and packaging the sardines.

Of course, we fished the living daylights out of the Monterey Canyon and by 1973 all 17 of the longstanding canneries had been shuttered. Thanks to some effective marine management since that time, however, Monterey Bay has returned to life. This would have been a source of pride for Ed Ricketts, Steinbeck's best friend and the inspiration for the "Doc" character in both *Cannery Row* and *Sweet Thursday*.

Steinbeck wrote with such simple elegance, believing that accessible words, short sentence structures and compelling narrative communicate best. Too much writing today is turgid and unnecessarily opaque, seemingly designed to hide meaning rather than reveal it. In that spirit, a visit to the National Steinbeck Center in the author's hometown of Salinas is a worthy destination for any student of literature.

Sunday, August 3, 2008
Love and Hate on the Diamond
Yankee Stadium
It is a cliché, no doubt, but these truly are hallowed grounds. The Red Sox are family for whom I have nothing but love and a rabid rooting interest. However, the bigger cliché is that one's love for the Red Sox automatically means hatred for the Yankees – or vice versa. I want to see the Red Sox crush the Yankees whenever they meet, but that does not reduce my independent capacity to recognize that the Yankees are a first-rate organization for whom it would be objectively impossible not to respect and hold in high regard.

The "Yankees Suck" moron screeds and t-shirts are an embarrassment. The treatment of Red Sox closer Jonathan Papelbon's pregnant wife by Yankee fans at the All Star Game is even worse. And to think that there have been several murders lately in Boston and New York involving people wearing the wrong team's paraphernalia. In this bitter rivalry, as elsewhere in life, too many people buy into utter nonsense and do no work whatsoever at developing or even questioning their outlook or the verbal and even physical violence that it sponsors. It seems when we lack for "tribes" to hate, we create them.

Just looking at the field below one sees ... Spike Lee. Yes, he's here. Ugh! In pleasant contrast, however, one also feels the memories of Yogi Berra, Joe DiMaggio, Whitey Ford, Lou Gehrig, Goose Gossage, Ron Guidry, Catfish Hunter, Reggie Jackson, Mickey Mantle, Roger Maris, Babe Ruth and, yes, Derek Jeter. How can this place be anything but great? As the new Yankee Stadium rises here by Jerome Avenue, however, it must also be said that it is sorely needed. Yankee Stadium and its neighborhood are much less comfortable and convenient than Fenway Park – and that's a mouthful! Without the winning tradition, this place would be mediocre at best.

Monday, February 11, 2008
Best in Show
New York City
I can now remove the Westminster Kennel Club Show from the list of the countless things I want to see, learn and do. I entered Madison Square Garden late this morning to join a world that too many of us only know from the pantomime that is the *Best in Show* (2000) movie. Well, actually, from my astonishingly accessible vantage point on the Garden's floor and in the staging areas, I have to admit that the movie and the real-life scene share much in common. The fussing and primping, the anxieties and adrenaline and the countless oddities were all in evidence. Oh yes, and then there were the dogs, too.

This 132nd edition of this extravaganza features 2,627 entries from among 169 breeds organized into seven groups such as herding or sporting. I looked skyward toward the Willis Reed, Walt Frazier and Bill Bradley banners at one point and thought, "I know nothing about this world." Of course, that's what makes it fun. That's why I'm here. Let the learning commence. I watched parades of dalmatians, sheepdogs, wolfhounds, bloodhounds, chow chows and even dachshunds with their hopeful, sometimes hilarious handlers.

So go ahead. Take a day and come to New York City for this extraordinary show. After all, one has to love a competition in which out-of-shape people are expected to compete on the floor of Madison Square Garden. And what's not to like about an event whose program unabashedly educates the reader about bitches?

As an aside, I'll finally be seeing Les Paul perform tonight at the Iridium. At age 92, this guitar and recording virtuoso is reportedly as strong as he is irreverent at these Monday night lovefests. Keith Richards once said that without Les Paul, generations of flash little punks like him would have been in jail.

Thursday, November 15, 2007
That's So Russian
Santa Monica
The St. Petersburg Philharmonic's stirring rendition of Prokofiev's *Romeo and Juliet* suite tonight at LA's Disney Center literally sent chills down my spine. Too bad we didn't hear more of it. For some reason, maestro Yuri Temirkanov chose to present only eight of the 52 pieces that comprise this Prokofiev masterpiece. Thirty minutes seemed far too brief a tribute to a great Russian composer by an equally venerable Russian orchestra.

The Philharmonic has what *The New York Times* critic Anthony Tommasini praised in a Carnegie Hall performance this month as an "earthy orchestral sound" that favors "sweeping organic interpretations" over "lighter textures and velvety sheen." This approach was much in evidence tonight, working well with Prokofiev but not so well with a lame interpretation of the more subtle Schumann *Piano Concerto*.

One hesitates to offer a stereotype, but the 205-year-old Philharmonic is just so traditionally Russian. Its members seem much older than those of other orchestras I have seen in recent years and there are very few women in its ranks. One is hard-pressed these days not to see a woman as the first or second violinist, and yet the Philharmonic's only two women violinists were to be found in the third row.

It Really Happened: Ruth Brown

The legendary R&B singer Ruth Brown died yesterday in Las Vegas. I had the privilege of seeing "the girl with the teardrop in her voice" perform several times, the most interesting of which was in the nearly empty basement lounge of The Viking Hotel in Newport, RI. It was the night before the 1997 Newport R&B Festival and, as tradition had it, some performers staying at The Viking would go downstairs late in the evening to jam with whomever showed up. Well, Ronnie Earl and The Broadcasters were playing for what seemed like family and friends when Ruth Brown walked onstage and absolutely enthralled us. She later joined our table and was as warm and gracious as her music.

Sunday, October 28, 2007
The Farnsworth Invention
New York City

The Farnsworth Invention opens November 14th at the Music Box Theater, a wonderful, intimate venue built in 1921 by Irving Berlin. This is an enjoyable account of the invention of television from Aaron Sorkin with Hank Azaria playing the lead role as RCA mogul David Sarnoff.

We saw the production today – happening to sit next to *Curb Your Enthusiasm's* Jeff Garlin – in previews and reminded ourselves that Broadway is back. While the saccharine, big-production musicals that chased many of us away from Broadway in the 1980s are still evident, one can readily find serious plays that, despite considerable license and historical inaccuracies, generate ideas and inspirations that are thought-provoking and meaningful. Witness last summer's *Frost/Nixon* performance, which garnered a well-deserved Tony Award for Frank Langella.

Philo Farnsworth is credited in many circles with "inventing" television. Actually, he invented the first working television using electronic scanning technology. However, as the play underscores, Sarnoff and many of Farnsworth's rivals were competing aggressively to be first to market. Indeed, Sarnoff used longtime Farnsworth rival Vladimir Zworykin to copy and implement some of Farnsworth's innovations, giving RCA certain advantages in the race to own the intellectual property supported by later court decisions that worked against Farnsworth. Coupled with his alcoholism and the death of his young son, the circumstances truly destroyed the brilliant Farnsworth.

By the way, a Saturday in New York City brings many delights. Add Keith McNally's Balthazar to my "best restaurants" list. We love the garlic escargot at this popular Soho bistro. We also enjoyed another Mary Cleere Haran performance at Feinstein's at the Regency, having seen her for the first time eight years ago at the Oak Room. In recent years, we have seen Keely Smith and Patti Lupone at Feinstein's, so give Michael Feinstein due credit for keeping the Great American Songbook alive and well in New York City.

Thursday, October 4, 2007
Ansel Adams & Clarity
Washington, DC
The Ansel Adams exhibit at the Corcoran Gallery here marks the third time in recent years that I have enjoyed the master's work in a museum setting. After early years shooting and printing in a romantic, soft-focus style, Adams found his trademark tonally rich, sharp-focus, glossy-paper approach under the influences of Paul Strand, Willard Van Dyke, Imogen Cunningham and the so-called "straight photography" movement. Of course, Adams was also substantially influenced by the great Alfred Stieglitz. I always got the biggest kick out of the fact that while Stieglitz rarely left New York City, his wife Georgia O'Keefe roamed New Mexico, sometimes in the company of Ansel Adams.

Adams achieved such formidable clarity in his trademark locations of Yosemite, Santa Fe, Taos, and Carmel. We all love *Moonrise at Hernandez* (1941) and *Mt. Williamson from Manzanar* (1944), but I had never before see the ghostly *Cemetery, Statue, and Oil Derrick* shot from Long Beach in 1939. The contrast among the three objects is striking and its potential for narrative is endless. Interestingly, Adams never even printed this image until the 1970s.

Adams viewed each of his images as movements in a larger symphony. That's why he shot and printed extended sequences of the same image, printed an image years after it was taken, or used very different printing methods for the same image. Each was a different work of art.

His marvelous *Surf Sequence* (1940) shot on Highway One near Carmel makes the point.

I discover something joyously new every time I consider Ansel Adams. I did not know until this show, for example, that he was a budding concert pianist early in his career.

Next up at the Corcoran, Annie Leibowitz. I was an avid *Rolling Stone Magazine* reader in the 1970s and '80s. Leibowitz's photography was one reason why. See you in DC in November.

Friday, September 14, 2007
Rumi with a View
Johns Hopkins University will host a three-day conference later this month on the 13th Century Persian poet, jurist and philosopher Rumi. It's not easy to go from Rickles (see below) to Rumi, but let's give it a try.

Rumi's work inspired the creation of the Sufi Mevlevi Order. Witnessing the ritual of these whirling dervishes in person, as Pat and I did in Washington several years ago, is a breathtaking introduction to the Sufi Path. That performance inspired us all the way to Istanbul later that year. I originally encountered the power of Sufi devotional music at a Nusrat Fateh Ali Kahn concert in the 1990s, having first heard the late Qawwali in some of Peter Gabriel's music.

Rumi possessed an astonishing ability to speak to the core of human longing. His gentle words shed light on the all-too-often darkness of humankind. His poetry conveyed the connectedness we should all feel to our land, our history and our fellow human beings. He intimately understood the central role of music, dance and poetry in leading a spiritual and spirited life. His was a world of love that seems desperately needed these days.

Monday, September 10, 2007
Rickles' Blog Entry
One can read Don Rickles' anecdote-driven memoir *Rickles' Book* (2007) in an afternoon. It's worth it for this one story. It seems he met a first date at the Sands one night, where he was doing a lounge act and Frank Sinatra was headlining. His date spotted Sinatra and his entourage in the corner

of the lounge after the performances, so he told her that Sinatra was like a brother to him. She asked whether Rickles could introduce her to Sinatra, propelling Rickles in the darkness to approach this superstar who, in truth, was a relative stranger to him. Sinatra said he'd think about it.

Sinatra kept Rickles waiting and sweating in anticipation until finally approaching their table and exclaiming, "Don, how the hell are you?" Rickles paused, looked annoyed, and turned to Sinatra, saying, "Not now, Frank, can't you see I'm with somebody." As is well known, Sinatra could have done virtually anything in that situation. What he did, however, was to double over laughing and fall in love with a guy he'd call "bullet head" for the rest of his life.

I was fortunate to see Rickles in the old Sahara in 1980. He first opened in Vegas in 1959, back when the Sahara defined that end of The Strip, and enjoyed many great runs there. I recall loving the show but praying that he would not come anywhere near my table in his capacity as "the merchant of venom."

Let's add Rickles to the list of legends such as Mort Sahl, Kirk Douglas and Les Paul, who we should appreciate while they are still with us.

Thursday, September 6, 2007
The Santa Fe Institute
Washington, DC
The Santa Fe Institute bills itself as the center of the intellectual universe for research in complex systems, be they in physics, biology or social science. I participated in the Institute's seminar here today on "Conflict, Creativity and Complexity," co-sponsored by the Chief of Naval Operations.

We were joined by author Richard Rhodes, the incomparable physicist Murray Gell-Mann and a host of leading scholars from the far corners of the complexity sciences. I was most intrigued by a presentation from Dean Simonton of UC Davis on creativity development as an evolutionary process.

Dr. Simonton says there are five sets of factors spurring the evolution of creative people: cognition, individual differences, developmental antecedents, creative careers and sociocultural phenomena. Two of these factors most interested me.

In cognitive terms, Simonton says that creative people make associations with stimuli further out in terms of remoteness from that stimuli. In other words, they let the stimuli take them to places most people literally can't imagine. He added that while subject-matter experts have disciplined focusing skills, creative people excel at "defocused attention." They pay attention to things that can seem undisciplined and irrelevant, but that sometimes produce pure creative genius.

As for sociocultural considerations, Simonton touts the relative creative advantages of political and cultural fragmentation if not some measure of civil conflict. Accordingly, the Golden Age of Greece and the Florentine Republic – abundant with creativity – were comprised of many diverse, competing power sources that drove heterogeneity. He added that 17th and 18th Century Germany produced so many great composers because of the agendas of its own competing princes. Simonton commented on his own research showing positive correlations between Japan's historic cycles of openness and subsequent rounds of creative productivity. On the other hand, he asserts that creativity subsides when a single political order ascends and drives the culture toward homogeneity. Fascists may make the trains run on time, but don't expect their citizens to flourish creatively.

Tuesday, August 28, 2007
Onward, Mort Sahl
I savored meeting Mort Sahl on Sunday and greatly enjoyed his performance at Jimmy Tingle's place in Davis Square, Somerville. At 80, Sahl hasn't lost much of the crispness of his delivery or potency of his message.

I'm on something of quest these days to experience the wisdom of the final life stages of great artists and influencers such as Mort Sahl. I won't be able to see Kirk Douglas (90) at a Boston event next week, but I intend to enjoy a Les Paul (92) performance at New York's Iridium this fall. What great contributions these men have made and continue to make to our lives. Yet, how sad it is that most people likely believe they are no longer alive, let alone still performing.

As has been said many times, Sahl upholds the traditions of Mark Twain, Jonathan Swift and Will Rogers in speaking truth to power and exposing the too-often vain and pathetic nature of politics and politicians. He is featured in the latest *Vanity Fair* in which writer James Wolcott dares to profess an admiration for Sahl over Lenny Bruce. Me too. I respected Lenny Bruce in some ways – not all – but greatly prefer what Wolcott calls Sahl's "snarky sophistication." Where Bruce chose heroin, obscenity and self-indulgence to express his anger, Sahl effectively uses conversation, jazz riffs and storytelling.

Sahl broke into an exploding stand-up comedy scene in the early 1950s, debuting at San Francisco's legendary *hungry i*. This was also the era when Sid Caesar, Carl Reiner, Mel Brooks, Jonathan Winters, Dick Gregory and so many other relevant comedians were starting, soon followed by Woody Allen, George Carlin, Bob Newhart, Richard Pryor and David Steinberg. Sahl was a liberal Kennedy loyalist and speechwriter who subsequently fell out of sorts with the clan when Jack and Bobby became exquisite grist for his pepper mill. They almost succeeded in destroying his career, too. Oddly, Sahl later became so obsessed with JFK's assassination that he actually joined District Attorney Jim Garrison's investigating team in New Orleans.

Sahl and others worry about the state of intelligent stand-up comedy these days. Wolcott writes that the audience's frame of reference has shrunk so much that fewer and fewer people today seem to "get" the more sophisticated jokes. Yesterday's show was a success, no doubt, but I had this dread sense on several occasions that people were missing Sahl's insights and humor. Inexplicably, Sahl supported the 1988 presidential candidacy of his friend, Al Haig. He told some Haig stories yesterday, along with cracks about other friends such as Woody Allen, Frank Sinatra and Adlai Stevenson. At one point, the woman next to me leaned over to her friend and asked, "Who's this Haig guy?"

Friday, August 17, 2007

The Oldest Sport in the World

Manchester, VT

Well, it had to happen. When you determine to try interesting things in life, you're bound sooner or later to encounter The British School of Falconry. I spent a marvelous day here with Rob Waite, who runs one of two facilities owned by Emma and Steve Ford dedicated to the art, science and sport of falconry as well as the preservation of these majestic raptors. The other facility is located in Gleneagles, Scotland.

Rob first introduced me to his birds in chambers – including a 24-year-old tawny eagle named Elsie – followed by field familiarization with a glorious Harris Hawk named Ethel. The broadwing Harris Hawks are native to North America, possess a gregarious, relatively social disposition and are the bird of choice in Anglo-American falconry. The long-wing falcon itself is the preferred bird in Arabian falconry. The hawks typically team with hunting dogs, pointers to mark game and spaniels to flush it out.

Rob then instructed me in the fine art of handling Ethel, releasing her into flight and then calling her back with the lure of raw meat. Hawks are extraordinarily efficient hunting machines. However, trained hawks are only as willing to hunt as they are hungry. So the key is to keep them on weight and, as a result, just a little hungry. This means that each bird's current and ideal weights are meticulously tracked by Rob and the British School staff.

Handling a hawk on your arm means making sure that he or she can always see you and that they always face the wind. That explains why I had to walk backwards into the chambers with Ethel to ensure that she remained calm. Otherwise, the hawks will "bate," which means they engage in temper tantrums that include hanging upside down on your arm like bats. Of course, the bating often starts anyway when they realize they are heading back to the chambers.

After our getting-acquainted session, Rob and I took to the forest for a one-hour "hawk walk" with two more raptors, Wallace and Haggis. The hawks followed us in flight, tracked and attacked prey in the canopy and on the forest floor and revisited with us every so often when we raised our gloved hands and placed raw meat on the top of our left thumbs. These marvelous creatures then soared through the forest and swooped gracefully onto our arms with abrupt landings that certainly get your attention. You can feel the pressure of their claws on your arm, which tighten when they hear certain high-pitched sounds – some of which, well, I couldn't help making myself.

Falconry probably originated in China around 2000 BC, reaching the United Kingdom around 860 AD. In 1486, *The Boke of St. Albans* organized the ownership of hawks and falcons by social rank. Falconry is an obscure art and sport, but I find this tutelage uniquely compelling. Perhaps it's something about that precarious relationship with a majestic raptor just one foot from your nose.

Sunday, August 5, 2007
A Bow to Bergman
Ingmar Bergman died this week. It seems cliché to comment on the bleak, depressing side of his films. Hey, I moved to Sweden in January one year, so I understand something of Swedish winters and all the dark metaphors they evoke. I discovered Bergman in the 1980s, repeatedly viewing *The Seventh Seal* (1957), *Wild Strawberries* (1957), *Persona* (1966) and *Cries & Whispers* (1973). The impact of these films was profound substantively and emotionally, but I have hardly viewed them again. I often wonder why.

Bergman's personal life aside, what's not to respect about a man who forced us to confront the most difficult issues of our time or any time – life and death, normality and insanity, right and wrong? What's not to love about a man who nurtured true cinema stars such as Max Von Sydow and Liv Ullman in whose shadows the likes of a Lindsay Lohan could not even comprehend let alone stand? One can also see Bergman's profound influence in filmmakers as diverse as Krzysztof Kie lowski, one of my favorites, or even Woody Allen.

It is remarkable that the great Michelangelo Antonioni also passed away this week. As with Bergman, Antonioni's work established a mid-century film aesthetic that lingers to this day in great films. His *L'avventura* (1960) is best known, of course, but his follow-on film *La Notte* (1961) is wonderful, too. Most folks might also recall *Blow-Up* (1966) with its fascinating photography motif.

Great filmmakers know how to tell a story, even a physically torturous one, without the need to depict every agonizing moment of the actual torture. The problem with some filmmakers today is that they feel the need to convey all the horror of, say, a political torture to make the most accurate point and convey the most powerful message. In my thinking, a little torture goes a long way. We get it, OK?

I was excited by the prospect of Milos Foreman's new film, *Goya's Ghost*, only to find that too much of it focuses on dreadful torture scenes that were endemic to the Spanish Inquisition. Goya is an artistic favorite of mine for his realism that bordered on photojournalism long before the invention of photography. I generally don't let reviews color my willingness to see a film, but the feedback on this film is simply tortuous.

Werner Herzog's new film *Rescue Dawn* provides plenty of opportunity for on-camera barbarism. It is the story of the escape of Dieter Dengler from a Laotian POW camp during the Vietnam War. Herzog told NPR's Terry Gross recently that he filmed all the requisite, flesh-crawling torture scenes and then dumped most of them in post-production. He said that a little went a long way and that he finally realized he didn't need to be so obviously brutal to make a brutal point. After all, many of us try to avoid needless torture fests, so if the idea is to make a political point it would be useful to get our fannies in the seats and our eyeballs on the screen, right?

Wednesday, August 1, 2007
Hip Hop Help
That's when it happened. The remake of the 1998 *Godzilla* movie had just been released and there were Jimmy Page and The London Symphony Orchestra playing the hip-hop, movie-theme version of the Led Zeppelin classic, "Come with Me," featuring Puff Daddy, no less. My familiarity with Zeppelin and the LSO served as an invitation, so I lowered my resistance to hip-hop music and its rap cousins and gave it a shot.

Yes, some hip-hop music is dreadful and much rap music is even worse. However, one can love rock, blues, jazz or classical forms and naturally understand that some groups, pieces or periods in those genres are terrible, too. To label all hip-hop with the gangsterish misogyny of its worst rap forms might suggest a closing mind. It might also beg the question, what else are those of us in our 40s, 50s and beyond possibly closing down?

Just as the 1960s horn sections in Blood, Sweat & Tears, Chicago and, later in my education, many of the Stax Records pieces served as my bridge to big-band music and then to jazz, the familiar in Jimmy Page and the LSO found me liking a Puff Daddy (as he was known then) song in 1998. And just imagine the purists who became nauseous at the mere mention of Jimmy Page and the LSO in the same breath. Jazz and the big-band sounds were not favorites among my childhood friends, but I felt some connection at the time among Glenn Miller, Louis Armstrong, Otis Redding and Al Kooper's vision for the BS&T horn section.

So what is it about human nature that has our interest end with the music of our youth or limited solely to our culture? Just look at the rage some Paul Anka fans expressed when he did his excellent album of 1980s and '90s covers last year? Isaac Hayes tells a wonderful story about getting dissed by his friends in the late 1960s for daring to like the white bread Glen Campbell song, "By The Time I Get To Phoenix." He delivered a powerful spoken-word version of the song one night at a club in Memphis, silencing the conversation and ultimately reducing his friends and colleagues in the audience to tears until they heard the line, "By the time I get to Phoenix."

Why wouldn't our curiosity pursue musical time forward and backward, understanding that one former avenue is now moving through a hip-hop moment and soon onto something else? Want to give it a try while still playing it safe? Check out Kirk Franklin's wonderful cover of the Earth, Wind & Fire classic "September." It really works.

Verge Records provides another useful place to start. The label has just released *The Wonderful Sounds of Rio de Janeiro*, which captures some of the terrific contemporary music emerging from Rio's favelas. It's a fusion of traditional Brazilian music with the hip hop and urban sounds of today. It's serious music and provides an even more meaningful and usefully optimistic bridge to understanding what works today in hip hop and even rap.

It's a joy to use what we know to discover what we do not yet know. In his latest book, *Five Minds of the Future*, Howard Gardener speaks to the power of the synthesizing mind that relishes such connections and interconnectedness. However, in their recent book, *Mistakes Were Made (But Not By Me)*, the social psychologists Carol Tavris and Elliot Aronson show why human nature seems to work overtime to confirm what we like and discredit everything else. "Most people will put a lot of energy into preserving their prejudice rather than having to change it, often by waving away disconfirming evidence." Please don't wave it off. Just go for it, instead.

Wednesday, July 25, 2007
Edward Hopper and Storytelling
The Edward Hopper exhibit at the Museum of Fine Arts in Boston is worth seeing. I enjoy the realism of Hopper, Caravaggio and Vermeer

and the Dutch Masters. This may qualify me for philistinism in some abstract art circles but, sure, I can appreciate Jackson Pollock and Jasper Johns, too. Like politics and just about everything else, art diminishes when it is reduced to warring camps.

Hopper's later work reminds me of simple (some might say simplistic) elegance of, say, Curt Swan's comic-book panels for National Periodicals in the 1960s. I guess it's a preference that helped steer me to a love of photojournalism 30 years ago. Even Hopper's fondness for acid yellows, burnt oranges and brick red colors reinforces this familiar warmth and depth.

We like to think of the frozen moments captured in Hopper's *Automat* (1927) or *Chop Suey* (1929), two of my favorites, as telling a story. And yet the MFA exhibitors suggest instead that, "He does not tell stories; he provides moments within them." Yes, why not? After all, we like to consider whether the two women in *Chop Suey* had just arrived or were ready to leave the restaurant. And why as John Updike famously commented did they both appear to be listening? And what about that seemingly lonely woman in *Automat*? Did she already eat and was that a last or first sip of coffee she was about to take? Hey, you don't even know she's in an old automat except for the title of the work. What are the stories behind these glimpses?

As I conjured my own stories about the lives of Hopper's subjects, I returned home to read a story about a new University of Maryland opera, *Later That Same Evening*. It seems that Maryland has teamed with the National Gallery of Art to bring subjects from five Hopper paintings to life and actually have some of them interact in storylines that start from the glimpse captured in each work, including *Automat*.

I stopped marveling about the constant serendipity of life many years ago and simply rejoice in its own delicious narrative.

Friday, June 8, 2007
Bravo, Frank Langella
New York City
Frank Langella's performance as the deposed Richard Nixon is a powerful tour de force in the new Peter Morgan production of *Frost/Nixon* here at the Bernard Jacobs Theater. Many fine actors such as Anthony

Hopkins have played Nixon well. Philip Baker Hall's one-man Nixon eruption in the 1984 *Secret Honor* was starkly engaging. After all, as far back as 1961 Phillip Roth said of Nixon as a character that he was, as he reiterated to *Slate* in 2004, "so fantastic, so weird and astonishing, that I found myself beginning to wish I had invented him."

Langella's work is far more compelling and, yes, strangely empathetic to the disgraced former president. The play was created by Peter Morgan, screenwriter for *The Queen* and *The Last King of Scotland* (both 2006), among other biographical works, and took 11 years to write. John Lahr wrote in an April *The New Yorker* that Morgan believes "the chemistry of opposition makes terrific drama." It certainly does in this case.

Michael Sheen is fine as David Frost, but the show belongs to Langella. Langella told Charlie Rose on April 23rd that he resisted playing Nixon because the character was simply not in his "bag of tricks." "He was not the sort of man I could find, play or inhabit," he added. Langella prepared thoroughly for the part, reading everything about Nixon, interviewing Nixon's close associates and visiting the Nixon Library. "I threw it all away. It had to be my Nixon. It had to be the essence of the man, rather than an imitation," Langella told Rose. He is nominated for a Tony Award, competing this year with Liev Schreiber for *Talk Radio* and Christopher Plummer for *Inherit the Wind.*

Interestingly, we attended the start of the Council on Foreign Relations Annual Meeting prior to last night's show. We saw former NPR and ABC reporter Bob Zelnick at the Council meeting only to arrive at the theater to realize that he had been part of David Frost's team for the Nixon interviews and was being played by the actor Armand Schultz. It all connects.

Friday, May 25, 2007
Weill Now, Pay Later
Charleston, SC
It's time for the Spoleto Festival USA once again. What a splendid event, and I have certainly been privileged to enjoy it along with the likes of the Aspen, Newport and Salzburg Festivals, too. I was fortunate to witness Messiaen's opera *Saint Francis of Assisi* when I was a Fellow in the Salzburg Seminar in 1998. What an appropriate kick-off we experienced

here last night in the classic Kurt Weill and Bertolt Brecht opera, *Rise and Fall of the City of Mahagonny.* The work may have debuted in Leipzig in 1930, but it holds up well as political theater and in testament to the dark side of human nature.

Weill and Brecht produced the blackest of black humor and did so in a truly subversive manner. It's no wonder the Nazis banned the work in their rise to power, since speaking truth to power always stirs the neuroses of authoritarians. With this opera, Weill and Brecht artfully and painfully illustrated our innate penchant for power and greed and how language is used to obfuscate reality and obviate responsibility. That's why this German opera of some 80 years vintage is as relevant today as it was back then.

Alas, lead character Jimmy Mahoney is sentenced to death not for manslaughter or the other criminal acts he committed, but because he is poor and cannot pay his bar bill. He dies at the hands of three corrupt rulers of Mahagonny, where greed, lust for power and hypocrisy reign supreme.

The highly personable Emmanuel Villaume was brilliant conducting the Spoleto Orchestra. You may know the wonderful "Alabama Song," which first appeared in this work and was covered over the years by David Bowie, The Doors and others. Richard Brunner played Jimmy very well, underscoring the extraordinary talent that comes with being both a leading operatic tenor as well as a comedic actor.

Saturday, March 31, 2007
Strategic Imagination
Creativity is central to solving today's most vexing problems. Our challenge is that so many of our leaders and institutions are locked into political, mechanistic structures that serve only short-term, narrow interests. It would be hard to devise less creative cultures than Congress or many of our largest corporations. Yet these are the very entities we expect to solve massively complex issues such as genocide or global warming.

What did the 9-11 Commission say prevented the US from anticipating the disastrous events of September 11, 2001? "The most important failure was one of imagination," they wrote in no uncertain terms in the

Final Report of the National Commission on Terrorist Attacks upon the United States.

Ten years ago, IMD in Lausanne teamed with the Danish company Lego to create a "science of serious play" to be used by organizations to engage in more effective strategic thinking and scenario planning. After all, young Lego enthusiasts and Hollywood film makers have been destroying model skyscrapers for play and entertainment for decades, but the idea was simply unimaginable to our leadership.

In the case of World War Two, the Allies' imaginative choice to launch D-Day at Normandy was deemed so implausible that the Germans left that part of the French coast relatively unprotected. Could such a surprise, high-stakes maneuver be even possible in today's politicized, media-frenzied, leak-riddled world?

Some see "strategic imagination" as key to unlocking the creativity needed in such complex, audacious times. These were the points raised by Alexander Manu, the founder and director of the Beal Institute for Strategic Creativity at the Ontario College of Art & Design in his 2006 book, *The Imagination Challenge: Strategic Foresight and Innovation in the Global Economy.*

This point is also well understood by the extraordinary people at the John D. and Catherine T. MacArthur Foundation. Earlier this week, the Foundation announced MacArthur Awards for Creative and Effective Institutions. My friend Aly Kassam-Remtulla helped create this new initiative for honoring small, agile organizations that use creativity to solve social problems.

When we lament the lack of leadership these days, we need to think small. Better said, we need to think small in order to think big. Small, dynamic organizations can have a gigantic impact by teaching our larger, lumbering leadership that complex problems are not insoluble. It just takes some creativity.

Wednesday, March 7, 2007
Bow Wow, Gertrude Stein
San Francisco
Have you ever read Gertrude Stein's poem, "If I Told Him"? Her Picasso tribute was first published in *Vanity Fair* in 1924. Have you ever heard

the piece read aloud? Well, we were driving today from Mendocino to San Francisco and happened upon a local radio station playing an old recording of Stein herself reading her work:

> *"If I told him would he like it. Would he like it if I told him. Would he like*
> *it would Napoleon would Napoleon would would he like it. If Napoleon if*
> *I told him if I told him if Napoleon. Would he like it if I told him if I told*
> *him if Napoleon. Would he like it if Napoleon if Napoleon if I told him.*
> *If I told him if Napoleon if Napoleon if I told him. If I told him would he*
> *like it would he like it if I told him.*
> *Now.*
> *Not now.*
> *And now.*
> *Now.*
> *Exactly as kings.*
> *Feeling full for it.*
> *Exactitude as kings.*
> *So to beseech you as full as for it.*
> *Exactly or as kings.............."*

It was on the Golden Gate Bridge, actually, where we concluded that the whole thing was utter nonsense. This surely must have been Stein's noted playfulness at work, right? Of course, the scholar asked to interpret the piece only made matters worse by seeming to read far too much into it. However, shame on me. It's entirely too facile to categorize something one doesn't accept or understand as "nonsense." After all, Stein was a literary lioness. Besides, such claims were made of the often impenetrable works of Picasso himself. Oh, so maybe that's the connection – a fractured, fragmented cubism of words, no less, which gave way to The Beats and the vocal histrionics of a Laurie Anderson.

Stein's stilted scat thrust itself at us in a manner also remarkably similar to the rap offerings of Bow Wow and Notorious BIG that we had been sampling earlier in our trip. The fact that Stein's performance had much of the same cadence, rhythm and even anger of a Bow Wow concoction was at once curiously revealing and absolutely disturbing.

Okay, take us out Bow Wow...

See man, Bow Weezy right here live and direct
I'm talkin to ya'll young'ns out there baby
I can't wait until I turn eighteen
I know it's the same for ya'll
Man, I know, I know
I'm talkin bout pullin up in them big cars on them 22's
Naw forget that, I'm talkin bout Charlie Woodsens man
I'm a pull up, I'm talkin bout 24's
It's a wrap for ya'll when I turn eighteen
Listen to the hook

Sunday, January 7, 2007
Neruda's Bedroom
Isla Negra, Chile
To stand in Pablo Neruda's bedroom here is to understand just why creativity so often needs that special place. Great artists will tell you of that singular location in their homes or studios where the light is just right and from which their creative energies can truly flow. The inspiration that is Neruda's bedroom starts with a wonderful panorama of the Pacific Ocean.

Neruda's design for the room borrowed from the mystical traditions of the Mapuche, Chile's native people. He positioned the bed so that the sunrise appeared through a window above his head and then traversed the bedroom until its dramatic setting over the Pacific.

The poet David Whyte in *The Heart Aroused* (1994) celebrates Neruda's "ability to treat life as a mystery to be lived rather than a problem to be solved." Indeed, Neruda's playful creativity is evident throughout his home. As we learn in Chile that true creativity is in the not knowing, in the childlike exploration of wonderment, Neruda's "La Poesia" rings true.

I didn't know what to say, my mouth
could not speak,
my eyes could not see
and something ignited in my soul,
fever or unremembered wings

and I went my own way,
deciphering that burning fire
and I wrote the first bare line,
bare, without substance, pure
foolishness,
pure wisdom
of one who knows nothing
and suddenly I saw
the heavens
unfastened and open.

Wednesday, October 18, 2006
Is It Asking Too Much?

"Gotcha journalism" is generally unfair and unwarranted. However, every once in a while, this "cheap shot" tactic is substantively and painfully necessary. Such is the case with Jeff Stein's work recently at the *Congressional Quarterly*.

Stein asked a handful of senior government officials leading US antiterrorism efforts some basic questions about, say, the differences between a Sunni and a Shiite, which branch Osama bin Laden and Al Qaeda follow or which sects dominate in Saudi Arabia and Iran. It would be akin to asking top officials at the Department of Health & Human Services the differences between Medicare and Medicaid.

Well, neither the top official at the FBI in charge of national security nor two members of Congress chairing House Intelligence subcommittees could answer these questions. Nobody can know everything, of course, but is it too much to ask that people in charge of specific functions know something about them? Knowledge and the curiosity that comes with it are – or should be – force multipliers.

Wednesday, October 4, 2006
A Cock and Bull Story

Bullfighting is a reprehensible spectacle. Cockfighting might even be worse. The former is bathed in art, history and high culture, while the latter, well, the latter just needs a good bath. Both are bathed in blood, no doubt, and both result in death.

A week at a bullfighting feria in Madrid back in 2000 did little to change my mind. I was trying to understand this garish display and, I admit, also attempting to recreate the sepia-toned photographs from Hemingway's *Death in the Afternoon* (1932). There is something undeniably majestic and eerily hypnotic about the corridas de toros, which are covered on the arts pages and not the sports section of the newspapers. It is far more dance performance than athletic competition, since the bull stands no chance. It's horrible, but who am I as a gringa to push that case too far?

Cockfighting is truly ghastly, even when a pleasant group of old men buys you – you guessed it, fried chicken and beer – to enjoy while watching two birds peck each other to death on a steamy night in San Juan, Puerto Rico. It was all sponsored by Marriott Hotels, too, which would make for an interesting Board Room discussion there.

In his study of the Balinese cockfighting culture, the legendary anthropologist Clifford Geertz wrote compellingly of the spectacle, "In the cockfight, man and beast, good and evil, ego and id, the creative power of aroused masculinity and the destructive power of loosened animality fuse in a bloody drama of hatred, cruelty, violence and death." Indeed.

Wednesday, November 14, 2007
Balboa Park
San Diego
Imagine being taught that Vasco Núñez de Balboa "discovered" the Pacific Ocean? This was the standard interpretation of history fed to so many of us without regard to the countless millions of native peoples from Chile to Alaska, let alone the mature civilizations of China, Japan and Russia who lived, worked and played in and around the Pacific Ocean. Ah, the myopia of ethnocentrism.

Balboa Park here is truly one of the nation's finest urban spaces. Originally developed for the 1915 Panama-California Exhibition, the park features many Spanish Revival-style buildings housing wonderful museums such as the landmark Museum of Man, Museum of Art, Museum of Photographic Art and even the Model Railroad Museum.

My Balboa discovery today was the San Diego Hall of Champions Sports Museum. Yes, it's an ironic name since San Diego has never won a Super Bowl, World Series or NBA Championship when either the Rockets or Clippers called this city home. Nonetheless, San Diego's sports history is rich and rewarding.

The Chargers did win the 1963 AFL title against the Boston Patriots and have long presented colorful, offensive-minded teams with great players such as Lance Alworth, John Hadl, Dan Fouts, Kellen Winslow, LaDainian Tomlinson and Junior Seau – now a darling of Patriots fans. The Padres lost two World Series bids, but have also showcased terrific players in Nate Colbert, Dave Winfield, Tony Gwynn and this year's NL Cy Young Award winner Jake Peavey. Plus, Petco Field in the Gaslamp District ranks among the finest facilities in baseball. For Red Sox fans, the old San Diego Padres of the 1930s Pacific Coast League produced future Boston stars Ted Williams, Bobby Doerr and Dom DiMaggio. Maybe being a champion does not always mean winning a championship.

CHAPTER 7

EDUCATION

Sunday, August 17, 2014

Now That's a Leader: Dr. Sylvia Earle

The documentary film *Mission Blue* debuted today. The film tells the story of our imperiled marine ecosystem through the lens of pioneering scientist, Dr. Sylvia Earle. Imagine what Dr. Earle had to endure in the 1960s and beyond as a so-called "girl scientist"? She led the first all-women's crew of Tektite II aquanauts who, in 1970, lived and worked submersed on the ocean floor for several weeks. The Tektite leaders chose an all-women crew to generate publicity, and so the media came in droves to report on "those attractive women" who are today's "mermaids." When somebody commented that she made being brilliant and beautiful okay – and yes, imagine that clumsy assertion – she said, "I never realized it wasn't okay."

This scientist, explorer, diver, inventor, entrepreneur, administrator, advocate, author and teacher has achieved more in one lifetime than most of us dare dream. This National Geographic explorer-in-residence and former Chief Scientist at the National Oceanic and Atmospheric Administration is passionate and tireless in her fight to protect and preserve our oceans and marine life. I recall being amazed by the beauty of the coral reefs while snorkeling off Huahine, French Polynesia in 2011 – where Walt and I were married. That night on our ship, however, I was told by veteran mariners that what we saw paled in comparison to what was there 10, 20 or 30 years earlier. How sad it was to see Dr. Earle's reaction in the film to dead coral reefs in Australia whose colorful life and vibrancy had delighted her decades earlier.

Dr. Earle is fighting the good fight and doing so against great odds. She tells anyone who listens that there is no Earth without healthy oceans. "No blue, no green," as she puts it. She's championing creation of dumping-free, fishing-free "Hope Spots," protected sanctuaries that now comprise three percent of the world's oceans.

Dr. Earle teaches us that it's all about balance. Of course, we need to fish the oceans. Of course, we need to conduct ocean-borne commerce. We just need to demonstrate the wisdom not to let greed, recklessness and callous indifference have us do so much of it that we bite off the hand that quite literally feeds us.

Thursday, July 17, 2014
Now That's a Leader: James MacGregor Burns - RIP
We lost a good one on Tuesday in this presidential scholar, Pulitzer Prize-winning author and longtime Williams College professor. I recall a day in 2006 when he was leading a seminar critique on the Clinton Presidency for 25 or 30 of us at Renaissance Weekend in Charleston. Guess who walked in part way through the proceedings? Bill Clinton, with coffee cup in hand. Professor MacGregor Burns was ever polite and respectful, of course, but he really let President Clinton have it on at least two occasions. The president sat there with the rest of us, sipped his coffee, asked a few questions, countered a few points and then told Professor MacGregor Burns that he ultimately had to agree with him on one particular bone of contention. It's odd to engage in a session on the Clinton Presidency with the president sitting right there, to say the least, but it sure was interesting. Not many people could have handled it with the grace and dignity of James MacGregor Burns.

President Clinton disappointed many of us who hoped for better things. Here we are at the 25th anniversary of Renaissance Weekends in Charleston, SC.

Wednesday, August 28, 2013
This Is the Problem
We entrust college professors to educate and inspire our children and, therefore, to ensure our future. Yet this is how New Jersey Governor Chris Christie (R) referred to college professors, as reported by Maureen Dowd in *The New York Times* yesterday: "College professors are fine, I guess. You know, college professors basically spout out ideas that nobody ever does anything about."

What a miserable viewpoint from a seemingly miserable human being. What a pathetic, painful cliché. What a slap in the face to amazing professors who change people's lives. And this from the chief executive of New Jersey's troubled higher education system.

Christie's use of a preposition to end a sentence is no big deal, especially since this was a verbal quote and trying to say it correctly can feel awkward. Still, it reminds me of a story. A young man arrives on the Harvard campus for the first time many years ago and encounters a tweedy professor. He asks, "Is this where Harvard Yard is at?" The professor observes him scornfully and says, "Young man. This is Harvard. We never end our sentences with prepositions." To which the visitor replies, "Oh, ok, is this where Harvard Yard is at, asshole?"

Friday, March 29, 2013
Cutting Comments
New Hampshire Governor Maggie Hassan (D) told our lunch group yesterday that the "previous Tea Party" legislature in her state had cut public university budgets another 50 percent from an already dangerously low point. She's inherited these Draconian cuts and wondered out loud why anyone should be surprised that businesses can't find enough skilled employees in her state.

Instead of attempting to reach an uneasy alliance with the wingnuts in their party, Republican business leaders should say, "No mas!" They cannot make intelligent, long-term investments in their enterprises and in their state without knowing they'll have access to a well-educated, high-quality workforce. Otherwise, they will and should move to states smart enough to protect their competitiveness by investing wisely in their own future. Enough with this nonsense, already.

Friday, October 26, 2012
A Lot of Baloney
Miami Beach
Today's *Miami Herald* invested six column inches on the arrival in town of the Oscar Meyer Wienermobile. I'm sure this brought tears of joy to OM's PR agency, but why not use that space instead to promote the amazing inspirational stories of students and teachers on display at the College Board Forum just down Collins Avenue? Is there any question that we don't have our priorities right as a society? It's a lot of baloney, no matter how you slice it.

It Really Happened: Even More Lost in Translation
I was on something of an educational odyssey in Tokyo, having spent the day in an ikebana (Japanese flower-arranging) class. I was taking a class the next day on the Japanese tea ceremony. I adjourned with my newspapers and magazines to the New York Bar atop my hotel, the Park Hyatt in Shinjuku. Yes, it's the hotel and bar made famous in *Lost in Translation* (2003).

The band (No, it wasn't Sausalito from the movie) took a break and the lead singer walked toward me, looked at my magazine and said, "Oh, *The Economist*. That gets the guys all the time." She asked me to join her at the band's table, likely feeling pity for me, and I did so. What the heck, right? I must have looked lost in translation myself.

Part way through the next set, the lead singer introduced the band members. She said something like, "I also have some great friends with me tonight," introducing visiting girlfriends from Los Angeles and Phnom Penh and, preposterously, me – by name. Each of us waved to the crowd.

The show ended an hour or so later and, as closing time approached, four hovering businessmen from Buenos Aires joined us at the table. We ordered more bottles of wine and one of the guys said we should hit the nightclubs. So, right out of the movie, the eight of us, open wine bottles in hand, took the elevators and then two cabs to a pulsating nightclub nearby that was, once again, right out of the movie.

These guys carried a statue of a Shinto deity for miles in this religious procession near Tokyo's Ryogoku Kokugikan (sumo wrestling arena). They invited me to join them for beer and cookies at the end of the event.

Thursday, October 25, 2012
Miami Dade President Invites Education to Join the 21ˢᵗ Century
Miami Beach
Eduardo Padrón, president of Miami Dade College (MDC), is something of a rock star in education circles. The Cuban émigré and self-described "American by choice" assumed his presidency in 1995 and has taken MDC to a position of national prominence. He opened the College Board Forum 2012 here last night with an unmistakable clarion call. "Most of us in education are stuck in the 20ᵗʰ Century," he told a packed audience of educators and administrators at the fabled Fontainebleau Hotel. "We're still working in the past and must ask how do we bring ourselves into the 21ˢᵗ Century?"

There were some nodding heads in the audience agreeing with Padrón. One got the sense, however, there were just as many people questioning, doubting or even resisting his premise that education is behind the times. Thus, the tricky crossroads that American education finds itself these days. He urged audience members to stop blaming one another for the troubles in education. "The colleges blame the high schools who blame the middle schools who blame the elementary schools," he said. Indeed, very few organizations exist like the College Board that could possibly address the problem systematically and holistically with all players around one table – though, of course, the politics are as thick as the Miami humidity.

Padrón was optimistic about the future in this regard. Once named among The Ten Best College Presidents by *Time Magazine,* he said, "Every human being should have an opportunity to get an education." He added, "This wasn't always so when education served the elites, but that's not the case anymore." He sent a good-natured jab toward "politicians who say that college education today is not for everyone; except they're not talking about their own kids." Interestingly, he labeled education "the most important civil rights issue of our time." Who's to question that assertion, since education is the gateway to most everything else in life?

Friday, September 14, 2012
What Price the Mind?
Minneapolis
It's far too easy for *Newsweek* to ask in blaring tones on this week's cover, "Is College Worth the Investment?" Yes, soaring college costs are alarming and seemingly continue to rise without any accountability. Certainly, colleges and universities must be more accountable and consumer-oriented. However, higher education is not a mercenary exercise. We run grave risks as a nation when higher education is seen merely or mostly as a narrow, technical transaction leading to a job. The world is too complex and our politicians too slippery for "we the people" not to be critical thinkers about life beyond ourselves and our paycheck. I think that's called civilization.

Tuesday, March 20, 2012
Education as a National Security Issue
I participated in a conference call this morning with Joel Klein, former Chancellor of the New York City school system, and Condoleezza Rice.

They're co-chairs of the Council on Foreign Relations' Task Force on US Education Reform and National Security. In addition to the usual and yet essential laments about the length of the American school year and school day remaining hostage to a centuries-old agrarian calendar, as well as the continued supremacy of teacher seniority over teacher excellence, Rice and Klein offered three useful insights for framing the issue.

First, they are right to examine US education – especially public education – through the lens of national security. Not accepting that the system is broken and that exceptional strategy, talent and resources are needed to repair it is, indeed, a clear and present danger. Next, Rice and Klein remind us that we are not attracting the best of our college graduates into the teaching ranks, unlike our competitors in Singapore, Taiwan, Germany, Finland and elsewhere. Yes, thankfully, there are many gifted, talented and committed teachers on these shores. There just aren't enough of them. Of course, it's not all about compensation. However, realizing pay scales that are at least a meaningful rounding error on what hedge-fund managers make would help. Finally, Rice and Klein speak to the essential role of education in restoring national purpose and cohesion. Is there any doubt that the decline in US K-12 education is contributing to the deterioration of our public discourse and the quality of those seeking higher office?

We wanted to hear more from the Task Force today on solutions, which always seem elusive. However, the compelling framing of the issue Klein and Rice offered could help bring us closer to tangible, productive outcomes.

Friday, November 12, 2010
School Reform: Balancing Pugilism with Patience
Cincinnati

Joel Klein's resignation as Chancellor of the New York City Public Schools, and that of Michelle Rhee in the comparable job in Washington DC, raise important questions about finding the right balance between the pugilistic determination and patient diplomacy necessary for achieving desperately needed school reform.

Basically, I've been a fan of both these leaders – though a guarded one. They've been unafraid to confront lethargic, insular and deeply entrenched systems that have been allowed to decay over many decades and, as a result, are doing such a disservice to children and our nation. Perhaps the best thing the Kleins and Rhees of the world bring to the task is to question existing orthodoxies and shake-up the status quo, which they can only do with healthy outside perspectives and the backing of a strong mayors such as Bloomberg in New York and, or so we thought, Fenty in DC. They also buoy so many individuals and institutions that had otherwise given up hope that real and lasting reform is even possible in large urban school systems.

Those who resist change and argue for gradualism in school reform are just wrong. Gradualism seems like a dilatory tactic by unions, opposing politicians, vendors and other vested interests designed to slow down if not entirely halt reform. What's needed instead is what organizational scholars call "punctuated equilibrium," and lighting rods. Klein and Rhee come with very big punctuation marks. That is to say, they enrage many people who stand to lose from rising performance expectations and other interruptions to business as usual.

Angering resistors can be a useful. albeit anecdotal, indicator of success, since nobody determined to overhaul something as sclerotic and frighteningly political as the New York or Washington systems will ever make friends. Just ask Mayor Fenty, who was tossed out of office in his recent re-election bid because he dared to support (one might say, create) Rhee and her reform efforts. It seems logical and even desirable that reform-minded leaders will make some enemies or otherwise risk not being effective on these brutal playing fields. Too much patience and excessive due process risk running out the clock, continually perpetuating systems that like to talk about change but have little authentic interest in actually doing so. Are Klein and Rhee divisive? Yes, of course. They absolutely must be, though they sometimes do get carried away.

The two outgoing chancellors are right to have brought a palpable sense of urgency to this seemingly impossible task. If a Taliban (or yesterday's bogeyman, a Communist) sleeper cell had somehow formed on these shores 40 years ago and conspired to create what we have had in the New York and Washington systems, well, we would be on a war footing right now to address it. It's that bad.

Having said this, however, Klein and Rhee often took matters too far. Teachers are not the enemy here. Most teachers are good, hard-working folks who are trying to do the best they can and often against all odds. Yes, union intransigence can be a serious impediment to progress, but that doesn't warrant stereotyping or vilifying teachers. Rhee told a group of us in Washington DC last week that she's learned some painful lessons in this regard, about the rightness, if not the utility, of treating people with respect, preserving the dignity of those who must change, communicating and collaborating across the board, and understanding that some inclusion, protocol and due process are necessary to ensure sustainable change. You don't have to be nice, but you do have to be smart about these things.

It's too easy to conflate these qualities and skills with simply "playing nice" or "being soft." Far from it. An effective leader can be firm and yet reasonable, tough and yet respectful, determined and yet diplomatic enough to not fear communicating and collaborating with some needed measure of inclusion. Otherwise, with little or no "buy in" from those being asked to change, the system will simply reject the foreign organism of change invading it like so many antibodies gathering in reflexive self-protection.

One gets the sense from Rhee that she sees matters of inclusion, respect and dignity as unacceptable forms of gradualism, despite words to the contrary. Instead, I might suggest she see them as the tools needed to achieve and sustain lasting reform. After all, the body politic in DC just rejected the Fenty-Rhee "organism," leaving her fans to wonder what they will have actually accomplished in the long term.

Perhaps another year or two of due diligence and due process would have preserved the Fenty-Rhee program and ensured that it actually succeeded in carrying out meaningful systemic change. Otherwise, what's the point? Opposition forces can simply wait it out until the flash-in-the-pan, disruptive leaders impale themselves on the sharp pickets of personal animosity and petty resentments that may never needed to have been so pointed in the first place.

Thursday, November 6, 2008
Crowing About Innovation
Houston
I found myself agreeing with virtually every word Arizona State University President Michael Crow said here at the College Board Forum about the lack of innovation in higher education these days. Not lacking in

self-confidence, and quite likely a difficult person with whom to work, Crow is pointed about the changes colleges and universities must embrace if they are to compete effectively in today's global economy. And he's right.

Crow is correct in arguing, for example, that most college vision and mission statements are bland, meaningless offerings that fail to differentiate one institution from another. He is right in stressing the importance of what he calls "intellectual fusion" on college campuses, exhorting rigidly separated academic disciplines to work together in an interdisciplinary manner that mirrors how the world actually works. He is absolutely right in calling for administrators to speed it up, considerably. He distinguishes between "university time" and "civilian time," urging colleges to move much, much faster in making and implementing decisions. Finally, Crow says we "need to quit patting ourselves on the back and get real" about the collective lack of innovation in higher education. Well, the data PBS essayist Richard Rodriguez's panel shared with us last night suggests Crow is right and the time to act is now – and real fast.

Wednesday, May 26, 2010
Will We Ever Reform Education, Really?
US Secretary of Education Arne Duncan says that desperately needed education reform in the United States is "this generation's Moon shot." Of course, that's precisely how Tom Friedman frames our equally desperate need for energy reform. Indeed, desperate times require too many desperate lunar analogies. Duncan spoke to a group of us at the Council on Foreign Relations yesterday.

Sure, the US remains the world's undisputed higher education leader. However, Yale President Richard Levin's article in the current issue of *Foreign Affairs* suggests it's just a matter of a decade or two before China catches up. Meanwhile, Duncan cited a sobering litany of US K-12 worldwide performance statistics. For example, we're 24th of 29 nations in one study of high-school math proficiency and 21st of 30 in a comparable study of science proficiency. Do we fully realize as citizens that the US is suffering a 27 percent high-school dropout rate, that as many as 40 percent of our college students need remedial help, and that we rank 10th in college completion globally, according to Duncan?

Remember that 1980s' music video in which Huey Lewis plunges his head into a sink full of ice water? *("I want a new drug; one that won't make me sick.")* Well, somehow, we the people need that kind of wake-up call. Every second we spend on peripheral "wedge" issues in this country, to serve narrow political agendas, is sapping our ability and willingness to solve the truly monumental challenges before us, such as real education reform.

In that context, Secretary Duncan speaks of the Obama Administration's "cradle to career" vision for education. It's nice rhetoric, as is his welcome alignment of cultural awareness and language proficiency with the "smart power" movement, but is it realistically achievable in four or even eight years? Instead, I'd prefer that the Administration be a little less grandiose in packaging concepts and more focused, for example, on attacking the structural and programmatic reforms that are needed before we can ever credibly dream of a "cradle to career" vision.

It Really Happened: The French Laundry
Walt and I have been fortunate to dine at some of the world's best restaurants. Thanks to our friend Ray, for example, we enjoyed a wonderful experience with another friend Kathy at Chicago's fabled Charlie Trotter's in its final weeks in 2013, touring the kitchen and chatting with the late Chef Trotter. The French Laundry was always on our list, too, but we didn't want to put the telephone time and energy into trying to secure a nearly impossible reservation.

My son Zack and I were dining at Frasca one night in Boulder, CO prior to a University of Colorado football game. Zack had a modest problem with one of his courses. We were pleasant about the whole thing, as was the Frasca team. Bobby Stuckey, who I knew was the brilliant Frasca sommelier, apologized for the problem, too. I did not realize it at that moment, but Bobby owns Frasca and had also been the celebrated wine director at The French Laundry. He's that good.

As our final course appeared, Bobby visited with us again and asked about our future travel plans. I mentioned to him that my husband Walt and I were heading back to Napa Valley soon, whereupon he asked if we'd ever been to The French Laundry. I told him that we had yet to dine there, but hoped to do so someday. He said, "No promises, but let me see what I can do."

The phone rang at home two weeks later. It was the French Laundry calling me! They made a Friday evening reservation available, concluding the call by saying, "Any friend of Bobby Stuckey's is a friend of The French Laundry." We had a superb experience there and, as we were departing, the maître d' invoked Bobby's name and escorted us to the kitchen for a tour – all because one of my son's courses at Frasca was not up to their otherwise excellent standards.

Thursday, October 30, 2008
Immelt Down
One can only assume that GE Chairman and CEO Jeff Immelt is accurate when he says in stump speeches that the United States graduates more majors in sports management than electrical engineering. If we are to compete effectively with China and India in the coming decades, we must understand the primary factors shaping economic competitiveness, acknowledge that these subjects are rigorous for very good reason and motivate young people to pursue them.

Sunday, July 6, 2008
Knowing That We Don't Know
Dublin
You can feel the weight of generations here at the Long Room in the Old Library at Trinity College. It's quite a place. One is reminded of the story of Umberto Eco's 30,000-volume library in which visitors often ask the great philosopher and novelist, "How many of these books have you read?" As the story goes, Eco tells his wide-eyed guests that the more interesting question is how many books he has not yet read.

His point is that the celebration of curiosity is a joyous, never-ending pursuit and that libraries are living, ever-expanding things. Eco seems to suggest that it is healthier to acknowledge the vast majority of knowledge that eludes us than to cling only to the narrow limits of what each of us already knows – or thinks we know. To paraphrase Petrarch of Arezzo, who wrote about the humility of unknown or yet-to-be-known knowledge, libraries are not unlearned collections, though they may belong to an unlearned people.

It Really Happened: Bobby Rahal

Bobby Rahal is one of the most successful drivers in Indy Car history, having won the Indianapolis 500 in 1986 among many other glories. I participated in a High Speed Performance School sponsored by Rahal Racing in 1995 at the Mid-Ohio Race Course. As I prepared to start racing in some kind of high-powered Honda, anticipating the ferocious hairpin at Turn #1, Bobby jumped into the lone passenger seat and said, "Let's go."

So, I found myself navigating hairpins and S-curves at fairly high speeds while Bobby chatted amiably and asked how my son Zack was doing. Zack was fine, but at that moment I was doing a white-knuckled 110 MPH on that long, back straightway as Bobby reminded me that he typically did over 200 MPH there. It must have seemed to him like we were standing still. I still marvel at driving a racing machine with one of the greatest racers in history in the passenger seat. In general, I cherish having attended many Indy Car races all over the country – including a few Indy 500s – up close and personal because of my former employer's sponsorship of and technology partnership with Bobby's team.

Monday, November 12, 2007
Now That's a Leader: William Durden
San Diego

We heard from Dickinson College President William Durden today, who can only be described as a force of nature. What a remarkable guy who seems intuitively to understand the role a great leader plays in personifying the brand, modeling brand behaviors and serving as a relentless communicator-in-chief. This makes him rare among people in leadership positions.

Durden was a keynote speaker on what he calls "deep marketing" at the American Marketing Association's annual Higher Education symposium. Put simply, he stole the show. The long-sleepy Dickinson has become a much more vibrant, visible and vigorous place since Durden assumed the presidency in 1999. He owes much of this success, he says, to the disciplined development and implementation of a bold and comprehensive brand strategy. Dickinson certainly owes much of this success, as well, for having chosen a high-energy, creative, humorous and highly substantive leader with Renaissance qualities that come from being a scholar, administrator, businessman, diplomat, soldier and linguist. Too many Boards of Trustees play it safe when selecting leaders and that's what they get in return – safe and average. Not Dickinson.

Durden contends that successful institutions with compelling brands are engaged in a powerful narrative, complete with protagonists, antagonists, plots and resolutions. He says that the "messaging should be so passionate that people want to be part of your narrative." He's right. Great leaders know how to embrace narratives and position themselves, their colleagues and their institutions in a drama designed to achieve something important. In Dickinson's case, it is to ensure a high-quality liberal education at a time of preoccupation with money, careerism and celebrity triviality. Ideally, the chosen narrative uses institutional history to provide context for future vision and current operations. For Dickinson this has meant the restoration of the school's founder, Dr. Benjamin Rush, who is also one of our nation's founding fathers.

When considering the future of liberal education in America, Durden rightly reminds us that the founding fathers bet this country's future on an engaged, energized and informed citizenry. This objective "demanded an education far different from the isolated, monkish, ivory-tower model" prevalent in Europe. Instead, an enlightened America was to have "an education that eagerly traversed the boundaries between classroom and community."

The revolution in American higher education envisioned by Rush, Jefferson and their colleagues found comfort in the academy and in practice communities alike, which is all too rare these days. It underscores the confidence that comes from appreciating multiple perspectives and participating in multiple communities, defying the insularity that Yale President Richard Levin has recently criticized. It is embodied by Renaissance leaders such as Durden who are able to portray their authentic selves, demonstrate comfort across diverse sectors and be allowed to get the job done unafraid of being different.

Durden certainly personifies the useful role of humor in successful leadership and storytelling, too. His funny, seemingly unassuming style warmly invites people into the Dickinson College story. I have seen far too many people use arrogance and personal insecurity to chase people away from working with the organizations they are entrusted to lead. My only suggestion for this terrific leader is that he make sure in future presentations that audience members understand he didn't craft the Dickinson story alone. By its very nature, an institutional narrative must have more than one character. Sometimes leaders can risk overwhelming their brand. And sometimes, brand personification can be taken too far.

Saturday, November 10, 2007
Levin Is Right
Yale President Richard Levin has it right. In our apparent desire to vote for politicians who are not elitist and with whom voters could imagine enjoying a beer, we must also demand that these would-be leaders are reasonably learned, well-read and globally oriented. The stakes are just too high at this critical national moment to indulge excessive on-the-job training or accept narrow world views born of inexperience or ignorance.

Levin is reshaping the Yale curriculum to require students to move beyond insularity and into the global marketplace of diverse ideas and peoples. He has also substantially increased the number of students from other nations in Yale's undergraduate population. He told *The Financial Times* earlier this month that, "A major motivation for this international-ism effort is to combat the tremendous insularity of leaders in America." This is tough stuff coming from a Yale president, since it generates for him and the institution he leads the predictable, stereotyped criticism of being elitist and unrepresentative of the real America. This is self-defeating nonsense, however, that too often comes from the very insular, narrow-minded thinking Levin is attacking.

The truth is that I do want my national leaders to understand the general patterns of world history, know where nations are located on a map and have visited some of them and be at least vaguely familiar with how the military actually works. I recall a Kennedy School seminar years ago in which a hot-shot rising politician proclaimed in a case-study discussion that he would land an AWACS on the nearby aircraft carrier.

Sure, one can always learn that landing AWACS on a carrier deck is a physical impossibility just as one can learn, Mr. Bush, that Greeks are not called Grecians and that there is a difference between Slovenia and Slovakia. However, wouldn't we be better served if on-the-job learning started at a more advanced state than this? So many of our contemporary foreign policy and national security issues are born of avoidable and almost willful ignorance.

Wednesday, September 5, 2007
Five Minds for the Future
Howard Gardner developed the theory of multiple intelligences (MIs) in the early 1980s. Gardner's teacher and great influence was the late Erik Erickson.

Long before the work of Daniel Goleman and others in emotional intelligence, Gardner was writing about the multidimensionality of human cognition. His most recent book, *Five Minds of The Future*, provides a broadly gauged but useful update to his earlier work.

Gardner suggests that we have find minds – disciplinary, synthesizing, creating, respectful and ethical – or at least that these five minds work in unison with one another to produce great thinkers, artists, professionals and leaders. Indeed, Gardner's quest is to explore how we should be producing minds, which often seems the antithesis of the teach-to-the-test rote learning of No Child Left Behind and other politically motivated educational initiatives.

Gardner is certainly correct when he says "that current formal education still prepares students primarily for the world of the past, rather than for possible worlds of the future." What those who diminish arts education miss, for example, is preparing young people to experiment, take risks, learn from failure, see abstract connections and engage in levels of subtlety needed to succeed.

Just skim Tim Weiner's deeply disturbing string of historic CIA failures in his book *Legacy of Ashes* and one readily sees the limits of incurious, one-dimensional and regimented learning. Keep in mind that the "smartest guys in the room" at the CIA put the Baathists in charge of Iraq with Saddam Hussein among them, created endless troubles in Iran after their unlawful Mosaddegh toppling, engineered the Bay of Pigs fiasco despite dire advance warnings of disaster, completely missed the Suez Crisis in 1956, did not anticipate the Soviet Union's demise and fabricated apocalyptic WMD predictions prior to the current Iraq War.

Yet it is likely that Alan Dulles, Richard Bissell and even George Tenet aced every standard test they ever took. "Reflective practitioners" they weren't – and aren't in the case of the Bush Administration – to use Donald Schon's term. And remember the DePaul University study that found current MBA students saying they want more technical and financial skills and less of the so-called "soft skills" involving leadership, creativity, empathy and communication.

I am most interested in Gardner's work on synthesis. It was as routine as it was predictable in my corporate career to witness the rejection of Gardner's synthesizing mind. All the value went to narrow, non-threatening expertise in financial, legal and technical subject matter. Take a current business challenge, give it a powerful historic metaphor, link it to certain cultural or scientific trends, imbue it with compelling narrative and watch employees and markets get very excited. And watch out, however, that your CEO and top-management peers will think you're some kind of intellectual, perish the thought. Gardner rightly says "the forces that stand in the way of synthesis are formidable." He adds that "as a species, we are predisposed to learn skills in certain contexts and to resist – or at least find challenging – their wider generalizations and broader applications." This underscores the power of Vartan Gregorian's call for a specialization as a generalist. We certainly do need far more curious, broad-minded generalists among our leaders today.

Gardner discusses another one of my concerns. Why is it that we drain ourselves of curiosity and childlike sensibility by the time we reach adulthood? What a loss. Gardner writes that "the mind of the five-year-old represents the height of creative powers." I never wanted to lose certain childlike behaviors – what embryologists call neoteny – and, well, people who know me say that I have not. Yet I certainly had to limit these curious, inquiring and playful tendencies in corporate life. Gardner writes that most corporations tout their creativity, but few actually demonstrate the courage of those convictions. He notes that great companies like 3M and GE have overcome such insecurities and are increasingly comfortable with real, raw creativity.

Finally, Gardner includes the ethical mind in his formulations crossing somewhat as it does beyond pure cognition and into the realm of affective and behavioral science. Why is such a claim paramount in today's ethically hobbled world? He quotes Rabbi Jonathan Sacks, who told him that, "When everything that matters can be bought and sold, when commitments can be broken because they are no longer to our advantage, when shopping becomes salvation and advertising slogans become our litany, when our worth is measured by how much we earn and spend, then the market is destroying the very virtues on which in the long run it depends."

Thursday, June 14, 2007
Erik Erikson & Play
Washington, DC
Dr. Carol Hoare of George Washington University spoke to our doctoral cohort today about the exceptional work of the late psychologist Erik Erikson. Carol's 2002 book, *Erikson on Development in Adulthood,* drew from her considerable research into Erikson's papers at Harvard.

I'm nearing completion of Walter Isaacson's massive biography *Einstein: His Life and Universe* (2007), with its many insights into Einstein's playfulness. What a joy it was to read Erikson's views on play, ideation and creativity. He is said to have once remarked at the Kennedy School's Godkin Lecture that "the opposite of play is death."

My favorite people intellectually are those whose confidence, vitality and individuality encourage them to play with words and concepts and question business as usual. Hoare echoes Erikson in writing that, "self-renewing adults somehow keep their internal youthfulness alive, contributing their energies to work; yet in the play and leeway of genuine work, they resist becoming a work's, an institution's or a superior's marionette."

This is a point that many organizations continue to miss. Playing with the unusual juxtositioning of ideas is great exercise for the mind and an incubator for original thinking, even when it occasionally feels subversive to the organization. Great leaders know how and when to encourage conditions for playful thinking and to reward its considerable harvest.

It Really Happened: Maurizio Pollini
I had asked my mother Doris to join me for a performance by the world-renowned pianist Maurizio Pollini at Boston Symphony Hall. "Who?" she asked. I gave her some background on Pollini, including the assertion that, "Ma, he's one of the world's greatest pianists." Knowing that I liked to joke with her, she heard this as "one of the world's greatest penises." We both laughed heartily and, once the momentary confusion was cleared, joked about this during the weeks prior to the concert.

After a marvelous performance, we want backstage to meet Pollini. I introduced him to my mother, "Maestro Pollini, this is my mother, Doris McWade. Doris, this is Maurizio Pollini, truly one of the world's greatest pianists." Of course, she heard "penises" again and started to giggle, tear up and then cough as Pollini looked puzzled and likely wondered what was wrong with her.

CHAPTER 8

ECONOMY & BUSINESS

Friday, January 27, 2017
Strictly for Amateurs

The White House is trying to flex its muscles with Mexico – amateurishly. This is regrettable for two of many reasons. First, slapping tariffs on Mexican goods will increase their prices and hurt American consumers. This is why Walmart and other retailers oppose the move. Second, and ironically, an even weaker Mexican economy will compel greater illegal immigration across our southern border.

Illegal immigration from Mexico has declined substantially in recent years, just as our investments in and success with improved border patrol have taken hold. The ill-conceived actions of an intemperate Administration will make matters much worse.

Wednesday, January 13, 2016
Politus Interruptus
Sydney

Men interrupt women in business meetings all the time. This is the part of the program where every woman now says, "No kidding," and most men say, "No we don't; no way." Actually, the woman says "No ..." and the guy interrupts her to say, "No we don't."

My advice to women who are so routinely interrupted is to keep talking. That's right, finish your damn sentence. Yes, this means two of you will be talking over each other, but you'll be amazed how this puts the blustery fellow chopping you off in mid-sentence in his place without appearing to be a jerk about it. Your thoughts and words have value. Don't meekly withdraw them because some guy across the table just wants to blurt something out.

On a separate note, thanks to Chef Tetsuya and his team for hosting Walt and I last night as we tour Australia for our fifth wedding anniversary, and special appreciation to our friend Ray, too, for introducing us to the great Tetsuya in the first place.

An indigenous Australian working the didgeridoo on Sydney's Circular Quay.

Friday, September 5, 2014
Oui ou non?
Detroit

Two interesting business stories out of France yesterday. One you can believe and the other is best served up as tripe. Or as French gourmands call one of their favorite stews, tripes a la mode de Caen.

I actually believe the voracious Bernard Arnault and his luxury giant LVMH are telling the truth in announcing that they are no longer trying to acquire Hermes. Actually, it was simply no longer possible for them to do so, given the well-orchestrated fight by Hermes. Chalk one up for the independence of a longstanding family-owned-and-operated businesses. The world is safe again for Kelly and Birkin bags. It is likely the LVMH won't make another run at Hermes for some time.

The announcement that the French government has decided to halt shipment of two Mistral-class warships to Russia is another matter entirely. The French are clearly buying time here, given the profound embarrassment of being seen as selling arms to Moscow amid Putin's malignant mischief, especially during the NATO summit in Wales.

It would be difficult to imagine the French failing to deliver on this order, given the inevitably expensive breach-of-contract lawsuits and the loss of revenue and jobs on future orders that would follow. The French economy is in terrible shape and President Hollande's political fortunes have been sinking like so many old Soviet Oscar class submarines. Ultimately, with Russian crews already starting the turnover process aboard these ships, Paris will find it very difficult to say nyet on this one. You showed some backbone in Mali, Francoise. It's time for some more.

It Really Happened: Super Bowl Sneaks

My friend and I were in Atlanta for the 1994 Super Bowl and without game tickets two hours before kick-off. Those were more innocent times before today's "see something, say something" security mania so, naturally, we decided to try to sneak into the Super Bowl.

My friend was bolder than me in getting us past the first two security rings, using fast-talk as well as media credentials and a sheriff's badge of dubious provenance. We had no idea what we were doing, of course, nor what it would take to succeed. Still, I was gaining confidence as we found ourselves approaching a fenced-in, tunnel area at the very moment a school bus pulled up to disgorge what I believe was called the Yellow Rose of Texas marching band. The band members were lugging their drums and tubas and decked out in canary yellow and black outfits, but they were escorted by men and women in civilian clothes – just like us. We jumped in among them and casually promenaded into the bowels of the Georgia Dome. Without Super Bowl credentials, however, our triumph was short-lived. Just ahead of us was a gate where each person's credentials were being examined.

That's when we saw a curtained area and decided to hide there to collect our thoughts. We looked out the other side of the curtain to see a throng of security guards lining the Georgia Dome basement corridor. We knew we needed to be more assertive at that point, as things seemed to be closing in on us, so I took the ridiculous badge from my friend and asked him to start limping as we emerged from the curtain. "Excuse me," I said to one of the security guards as I flashed the badge. "The sergeant here has twisted his ankle. Can you direct us to First Aid?" The woman could not have been sweeter, putting us on a small elevator and pressing a floor number to take us to First Aid.

Once the doors closed, I chose a different floor number. We alighted from the elevator to confront the Vince Lombardi Trophy and a few friendly security guards minding it. We gracefully but purposefully returned to the elevator, chose another floor and found our way into the stadium itself, spending the entire game sitting in aisles or standing in concourses. I've been lucky to attend five Super Bowls, and this one was both the least comfortable and most adventurous.

Sunday, May 18, 2014
Acquiring Minds
Washington DC
Mergers and acquisitions can be illusory. I was directly involved with 50 or 60 completed acquisitions in my corporate years, some of them blockbusters such as Raytheon's acquisition of the Hughes Aircraft Company. We labeled some of these purchases "mergers," occasionally using the "of equals" sobriquet to conceal our real intentions to debone the

acquired firm. If you ever find yourself in a firm being acquired under this "merger of equals" rubric, head for the hills unless, of course, you're a sizable shareholder.

The Economist for May 3rd reports that global M&A activity in 2014 is off to its hottest start since 2007, with some big brand names in play, such as Pfizer and AstraZeneca, AT&T and DirecTV, Time Warner and Comcast, GE and Alstom, and Omnicom and Publicis. How strange it was to learn, however, that the much-ballyhooed $35 billion engagement between these last two advertising and communications behemoths was abruptly scuttled. Each party is blaming the other, off the record, of course, and both are citing "cultural differences" as well as regulatory delays as two causes of failure. Sure.

In writing about the proposed Omnicom-Publicis deal this month, *Forbes'* columnist Avi Dan is correct in stating that "there was nothing in it for the clients," and that "scale is not as relevant as it once was." Regrettably, these are not new phenomenon. Every time we acquired another firm in my banking days, for example, we positioned the deal as benefitting our customers. In truth, this was rarely the case. Most deals were attempted then (and still) under customer-indifferent market pressures to get bigger and bigger. Size is certainly an asset in some markets at some times. Size matters most, however, when it enables agile, innovative smaller firms to play Davey to stumbling, lumbering Goliaths focused inward. Of course, deals are often forged to help a small number of shareholders get wealthier, too, not that there's necessarily anything wrong with that.

How is it that the world's best branding and public relations minds at Omnicom and Publicis could so mishandle their proposed "merger"? Publicis' Maurice Levy and Omnicom's John Wren spent nine months and a reported $100 million in fees to create impossible expectations about an unworkable deal that would have been of little true merit to their customers. Here's where *Forbes'* Avi Dan is wrong, however, in downplaying the role of clashing egos in the demise of the deal. It's beyond me how Levy and Wren let so much time pass without deciding which of them would be the boss and for how long. These co-called "social issues" were most definitely at play here. They almost always are. Their own investor relations experts would have advised them to have these difficult, ego-laden arrangements worked out before going public with the deal. Now, they are left with nothing but embarrassment and legal fees.

Tuesday, May 6, 2014
Now That's a Leader: Eric Dawson
Philadelphia
Congratulations to Eric Dawson for being named by *Boston Magazine* as one of Boston's top 100 "visionaries, idealists and thinkers." An old friend of mine, Eric is president and co-founder of Peace First. *Boston Magazine* rightly lauds Peace First for helping young people develop peacemaking skills. The Clinton Global Initiative has embraced the work of Eric, Karen Grant and their team, serving as the platform last year to announce the first-ever national Peace First Prizes. Thank you, Eric, for your wisdom, determination and commitment. This recognition is richly deserved.

It's mildly irritating, however, that these magazine and newspaper lists touting leaders, thinkers and doers are often guilty of, in the words of the immortal Captain Louis Renault from *Casablanca* (1943), rounding up the usual suspects. Do we really need the governor, mayor, US senator, cardinal, secretary of state and the predictable power-broker CEOs on the list again and again? Sure, the recognition is deserved in some cases. And yes, the publishers need to sell magazines and that means celebrating celebrities and those who lead organizations with large advertising budgets. Still, we're always better off knowing more people like Eric Dawson who are improving our lot and actually in need our recognition and support.

It Really Happened: Spies Like Us
Aboard The World off the coast of Da Nang, Vietnam
I was assigned to NATO in 1986 to support exercise Northern Wedding in Norway. My hardship duty included a stay at the Park Hotel in the lovely, southern port town of Sandefjord, which was the location of the Allied Press Information Center. One night at the bar I was approached by a rather garrulous guy who wanted to be my best friend. He bought me a glass of wine and we talked about life until he started to make his move.

He was obviously an amateur because he was working the wrong person in trying to elicit classified information from me because, in truth, I didn't know anything of value. Plus, he was so obviously up to no good that it all felt like a scene from one of the Pink Panther movies. None of this prevented me from enjoying the occasion, however, as I filled this guy up with useless trivia of no importance whatsoever.

My colleague Dennis and I knew we had to report the incident to Allied intelligence at Torp Airfield. The Norwegian naval intelligence officer there refused to believe us, however, repeatedly claiming that it would be absolutely impossible for Warsaw Pact charlatans and characters to be milling around the headquarters hotel for a NATO exercise. Two days later, we learned that a "trade" delegation from East Germany staying at the hotel had been asked to leave.

Boys at the extraordinary Han Market in Da Nang, Vietnam.

Sunday, November 24, 2013
Now that's a Leader: Tommy Cooney
Eleven-year-old Tommy Cooney can teach us a thing or two about leadership and wisdom. He learned that six-year-old Danny Keefe was

being bullied because of a speech condition that makes it difficult to understand him. Danny was also being unmercifully teased by kids in Bridgewater, MA because, for whatever reason, he likes to wear suits and ties to school – the same school Cooney attends. It seems that Cooney recently organized 45 boys to attend school in suits or shirts and ties to show Danny "that he was loved." What an inspiration at a time when playground and workplace bullying continue to rear its ugly head.

And what a contrast to some who occupy leadership positions – one should never confuse them with actual leaders – such as disgraced Lawrence, MA Mayor William Lantigua. Lantigua cast considerable shame on his city in recent years, lost an election this month, demanded a recount, got the recount and lost again, and is still refusing to concede defeat. How can we even admonish Lantigua or Toronto's buffoon-in-chief Rob Ford to "stop acting like children," since children like the Tommy Cooneys of the world are so much better than that?

Sunday, April 14, 2013
Florida in Detroit
Miami
I have long rooted for Detroit – old Tiger Stadium, new Comerica Park, the auto shows, the Lions moving downtown, restored Fox Theater and, yes, those pistachio baskets at the Astoria Bakery in Greektown. Besides, I like underdogs. And yet is Richard Florida too optimistic in today's *Financial Times* about the role of Detroit's new "creative class" in the revitalization of a city on the edge of the abyss?

Sure, what he describes as an emergent, youthful technorati is hopeful, but this is the easy part. Young, hip pioneers will always reclaim the best of decayed but worthy urban spaces, especially in Detroit's "post-government" era. The key to long-term growth will be connecting these successful, albeit, small private initiatives to the larger, longer and tougher public-private partnerships needed to move Detroit forward in more than a boutique manner. Still, you have to start somewhere.

It Really Happened: I'm Serious, Ma!
Our mother Doris often accompanied Pat and me on many adventures. The three of us saw Dizzy Gillespie perform one evening at Washington

DC's Blues Alley. I enjoyed making my mother laugh, which she sorely needed and wanted after many very tough years. I told her that she was going to lose it when Dizzy played his horn and his cheeks puffed out like a hamster on steroids – a silly post-hypnotic suggestion on my part. We sat at table directly in front of the stage and, when Dizzy demonstrated his trademark facial elasticity, Doris burst into laughter and then tears. When Dizzy looked at our table, I almost imagined he was thinking that somebody needed to help that poor, distressed woman.

"I'm serious, Ma," I said to Doris in inviting her to join me at an event honoring former President Gerald Ford. "The president was asking for you the other day on a conference call," I added, to which she justifiably replied, "I never know when you're kidding me or not." I was kidding, of course. As we entered the hotel and made our way to a private reception, I reiterated that the president would be glad to see her and that I had told him all about her. We turned the corner into the reception and, of course, walked right into former President Ford and his small entourage. "Hello, Mr. President," I said, teasingly adding, "You know my mother, Doris." Now Gerald Ford was not only a politician, but he was a friendly, decent man, too. "Yes of course, Doris, it's so wonderful to see you," making her feel as if they had met in the past. After he departed, my mother turned to me and queried, "Had he really been asking about me?"

We hosted many heads of state and government over the years at the World Affairs Council of Boston. As Council president, I once had the honor of presenting Ireland's Taoiseach Albert Reynolds with our Christian A. Herter Award. I was inspired to invite him after participating in a British-American Fellowship to Belfast, Northern Ireland just as the possibility of peace started to emerge from The Troubles. I greeted Reynolds when he arrived at the hotel amid the swirl of security, whisked as we then were onto a secure elevator. I briefed him on the proceedings, adding at the end of my report that, "Of course, sir, you'll have to meet my mother, too."

He barely reacted, so I disposed of that thought. The event went well and we reversed our path through the gauntlet and toward his limousine when he abruptly stopped short, with all of us reacting like the cartoon Road Runner screeching to an immediate halt. The prime minister looked at me and asked in exclamatory fashion, "Where's your mother?" I can only imagine the look on Doris' face when two Secret Service agents found her upstairs and escorted her to the basement to meet the leader of Ireland.

Thursday, March 28, 2013
Brain Gain
Congressman Ed Markey (D-MA) told us yesterday that 10 percent of MIT students come from Massachusetts, but that 35 percent of them remain in the state upon graduation. So how are colleges and universities working with state and regional economic development authorities to boost these kind of "brain gain" numbers? Should a university's Career Development Office see this as part of their mandate? Yes. Are they doing so or empowered to do so? Of course not.

The issue is especially acute when it comes to retaining brilliant immigrants, since our federal government makes this so perplexingly difficult to do. Markey cited a study by Harvard, Duke and the University of California at Berkeley reporting that twice as many immigrants apply for patents than native-born US citizens and that immigrants are responsible for 25 percent of all US patents.

Monday, April 6, 2009
A Saab Story
San Francisco
How the mighty are falling. I remember spending several days at Saab-Scania headquarters and at various manufacturing facilities in and around Stockholm as a graduate student at the Stockholm School of Economics in 1980. Saab-Scania enjoyed both a rich history in automobiles, trucks, engines and airplanes as well as a distinctly bright future. The company was nimble and technologically innovative, and it seemed to value its employees.

Saab-Scania was ultimately split up in the mid-1990s and, left to the vagaries of the global automobile market, Saab Automobile AB began its long slide into oblivion. The company's deterioration was predictably exacerbated when General Motors acquired a major stake in the firm at the same time. Now, having lost $343 million last year, Saab Automobile is on the brink of failure.

The intriguing part of this sad tale is that the Swedish government has no intent of bailing out the company, despite French, German, British and American government support (actual or intended) for their own ailing automotive firms. This is not to say that a bailout is the right thing to do; it all depends upon the circumstances. But who would have imagined that Sweden would be the nation to say, "Nej, tack." After all, the traditional Swedish "third way" between capitalism and socialism was supposed to present capitalism with a human face. One might wonder what will now happen to those workers in Saab company towns like Trollhattan.

The center-right Swedish government seems to have drawn a line in the sand on this issue, citing the usual mush about market forces taking care of themselves. They won't. Enterprise Minister Maud Olofsson told *The New York Times* last month that, "The Swedish state is not prepared to own car factories," although they were prepared to own the failed banks they nationalized in the recent past. So Saab may well fail someday very soon.

GM has indicated that it will pull out of Saab by the end of this year, further infuriating Minister Olofsson. "They're washing their hands of Saab and dropping it in the laps of the Swedish taxpayers," she said. Hey Maud, it's GM. What did you expect?

Wednesday, March 11, 2009
Bernanke Speaks
Federal Reserve Chairman Ben Bernanke joined us this morning for a conversation at the Council on Foreign Relations. He called for "consolidated government supervision" of financial institutions, underscoring the need to deter efforts by companies in the future to shift excessive risks from more to less regulated markets. If human nature is any guide, we will be reading stories in the not-too-distant future of corner-cutting financial buccaneers trying to shield themselves from appropriate risk regulation and ultimate accountability.

The Chairman also contended that the current financial crisis should, once and for all, end the unthinking, clichéd view that markets somehow fix themselves. Markets can profoundly screw themselves up, especially with government complicity. However, most markets in current (and many other) conditions can and will not correct themselves naturally, at least not in time to prevent outright disaster. There is simply no such thing as pure, market-trusting laissez-faire capitalism, though some cling to the view for ideological reasons. Indeed, most of us are Keynesians during perilous moments such as this one.

Bernanke also spoke of the lamentable pro-cyclical effects of poor government regulation. He is pointing here to our all-too-human bandwagon tendencies to stimulate even greater access to credit in boom times, when excessive credit is unneeded and unhelpful, while slamming credit availability shut during credit crunches when it is otherwise so desperately needed. It's easy to lend in good times and to bolt the doors shut in tough times, although the effects of doing so can be catastrophic. I have sat in my share of credit committees over the years. Real leadership emerges when, for example, bankers understand an innovative vision in tough times and carefully finance it in the midst of economic distress. Lemmings need not apply.

This is what we did with the $6 billion BankBoston Credit Initiative in the early 1990s. Of course, we also reaped a windfall of favorable publicity since few institutions were lending during that severe and self-fulfilling credit crunch. I remember then-Congressman Joe Kennedy (D-MA) marveling at the global publicity we received for an action that he said was akin to Star Market announcing they were selling bananas.

Anyway, Bernanke, a scholar of the Great Depression, cited two lessons from the 1930s. First, he reiterated that monetary policy needs to be supportive and not restrictive in a crisis. The Federal Reserve Bank during the Great Depression spurned easing credit and was far too conservative in its approach. By contrast, today's Fed has been aggressive with interest rates and other countries are now following suit. Then, he added that the Fed of the 1930s also chose not to intervene in bank failures, a hands-off attitude that exacerbated the contagion of fear and added to our illiquidity.

Saturday, March 14, 2009
Remember the Customer
Market downturns often find old-line businesses rediscovering their customers. The fear and insecurity created by a recession can return senior executives to common-sense principles and remind them why their institutions are doing business in the first place – or at least they should. Now is the time when organizations become awash in "back to basics" and "customer delight" mantras that risk being temporary, clichéd and insincere.

I lived through successive rounds of customer rediscovery – as if customers ever went away in the first place – in my commercial banking days. In an attempt to prevent another embarrassing declaration that a certain year would be proclaimed, "The Year of the Customer," I once floated the idea at my global bank-holding company that we appoint a Director of Common Sense to help prevent or at least mitigate these bad ideas. I was only half joking, but the suggestion never flew. Only years later did I figure out why. It seemed to me that nobody wanted to be held to any common-sense standards. I don't think people resisted the appointment of such a mythical director that in its very creation would then, and now, earn a *Wall Street Journal* headline. Instead, they likely feared the ridicule that would come the very next day and for days, months and years thereafter when common sense would certainly be violated.

This is why it is so painful now to hear top executives in financial services and elsewhere brag about their movement back to the customer. A top New England banker I do not know and have never met just told *The Boston Globe*, "When things are difficult, you go back to your customer focus, and that's what we're doing." It is likely that this official does not understand the exasperatingly revealing nature of this statement. If institutions actually wanted to acquire and retain customers, they would hire, train and fairly pay customer-service specialists who understand the primary language of the country they serve and are truly knowledgeable about the institution. These folks would be ready, willing and able to relay, remedy and reward customers who call, write or e-mail the company. In doing so, these firms would rip out the front-end, voice-mail-hell to which many of them now subject their customers.

When mediocre leaders enjoy good times, they move away from customers and take them for granted. Their focus moves to mergers and acquisitions, the usual musical-chairs, who's-on-first office politics, and all manner of luxuries and even banalities that would not be tolerated in tough times. Perhaps they could eliminate or at least reduce trouble if customer focus was not so situational and variable.

Thursday, October 4, 2008
Barking Up the Wrong Tree
Can it possibly be true as Tom Friedman tells us in his new book *Hot, Flat and Crowded* that the American pet food industry spends more on research and development than this country's power companies? I think we're going to the dogs.

Sunday, November 18, 2007
Now That's a Leader: General Wes Clark
Santa Monica
General Wes Clark is a good man. He was among my choices for president last time, at least as far as he went, and he would be again. It seems that he is positioning himself – and being positioned by others – as a potential running mate for Hillary Clinton. His Arkansas ties with the Clintons run deep.

General Clark is in town for a series of fundraisers, speeches and media appearances. As I review the *Los Angeles Times'* coverage of his trip here, I fondly remember an encounter with General Clark last year at the Renaissance Weekend.

I mentioned to General Clark that I had once served as a reservist in his NATO command in Brussels. He smiled, looked me squarely in the eye and wanted to know with seemingly sincere interest what I thought of the experience. Then, as he moved on, he said, "Thank you." No sir, thank you for being a thoughtful, insightful gentleman warrior with an understanding of the few benefits and many costs of warfare that has been utterly lacking in the White House and Congress.

General Clark's new book is entitled *A Time to Lead*. It sure is, General. Know any good leaders?

Saturday, April 07, 2007
Urban Myths
Mercer Human Resources has released its latest list of Top 50 Global Cities for Quality of Living. Once again, the work serves as an eye-opener for Americans. While the Canadian towns of Vancouver, Toronto, Ottawa, Montreal and Calgary all rank among the leading 25 cities, no American city appears until Honolulu (27), San Francisco (28) and Boston (38). Really? Ottawa is lovely, sure, but there are few cities anywhere that can rival San Francisco.

Still, we Americans must marvel at a world around us that is bristling with energy, culture and opportunity. Regrettably, so few of us ever experience it. Indeed, only 25 percent of Americans have ever applied for a passport, according to workpermit.com. It would seem that global travel joins quality relationships with diverse people, engaging conversation, community service, fine art, quality music and good books framed in intellectual curiosity, spirituality, humility and humor as pillars of an examined life.

One wonders what our urban policymakers can learn from places like Zurich (1), Geneva (2) or Bern (9); Auckland (5) and Wellington (12); or Dusseldorf (6), Frankfurt (7), Munich (8) and Berlin (16).

On a separate subject, it is dizzying to realize that the 25th anniversary of the Falklands, er, Malvinas, War is upon us. I recall happening upon a 10th anniversary commemoration just outside the Cinco de Mayo Plaza in Buenos Aires one day. The weather was as beautiful that day as the mood was dark, somber and resentful.

Wednesday, January 14, 2004
Two Americas on Four Wheels
Detroit
The Boston Globe
Even the most casual observer here at this week's North American International Auto Show can't help but notice the schizophrenia that marks the auto industry. American automakers are moving in two extreme and opposite directions that seem to mirror competing and often contradictory visions for America itself.

Just beneath the glitz that permeates every aspect of the nation's largest auto show lie some fundamental questions about America's view of itself. Of course, Detroit has long served as a powerful metaphor for America. As our election season heats up, however, this year's auto show offers a compelling glimpse of the "two Americas" that emerged from the 2000 election. Call it "Red and Blue America," conservatives versus liberals, the heartland versus the coasts, or Bush lovers versus Bush loathers, the politics of division are readily apparent in Detroit this week.

On the one hand, there is the proud and loud America that likes to flex its muscle. This America is easily provoked by real or perceived infringements on its individual rights. This America will fight to its last breath to ensure that we are free to drive gargantuan earthmovers that pass these days as SUVs. In this America, size and muscularity really do matter. And boasting about size matters, too. Is it any wonder that the new Ford Freestyle SUV has 12 cup holders or that the company claims its new Five Hundred sedan can hold eight golf bags? Who needs 12 cups of anything in their car, let alone eight golf bags?

It's reminiscent of gangster-turned-car-salesman Robert DeNiro's line in the movie *Analyze That* (2002): "Look at the size of that trunk; you could put three bodies in there."

It's also the automotive equivalent of the Bush doctrine of preemptive war. A kind of feel-good security comes to those who anticipate trouble, whether it has a real chance of occurring or not, and through great size and power seek to make themselves safer. Too bad that SUV accident and injury statistics tell a different story of death and destruction. Still, the "proud and loud" approach feels and sounds good, and besides, most of its downsides won't be felt for years to come.

On the other hand, there is the sensitive America that thinks much more about our collective good, our threatened environment, and our finite energy resources. This America worries and occasionally whines about the need to balance individual rights with individual responsibilities. This America also likes to condemn the other America without making much of an effort to understand it.

For this America, the auto show has newfound appeal. There are numerous hybrid vehicles on display here touting the advantages of a combined gas and electric fuel system. Promotional materials for the hybrids underscore the societal benefits of low-emission, fuel-efficient vehicles, while these same vehicles are displayed adjacent to the gigantic, gas-guzzling land yachts. Automakers are also showcasing experimental hydrogen-fueled vehicles in Detroit this week.

They're teasing the sensitive America with images of an environmentally safe, post-hydrocarbon world where we will finally be free of our reliance on foreign oil. Of course, that's about the last thing Detroit really wants to see happen. Some claim that the automakers are touting hybrids and hydrocarbons, as well as small cars and vehicles made from recyclables and agricultural byproducts, simply because it's good PR. Sure, it helps them with lawmakers, regulators, environmental groups, and skeptical journalists, but there's more to it than that.

Detroit is finally starting to take this other America seriously. Why? Money! American automakers see a growing market for high-quality, low-emission, and energy-efficient vehicles that can actually fit on our streets and in our parking garages. With so much trouble in the Middle East foreshadowing another energy crisis, they don't want to be left out of this potentially lucrative market.

Besides, their remarkably successful run with SUVs and light trucks is coming to an end. With so much competition from the Japanese and others in these markets today, American automakers can no longer generate the record revenue and profit margins they once made from SUVs and light trucks.

The simple truth is that Detroit is schizophrenic because we are schizophrenic. We are every bit "two Americas" when it comes to buying vehicles or, for that matter, in choosing our political candidates, reading material, or popular music. Until the next energy crisis forces our hand collectively, however, it will be up to each of us to look at ourselves in that rear-view mirror and decide how best to balance our own rights and responsibilities.

Friday, February 23, 2007
Cafe au Lloyd
Rochester, NY
Do you know the nature of the original Lloyd's of London business? Well, it was a coffee shop. It seems that Edward Lloyd opened a fashionable

coffee house in 1688 not far from London's bustling seaport. Centuries before Starbucks marketed itself as "America's third place," Lloyd's became a social crossroads for ship owners, captains and assorted merchants who grew to rely on Lloyd's ever-so-reliable weather and shipping news. Soon, good old Lloyd was using his proprietary knowledge base and customer relationship management skills to transform his coffee joint into what became the most storied insurance brand in history. With whole beans, can whole life be far away?

ABOUT THE AUTHOR

Photo Credit: Sandie Allen

Jessica C. McWade, Ed.D. is President of McWade Group, Inc., specializing in leadership, strategy and message development. She has consulted for many corporations, colleges and universities, non-profit organizations and government agencies. Jessica previously led global communications and public affairs for three Fortune 200 corporations and served as President of The World Affairs Council of Boston as well as a Commander in the U.S. Naval Reserve, which took her on assignments around the world many times.

She is a member of the Council on Foreign Relations and trustee of the SEA Education Association. She has also served as a Fellow to the Salzburg Seminar and a British-American Fellow in Northern Ireland. Jessica earned an Ed.D. in leadership and organizational development from George Washington University. She also holds degrees from Harvard University's Kennedy School, New York University's Stern School and Boston University's College of Communication and studied at the Stockholm School of Economics in Sweden.

Made in the USA
Middletown, DE
11 April 2017